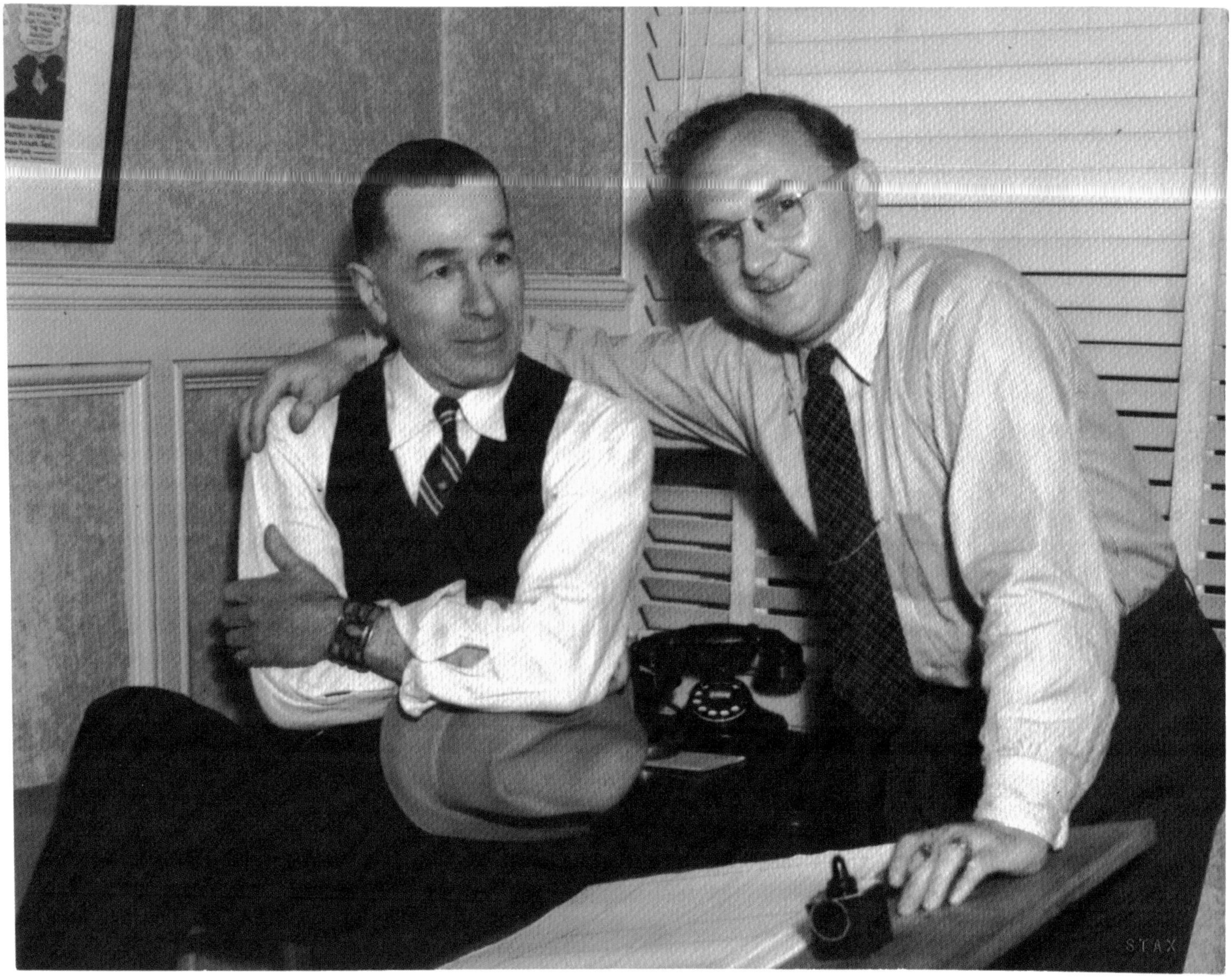
STAX

George Herriman, c. 1940, possibly in his home studio, with a "Carroll W. Funk," about whom nothing, at least at this moment, is known, though he may have been an employee of the Hal Roach studios, as other photographs which appear to have been from this same session include Roach employees. Ruled-out but undrawn *Krazy* dailies await Herriman's pen on the desk and comic strip scholar Rick Marschall interestingly identifies the framed comic strip on the wall as likely being by Jimmy "They'll Do It Every Time" Hatlo. From the collection of, and many thanks to, Rob Stolzer.

KRAZY & IGNATZ.

by George Herriman.

"A Ragout of Raspberries."

Culling Together the Complete Full-Page Comic Strips,
with Addenda.

1941-42.

Edited by Bill Blackbeard
with an Introduction by Jeet Heer.

Fantagraphics Books, SEATTLE.

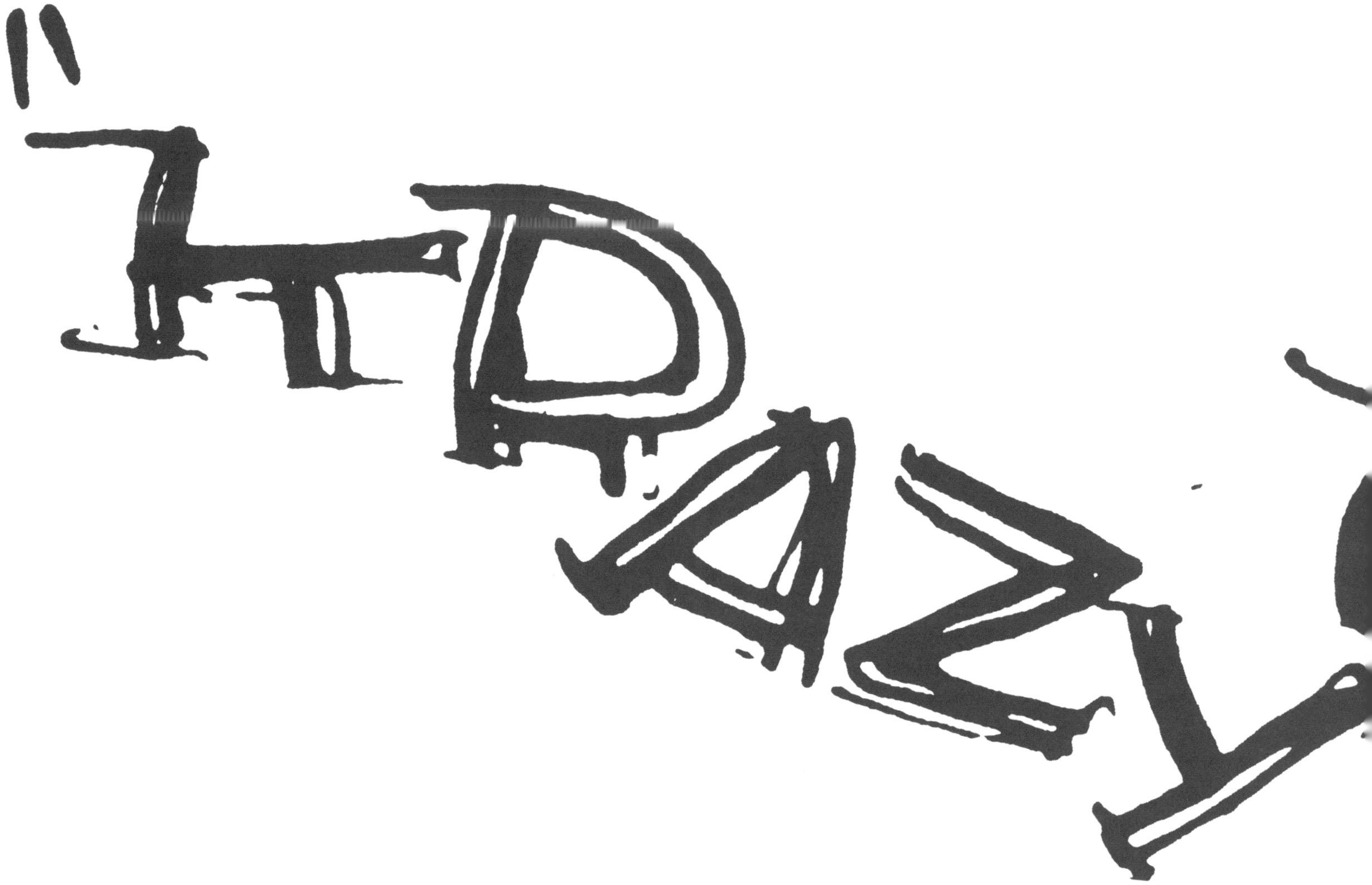

Published by Fantagraphics Books.
7563 Lake City Way North East,
Seattle, Washington, 98115, United States of America.

Edited by Bill Blackbeard.
Except where noted, all research materials appear courtesy of the San Francisco Academy of Cartoon Art.
Additional research by Jeet Heer.
Design, decoration, and occasional cutlines by Chris Ware.
Production assistance and scanning by Paul Baresh.
Promoted by Eric Reynolds.
Published by Gary Groth and Kim Thompson.

First Fantagraphics Books edition: December 2007.

ISBN13: 978-1-56097-887-9.

Printed in Korea through Print Vision.

Special thanks to Derya Ataker, Erich Brandmayr, John Fawcett, Rick Marschall, and Rob Stolzer.

"KRAZY KAT"

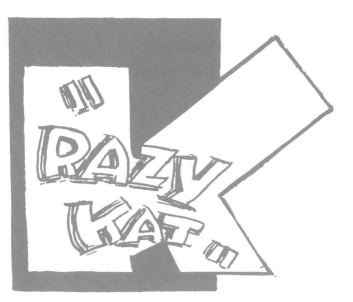

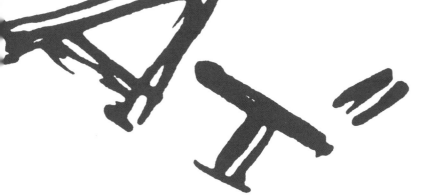

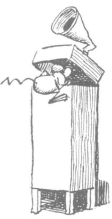

KRAZY & IGNATZ.

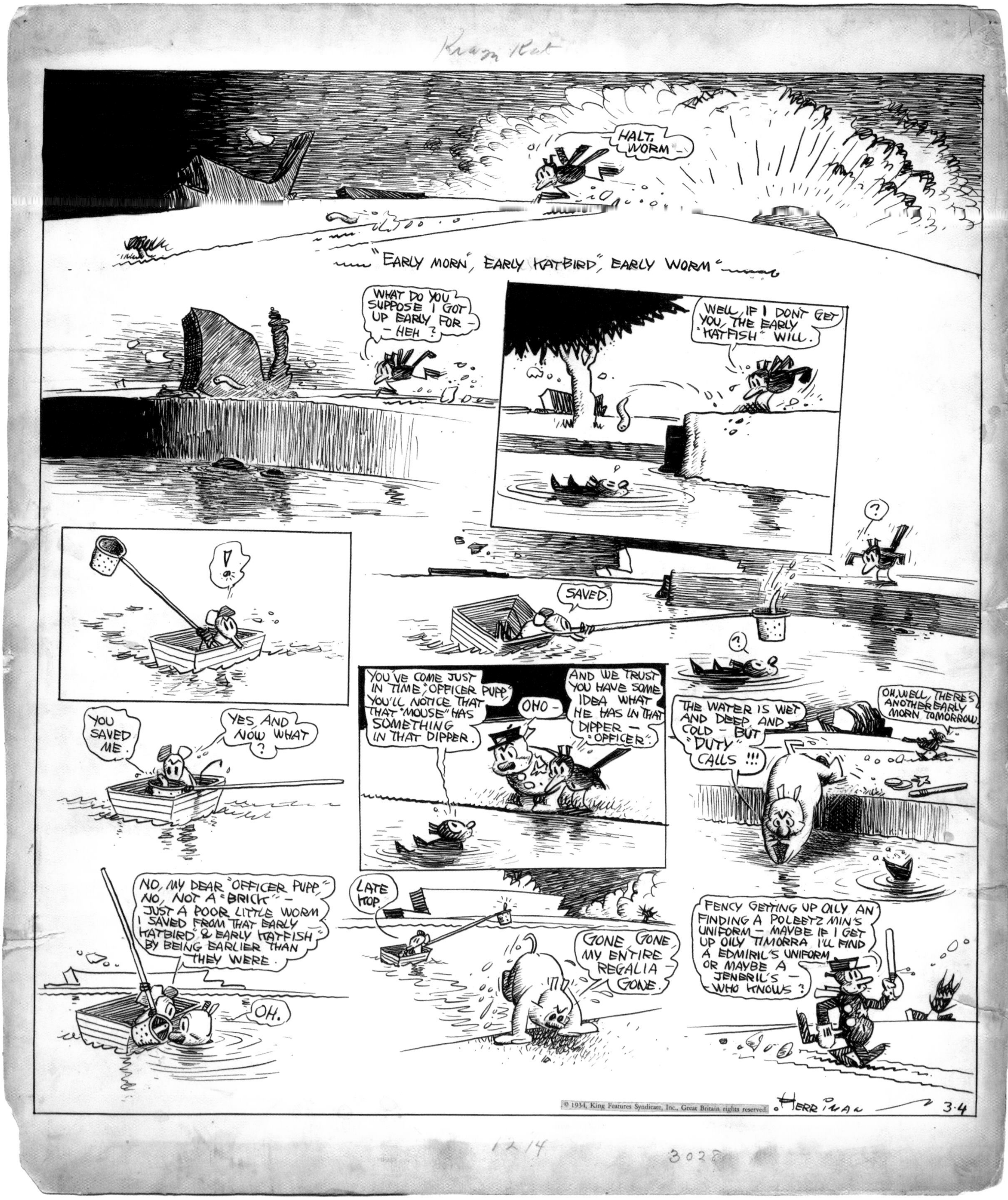
Krazy Kat
HALT, WORM
"EARLY MORN", EARLY KATBIRD", EARLY WORM"
WHAT DO YOU SUPPOSE I GOT UP EARLY FOR – HEH ?
WELL, IF I DON'T GET YOU, THE EARLY "KATFISH" WILL.
?
!
SAVED.
?
YOU SAVED ME.
YES, AND NOW WHAT ?
YOU'VE COME JUST IN TIME, "OFFICER PUPP" YOU'LL NOTICE THAT THAT "MOUSE" HAS SOMETHING IN THAT DIPPER.
OHO –
AND WE TRUST YOU HAVE SOME IDEA WHAT HE HAS IN THAT DIPPER – "OFFICER".
THE WATER IS WET AND DEEP AND COLD – BUT "DUTY" CALLS !!!
OH, WELL, THERE'S ANOTHER EARLY MORN TOMORROW.
NO, MY DEAR "OFFICER PUPP" NO, NOT A "BRICK" – JUST A POOR LITTLE WORM I SAVED FROM THAT EARLY KATBIRD & EARLY KATFISH BY BEING EARLIER THAN THEY WERE.
OH.
LATE KOP.
GONE, GONE MY ENTIRE REGALIA – GONE.
FENCY GETTING UP OILY AN FINDING A POLEETZ MIN'S UNIFORM – MAYBE IF I GET UP OILY TIMORRA I'LL FIND A EDMIRIL'S UNIFORM OR MAYBE A JENERIL'S – WHO KNOWS ?
© 1934, King Features Syndicate, Inc., Great Britain rights reserved.
HERRIMAN
3-4
1214
3028

Original for a *Krazy Kat* page, March 4th, 1934, from a less often seen period of Herriman's work. Readers can compare this with the version that appeared on page 93 of *Krazy and Ignatz: 1933-1934*, a guessed-at reconstruction from a bastardized version which was the only one available to the publishers at the time. Many thanks to Erich Brandmayr. Collection C. Ware.

KAT GOT YOUR TONGUE:

Where George Herriman's Language Came From.

Introduction by Jeet Heer.

The year is 1909 and you've just walked into a fraternity house at the University of California in Los Angeles. The boys are gathered around the piano, smoking cigars, horsing around. Recorded music is still a new-fangled invention, so most of the songs being boisterously belted out aren't slick tunes but improvised limericks of uncertain origin. One song sticks in your mind, as ditties sometimes do for mysterious reasons. The melody is simple (two notes) and it is sung slowly in unison, like a dirge (albeit with a comic twist). It goes like this:

The steward went below
Whoo-oo-oo
To light the cabin lamp
Whoo-oo-oo
The lamp it would not burn
Whoo-oo-oo
Because the wick was damp
Whoo-oo-oo, whoo-oo-oo.
The captain went below
To kick the steward's ass
Fire up, you son of a bitch,
The Golden Gate is past.

George Herriman never went to college but he must have heard this song in some manly, sodden social gathering because he reproduced it, in garbled form, in a *Krazy Kat* daily strip that ran on March 23, 1916. In the Herriman version, a cheeky dog obliviously sings to himself:

Oh, the captain went be-low,
To light the cab-in lamps,
Fi-yer up — y'rannigazoos,
The Gold-din Gate is passed.

There are multiple ironies built into this strip. The canine who chants this roughneck ballad is "a son of a bitch" (as all dogs are) but he can't use that phrase because he's appearing in a comic strip that runs in family newspapers, hence the euphemism "rannigazoos." Appropriately enough, this dog gets pricked in the hind-quarters, a variation on the ass-kicking that is mentioned in the original song but glided over in the carefully refashioned newspaper rendition.

Herriman's use of this frat house beer song illustrates the social roots of his linguistic playfulness. Cartooning is an inherently hybrid art, a mixture of words and pictures. Much has been written about Herriman's peerless drawing skills, while his writing tends to be scanted. Herriman was as much a master of language as of drawing. His words are as full of vim and vitality as his fluid pen work.

Where did Herriman's colorful language come from? To a striking degree, Herriman drew on the rich oral culture of early 20th century America. Herriman was a cultural magpie, taking his words from diverse sources far and wide, ranging from popular songs to political speeches to the Bible to medical and scientific discourse.

In describing Herriman's literary skills, it's easy enough to classify him as a nonsense poet, a coiner of nonce-words and playful gibberish in the great tradition of Lewis Carroll and Edward Lear. But if you pay close attention to Herriman's language, what becomes evident is that he

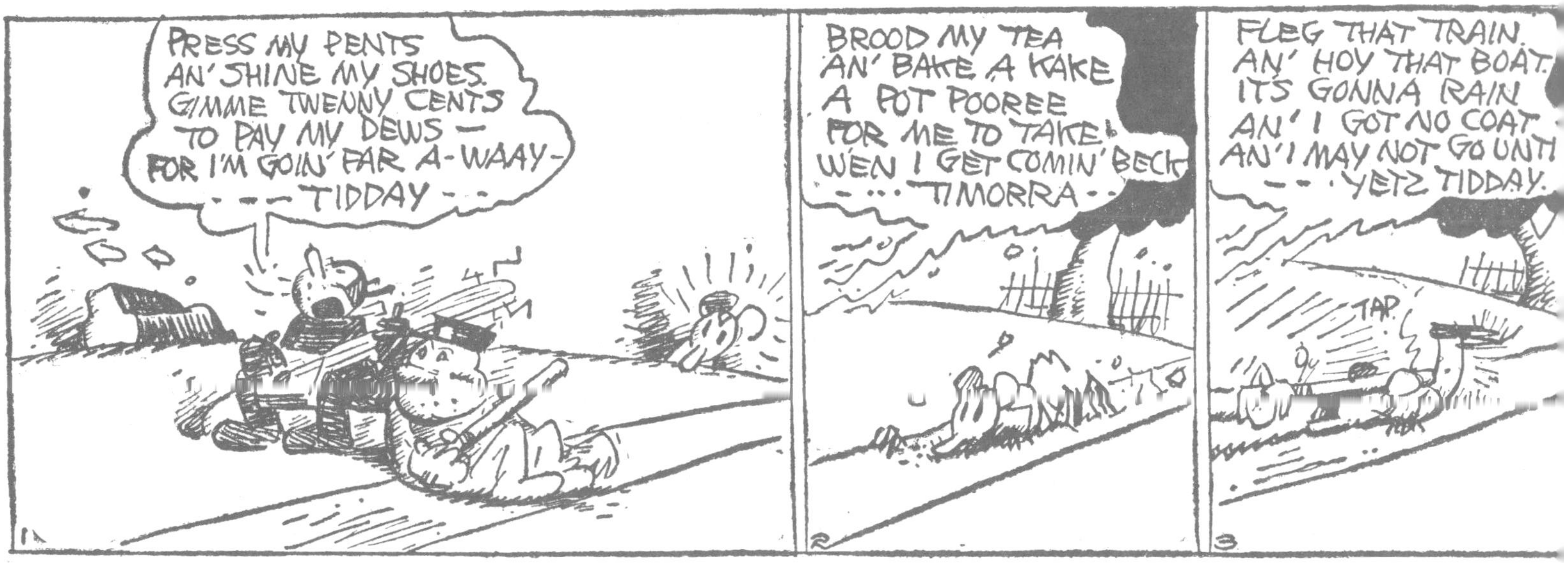
PRESS MY PENTS AN' SHINE MY SHOES. GIMME TWENNY CENTS TO PAY MY DEWS — FOR I'M GOIN' FAR A-WAAY- - - - TIDDAY - - -
BROOD MY TEA AN' BAKE A KAKE A POT POOREE FOR ME TO TAKE! WEN I GET COMIN' BECK - ... TIMORRA - -
FLEG THAT TRAIN. AN' HOY THAT BOAT. IT'S GONNA RAIN AN' I GOT NO COAT AN' I MAY NOT GO UNTI - - YETZ TIDDAY.
TAP

usually doesn't make words up, however much he might twist them around. Rather, Herriman had a great ear for speech, for the endless mutations and variations of language as garbled by the human tongue. Herriman's language was not something he invented in his head; it can be traced back to the world he lived in.

The America Herriman grew up in was much more oral than anything we're used to. For us, music is something that comes out of a c.d. player or an iPod. In Herriman's world, people could break out into song all over the place: at parties, at picnics, and in church. All the characters in *Krazy Kat* are tuneful, especially the eponymous heroine. These songs come from all sorts of genres, ranging from traditional hymns (such as Krazy's familiar refrain that "there is a heppy land, fur, fur a-wa-ay") to frontier anthems ("home on the range" gets a workout on July 26, 1942) to bluesy lamentations (when Krazy sings "Press my pents an' shine my shoes" on July 22, 1935). Herriman also brings in songs from other languages. On July 29, 1941 we hear Ignatz sing to himself "Adios, Chaparrita Chula." These words (which could be translated to mean "goodbye insolent darling") are taken from the traditional Mexican lover's lament "Adios, Mariquita Linda."

In the early 20th century, listening to long speeches was a common experience, whether in the form of uplifting sermons or smooth-flowing lectures by professional elocutionists. Our ancestors had more patience than we do and were more attuned to the rhythm of long talks. The preferred mode of oratory was orotund, ornate, and elevated, as in the speeches of William Jennings Bryan or Woodrow Wilson. In the workplace, all sorts of trades depended upon a glib and copious tongue, whether it be the sing-song patter of carnival barkers (a profession Herriman took up in his wayward youth), the attention grabbing shouts of street urchins hawking newspapers, the hyperbole-laden hyperventilization of sports announcers, or the oily and ingratiating words of a travelling salesman. This sort of exhibitionist speechifying is a recurring feature of *Krazy Kat*, as seen in strips showing a politican trumpeting the importance of trumpets (November 8, 1942) or a boxing announcer excitedly describing a battle between a mouse and a brick (August 3, 1941).

The sonorous cadences of the King James translation of the Bible are a constant resource for Herriman. Whatever his religious beliefs may have been (a topic we'll take up in another essay), Herriman liked to evoke the heightened tone of Biblical phrase-making. Listen to Officer Pupp as he gives a high-minded warning to Ignatz: "Whither you go, 'Mouse', there do I also go. That I do for the good of the law. And if my eyes offend you, I bid you bind them, seal them" (April 20, 1941).

Here we have two starkly opposite biblical passages merged into one. Pupp starts by evoking Ruth's beautiful words to Naomi: "For whither thou goest, I will go; and where thou lodgest, I will lodge: thy people shall be my people, and thy God my God" (Ruth 1:16). But of course Ruth's words were ones of devotion and duty, whereas Pupp speaks as an officer of the law, merciless in pursuit of the miscreant mouse. The passage also calls to mind Jesus' stark warning against a lustful heart: "And if thine eye offend thee, pluck it out" (Mark 9:47).

Krazy Kat

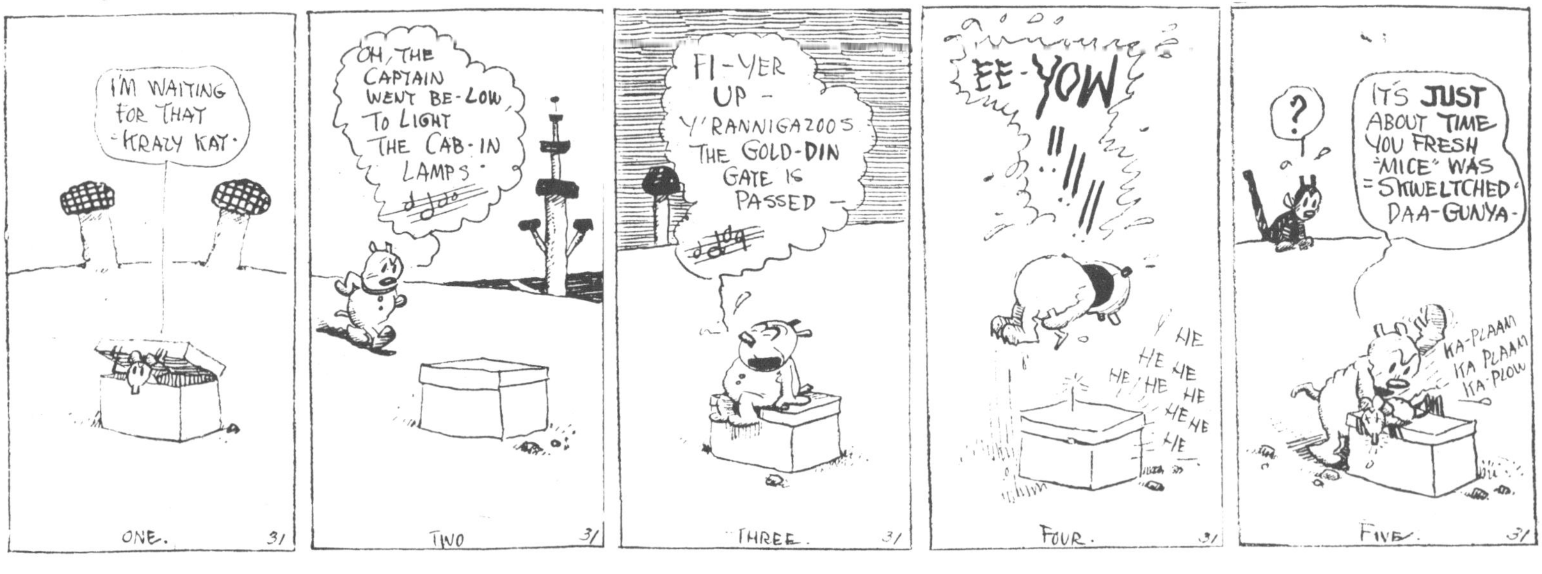
I'M WAITING FOR THAT KRAZY KAT
ONE.
OH, THE CAPTAIN WENT BE-LOW TO LIGHT THE CAB-IN LAMPS
TWO
FI-YER UP - Y'RANNIGAZOO'S THE GOLD-DIN GATE IS PASSED —
THREE.
EE-YOW
HE HE HE HE HE HE HE HE
FOUR.
?
IT'S JUST ABOUT TIME YOU FRESH "MICE" WAS =SKWELTCHED= DAA-GUNYA-
KA-PLAAM KA-PLAAM KA-PLOW
FIVE.

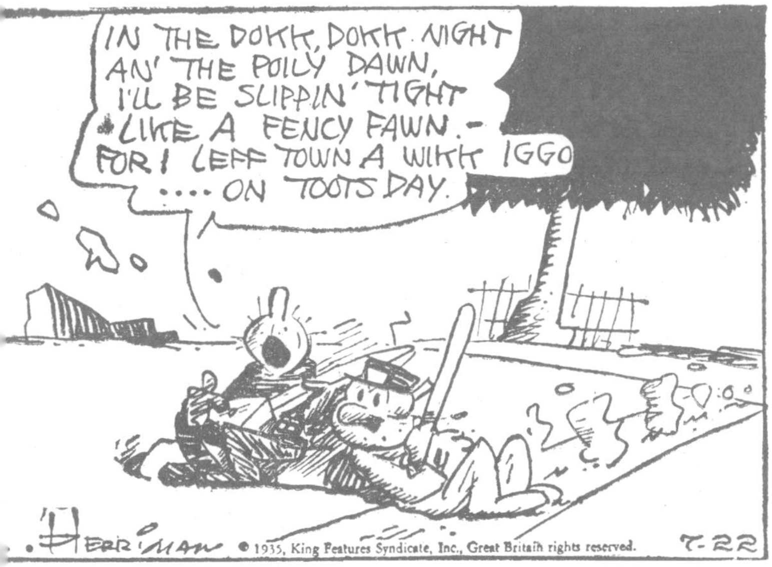
IN THE DOKK, DOKK NIGHT AN' THE POILY DAWN, I'LL BE SLIPPIN' TIGHT LIKE A FENCY FAWN.- FOR I LEFF TOWN A WIKK IGGO .... ON TOOTS DAY.
HERRIMAN
© 1935, King Features Syndicate, Inc., Great Britain rights reserved.
7-22

Again, as with the Ruth's words, the original passage is subtly inverted: the harsh Gospel command of eye-plucking is softened into covering the eyes with cloth. The inward command of self-discipline is turned into a comic outward display.

Poetry was also a source of inspiration for parody. Herriman lived in a time when poetry reading was still a public activity rather than a private hobby. Memorizing and reciting poetry was a part of the education, and many students carried scraps of half-remembered verse into their adulthood. Newspapers in Herriman's time still printed occasional poems sent in by readers.

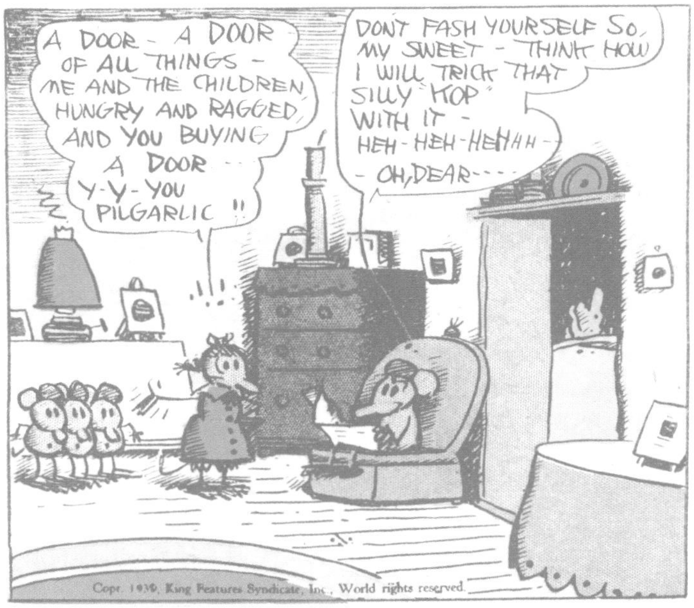
A DOOR - A DOOR OF ALL THINGS - ME AND THE CHILDREN HUNGRY AND RAGGED, AND YOU BUYING A DOOR -- Y-Y-YOU PILGARLIC !!
DON'T FASH YOURSELF SO, MY SWEET - THINK HOW I WILL TRICK THAT SILLY KOP WITH IT - HEH-HEH-HEHAH - OH, DEAR
Copr. 1939, King Features Syndicate, Inc., World rights reserved.

That Herriman expected that some of his readers would be poetry readers can be seen in the episode of October 5, 1941. Here Officer Pupp says of himself that "Like Mr. Lochinvar 'Mousie', I come out of the west." This is an allusion to Canto 5, verse 313 of Sir Walter Scott's once-famous poem *Marmion* (1808): "O, young Lochinvar is come out of the west,/Through all the wide Border his steed was the best."

In another strip, Officer Pupp hears Krazy singing and asks "Who sings today, by the blue bean bush? Who croons the haunting lay?" (March 8th, 1942) This calls to mind William Wordsworth's classic poem *The Solitary Reaper* (1798), where the poet hears a peasant girl singing and asks:

Will no one tell me what she sings?
Perhaps the plaintive numbers flow
For old, unhappy, far-off things,
And battles long ago.
Or is it some more humble lay
Familiar matter of today?

Starting in the late 1930s, Herriman became increasingly attentive to scientific and medical terminology. In the strips reprinted in this book, we see Officer Pupp suffering from diplopia (January 5, 1941) and Ignatz coming down with the mumps (September 14, 1941). Like doctors, Herriman's characters love to use fancy, Latinate words to describe simple actions: nictating for winking (September 16, 1942). Changes in Herriman's health might have had an impact in making him more aware of medical terms. During these years he started to feel the effects of old age and had some major surgery.

The interest in science might also be due to the fact the real world Coconino County, where Herriman liked to vacation, was becoming a major site for geological research. In one *Krazy Kat* strip, a professor reconstructs fossil skeletons of an ancient cat from "the mires of the Miocene, from the silts of the Silurian, from the jungles of the Jurassic. (July 6th 1941). As with biblical language, Herriman is subtly subversive: undermining the gravity and seriousness of scientific discourse by putting it in the mouths of talking animals.

Aside from Krazy herself, all the animals in Coconino have faith in science and technology and they use it for their ends. Ignatz occasionally uses science to aid his brick-throwing, just as Officer Pupp tries to get technology to ease the act of mouse-catching. Joe Stork now delivers babies with a plane and a robot perambulator — called the "perobotambulator" (August 24, 1941). Colin Kelly starts using mass production techniques to make bricks on a big scale (September 27, 1942).

What's striking about Herriman's language is how precise it often is. Completely made up words like "rannigazoos" are rare. Rather, Herriman often adheres with nearly dictionary exactness to the specific meaning of words, albeit unfamiliar and arcane terms. Once, when Officer Pupp is chatting with Mrs. Kwakk Wakk, he says in exasperation, "Have done with gammer, woman" (June 22, 1941). The verb "gam" is old whaler jargon for a friendly or inconsequential conversation. Herriman, as was often his wont, turned the verb into a noun, meaning that Pupp wanted Kwakk Wakk to be done with shilly-shallying and cut to the chase of the talk. On another occasion, Ignatz says to Krazy: "Don't fash yourself so, 'Kat'" (October 19, 1941). "Fash" is a Scottish term for vex or bother (possibly also related to the homonymous French word "fâcher," to anger). Herriman liked to be consistent in the diction he gave his characters, using words to define their personalities. Hence there are other occasions where Ignatz says "fash" and Pupp "gam" (January 15, 1939; August 3, 1941).

Words aren't stable, fixed things. They have shades of meaning and shifting connotations. Herriman was supremely alert to the slipperiness of language. Listen to how Ignatz tries to sweep aside Mrs. Kwakk Wakk: "Away, woman away with your gabble and gossip" (May 25, 1941). Gabble is the perfect word because it denotes both meaningless speech and the low jabber of a duck (which is of course Mrs. Kwakk Wakk's species).

In one Sunday strip, Ignatz tries to write a poem, but is frustrated by his inability to come up with words that rhyme with brick. "Foowy," the mouse complains. "Where'd I get the idea I'm a poet? Fuwi." (March 15, 1942) Ignatz might not have been a poet but his creator certainly was. Herriman had a poet's ear for linguistic diversity, a poet's sensitivity to diction, a poet's feel for rhythm, and not least, a poet's ability to have fun with words. More than any other cartoonist, Herriman can be enjoyed for his words, which he took from every available source in the world around him.

Clockwise, from upper left: A *Krazy Kat* daily from July 22nd, 1935, a panel from the January 15th, 1939 Sunday page, and another daily from March 31st, 1916.

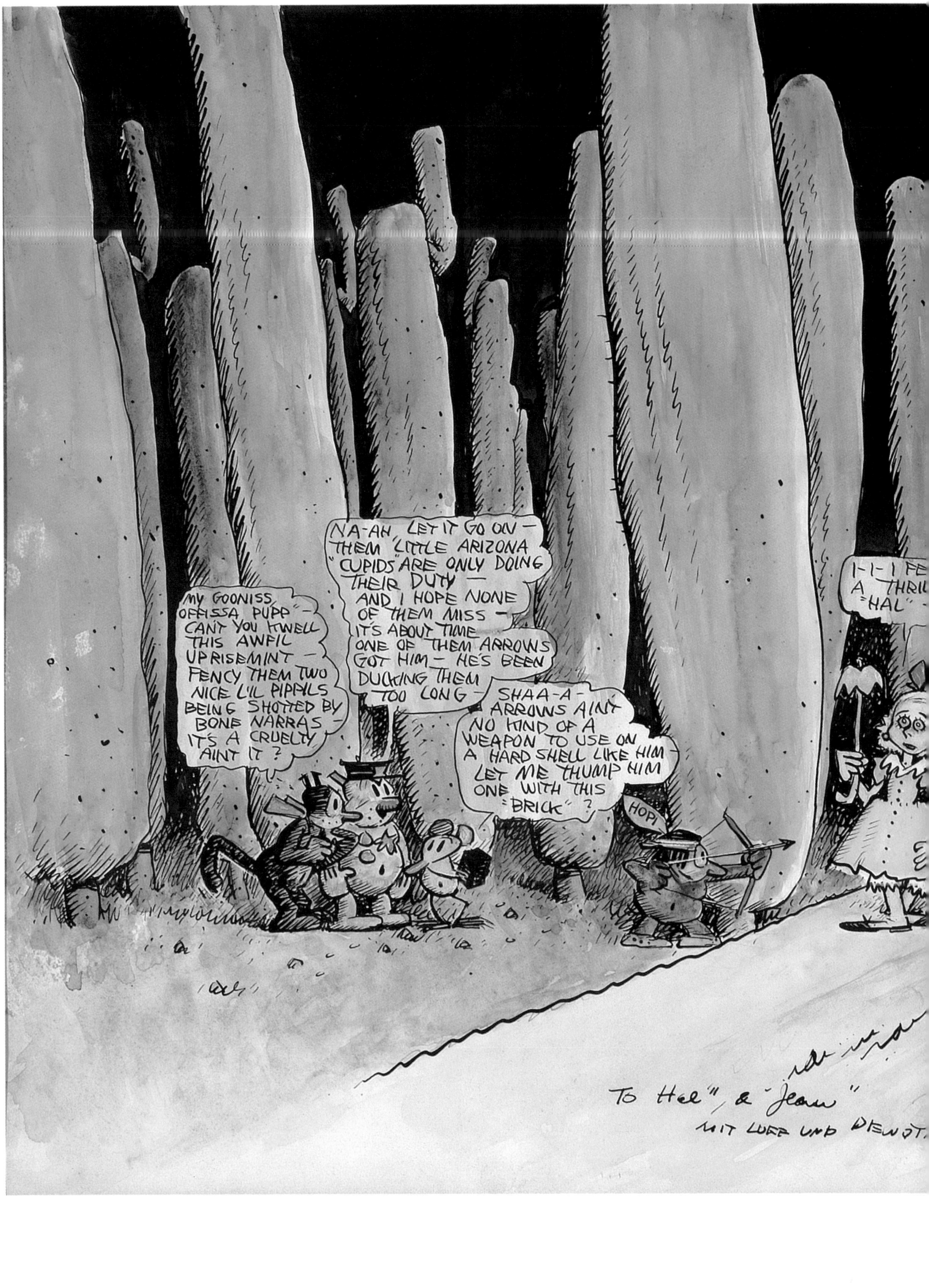
MY GOONISS, OFFISSA PUPP – CAN'T YOU KWELL THIS AWFIL UPRISEMINT – FENCY THEM TWO NICE L'IL PIPPILS BEING SHOTTED BY BONE NARRAS – IT'S A CRUELTY AINT IT ?
NA-AH LET IT GO ON – THEM "LITTLE ARIZONA "CUPIDS" ARE ONLY DOING THEIR DUTY – AND I HOPE NONE OF THEM MISS – IT'S ABOUT TIME ONE OF THEM ARROWS GOT HIM – HE'S BEEN DUCKING THEM TOO LONG –
SHAA-A – ARROWS AINT NO KIND OF A WEAPON TO USE ON A HARD SHELL LIKE HIM – LET ME THUMP HIM ONE WITH THIS "BRICK" ?
HOPI
I-I-I FE
A THRIL
"HAL"
To "Hal" & "Jean"
MIT LUFF UND DEWOT.

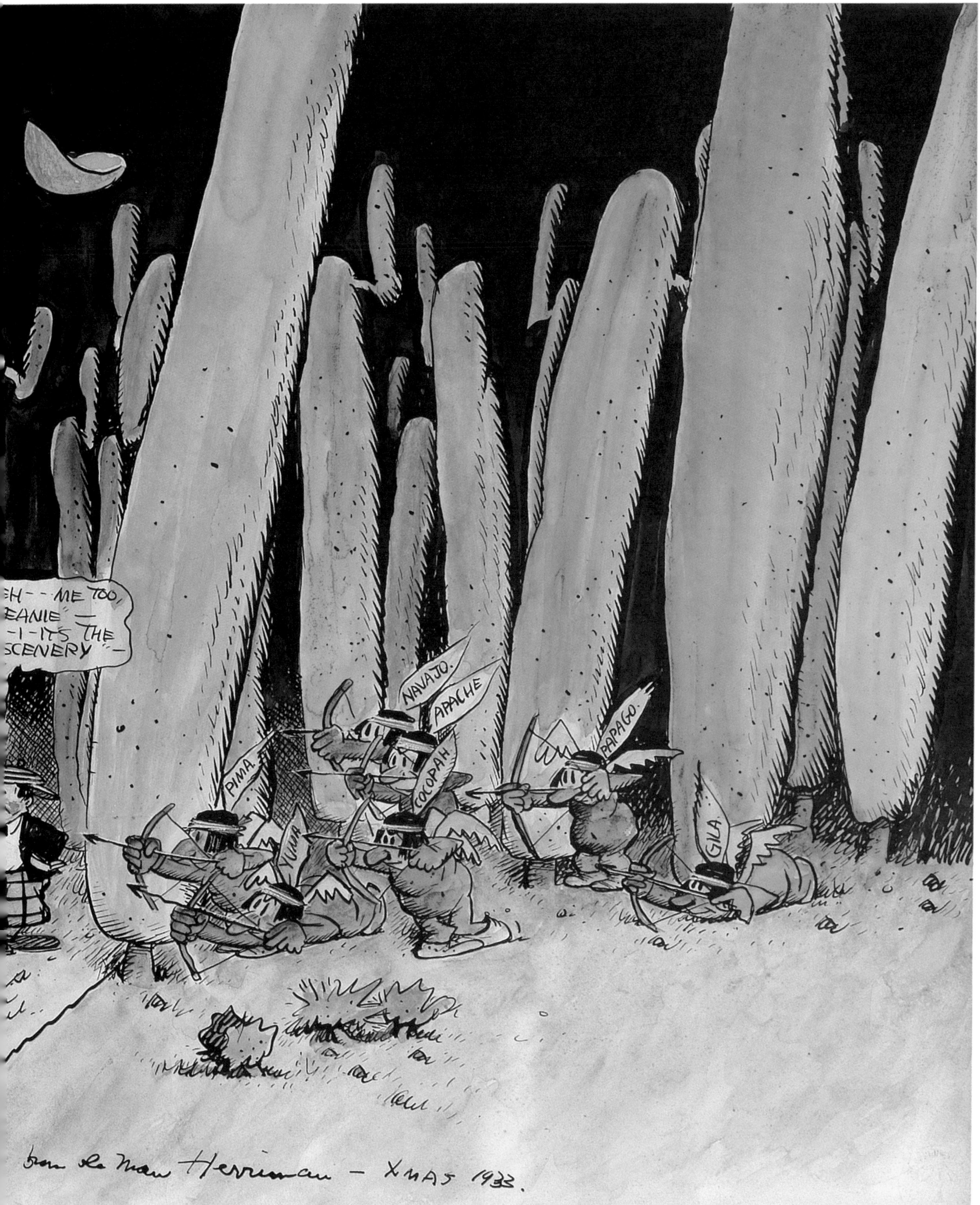
H-- ME TOO,
EANIE —
-I-IT'S THE
SCENERY
NAVAJO.
APACHE
PAPAGO.
PIMA.
COCOPAH
YUMA
GILA
Herriman – XMAS 1933.

This presentation piece was done in 1933 as a gift to Jean Harlow and Hal Roach, but when she and Roach broke up, Harlow passed it on to her maid, who then sold it to an art dealer, where it was eventually sold to collector John Fawcett. Thus, many thanks to, and courtesy of, John Fawcett. The size of the original art is 22 1/4" x 13 1/2".

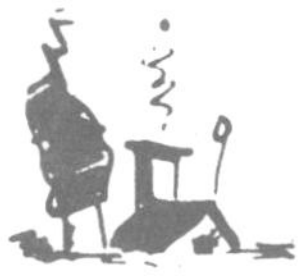

1941.

Readers, please note: an Ignatz "dingbat" placed below a strip indicates a relevant or related footnote at the volume's end for that particular selection, all to be found in the "Ignatz Debaffler" section.

DOUBLE "KATS" — A PRETTY SIGHT, BUT IT IS NT RIGHT.
KRAZY KAT
Registered U. S. Patent Office
DOUBLE ME -- THAT'S WRONG TOO.
DOUBLE "MICE," I'D LIKE TO ARREST THEM BOTH -- B-BUT -
DOUBLE "BRICKS" THAT SETTLES IT --- I'M A SICK "COP."
"DOC." "DOC." OH-H, "DOC."
WHAT IS IT, "DOC." ? - I-I-I MEAN, "DOCS" -
"DIPLOPIA" - DOUBLE VISION ---- I'LL FIX YOU UP.
DOUBLE "DOCS," DOUBLE FEES, BUT HE GOT ME SEEING SINGLE AGAIN
AH, THE RIGHT NUMBER OF "MOUSE" - THE RIGHT NUMBER OF "BRICK" - AND THE RIGHT NUMBER OF "KAT" "DIPLOPIA," I HAVE DEFEATED YOU.
ZIP
POW
"DIPLOPIA" - "OPTIC BOON" — A MOST PLEASANT AFFLICTION - AH-H-H ME.
?
JAIL
JAIL
Copr. 1941, King Features Syndicate, Inc., World rights reserved
HERRIMAN 1-5
TWO OF HIM HOW AWFUL -
TWO OF HIM - HOW HORRIBLE
TWO OF HIM - HOW NIZE.

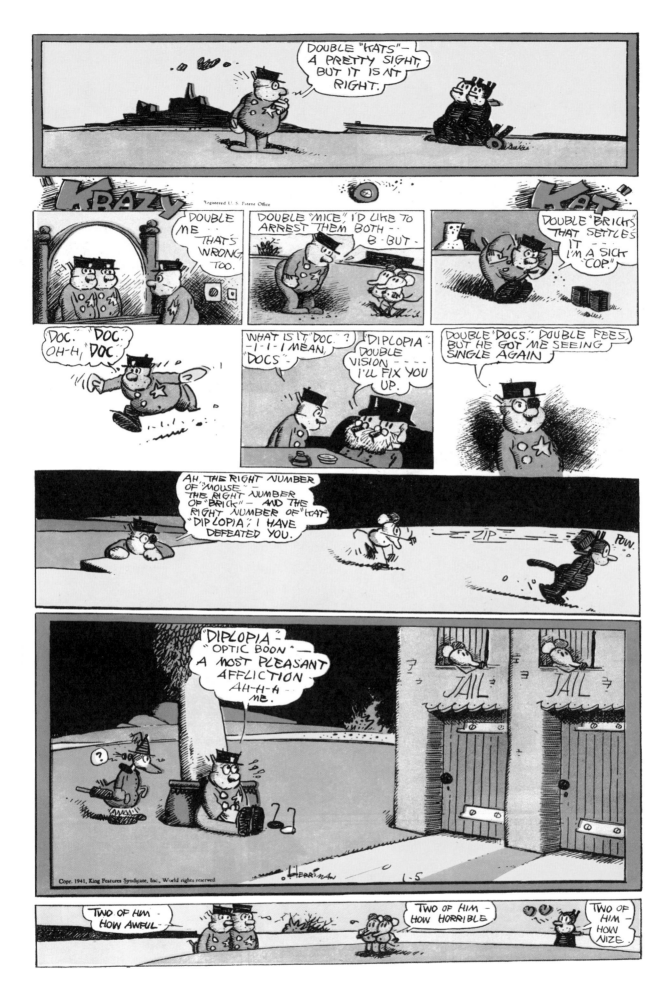

January 5th, 1941.

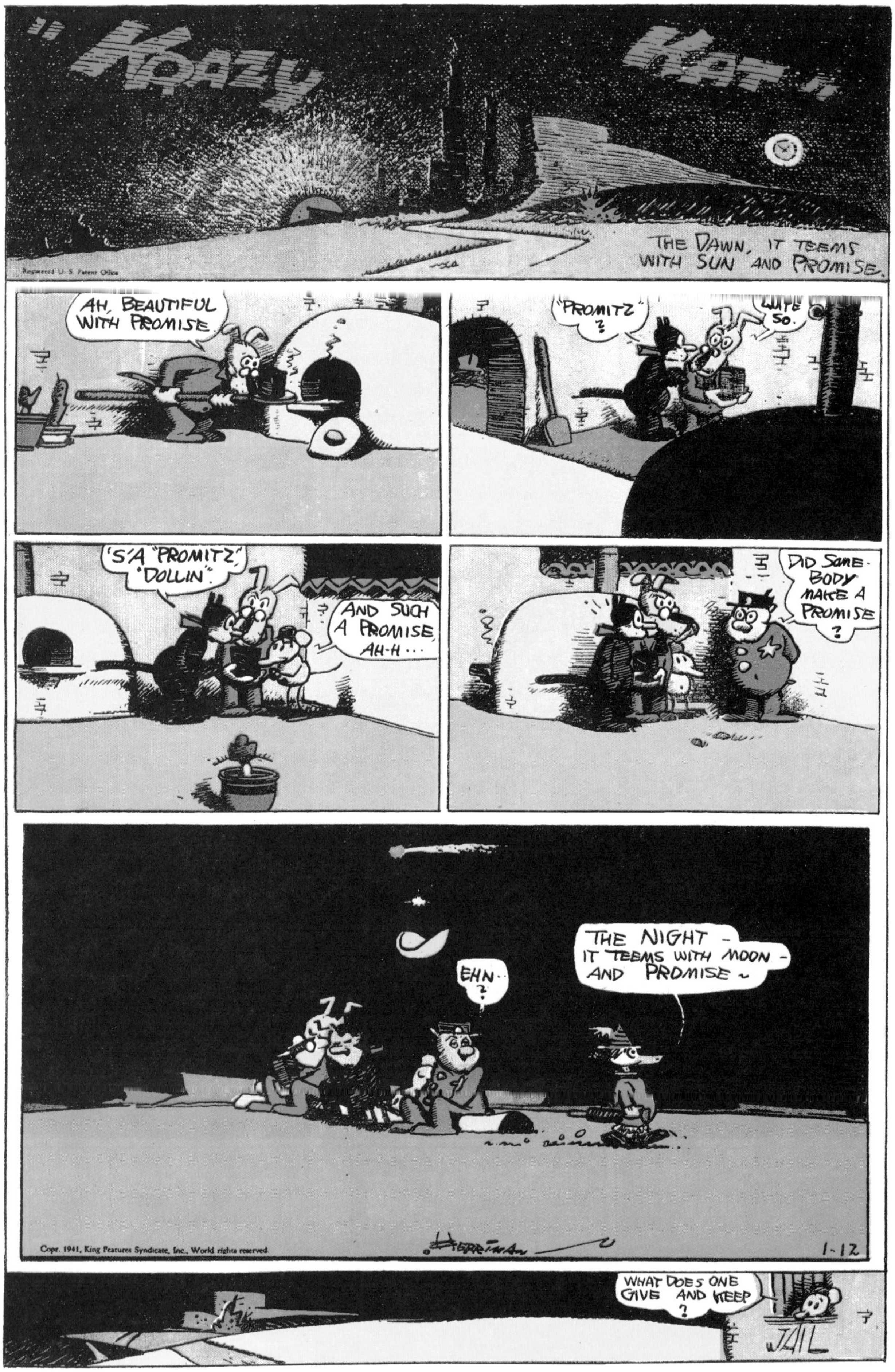
"Krazy Kat"
THE DAWN, IT TEEMS WITH SUN AND PROMISE.
AH, BEAUTIFUL WITH PROMISE
"PROMITZ" ?
QUITE SO.
'S'A "PROMITZ" "DOLLIN".
AND SUCH A PROMISE AH-H...
DID SOME-BODY MAKE A PROMISE ?
EHN ?
THE NIGHT - IT TEEMS WITH MOON - AND PROMISE ~
Copr. 1941, King Features Syndicate, Inc., World rights reserved.
1-12
WHAT DOES ONE GIVE AND KEEP ?
JAIL

January 12th, 1941.

"MOUSE" - BUCKET - HASTE - ADVENTURE
KRAZY KAT
Registered U. S. Patent Office
ADDED ATTRACTION - "HOP" -
"HELLY" IT IS I - YOU KNOW ME
TOSS OVER A DIME -
RAP RAP RAP
LOOK OUT FOR L'IL FINNERS, IT'S HOT
I - I -
I - I - I.
GOT IT.
TO TELL THE TRUE, OFFISSA "PUPP" I'M LOOKIN FOR A "EDWENTURE"
OOH, GOODY - RIGHT OVER BY THE BLUE BEAN "BUSH" YOU'LL FIND A "MOUSE" - HAVING ONE WITH AN EMPTY BUCKET
Y - YEH - H -
Copr 1941, King Features Syndicate, Inc., World rights reserved
HERRIMAN
1-19

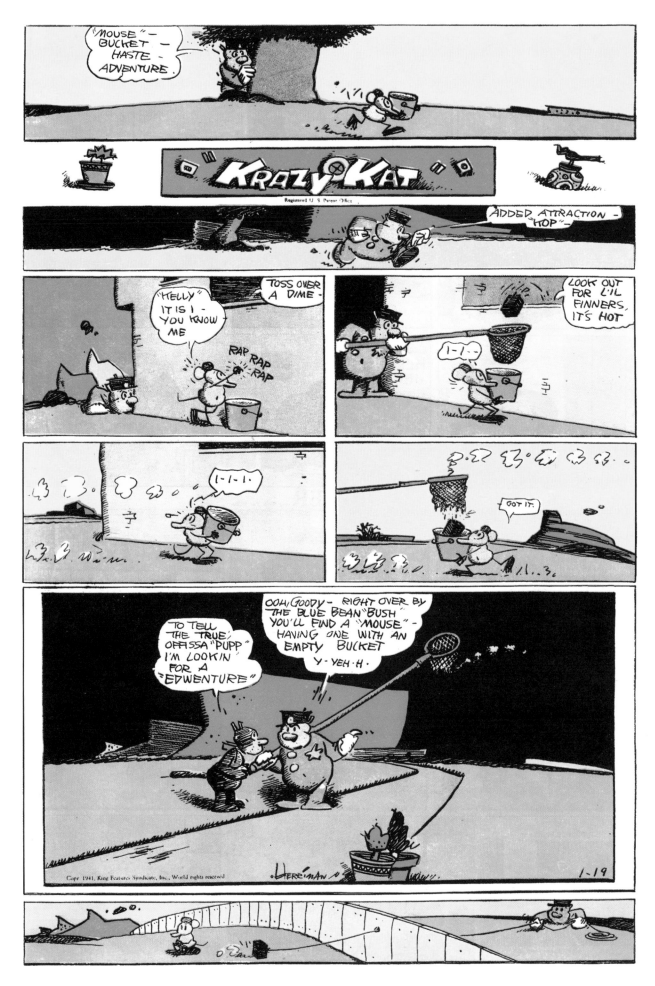

January 19th, 1941.

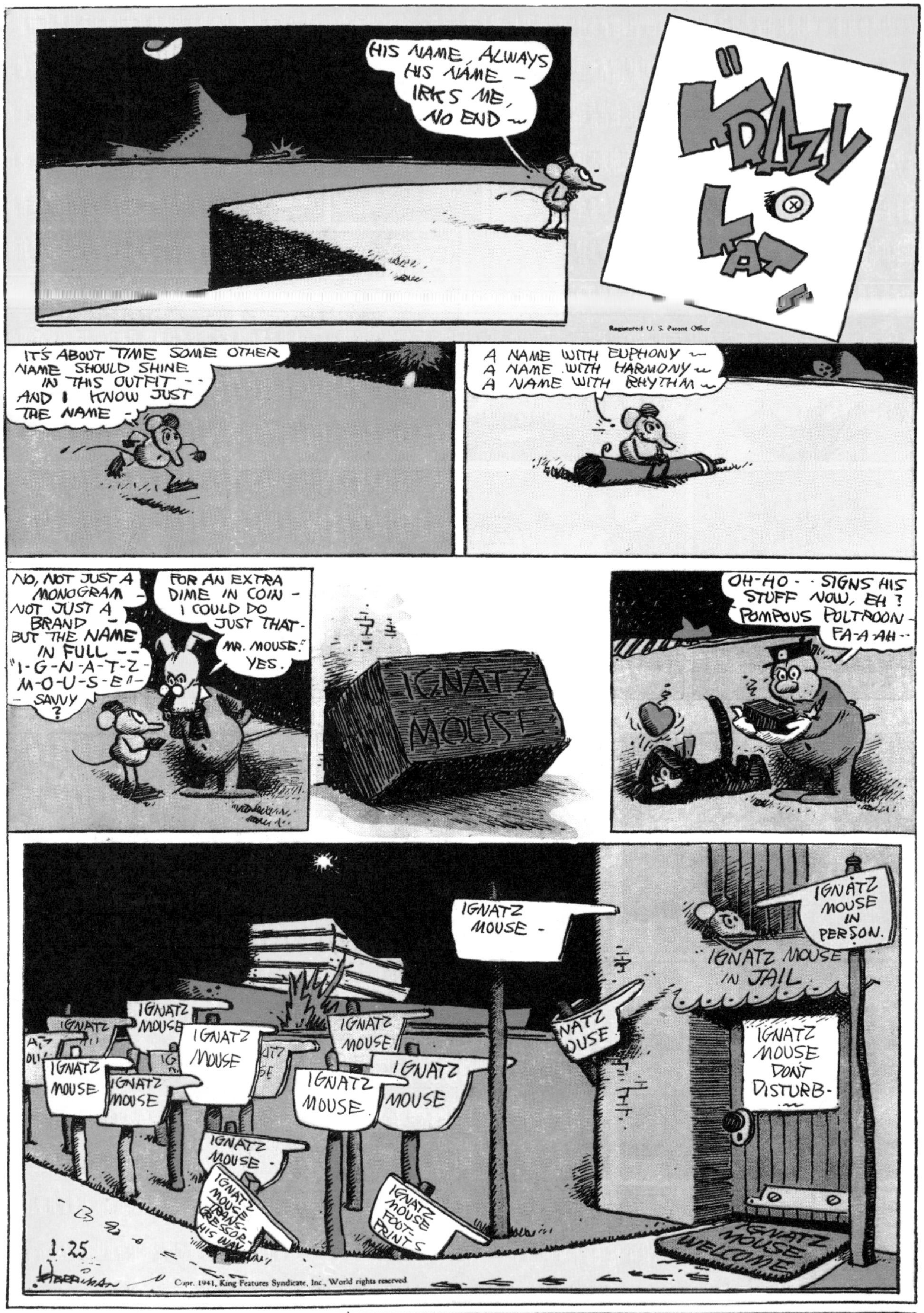
HIS NAME, ALWAYS HIS NAME - IRKS ME, NO END ~
"KRAZY KAT"
Registered U. S. Patent Office
IT'S ABOUT TIME SOME OTHER NAME SHOULD SHINE IN THIS OUTFIT -- AND I KNOW JUST THE NAME -
A NAME WITH EUPHONY ~ A NAME WITH HARMONY ~ A NAME WITH RHYTHM ~
NO, NOT JUST A MONOGRAM - NOT JUST A BRAND - BUT THE NAME IN FULL -- "I-G-N-A-T-Z M-O-U-S-E" - SAVVY ?
FOR AN EXTRA DIME IN COIN - I COULD DO JUST THAT -
MR. MOUSE! YES.
IGNATZ MOUSE
OH-HO - SIGNS HIS STUFF NOW, EH? POMPOUS POLTROON - FA-A-AH --
IGNATZ MOUSE -
IGNATZ MOUSE IN PERSON.
IGNATZ MOUSE IN JAIL
IGNATZ MOUSE DON'T DISTURB -
IGNATZ MOUSE
IGNATZ MOUSE TRANS-GRESSOR HIS WAY
IGNATZ MOUSE FOOT-PRINTS
IGNATZ MOUSE WELCOME
1.25
Copr. 1941, King Features Syndicate, Inc., World rights reserved
OLD SUPER KOP
OFFICER B. "PUPP"

January 25th, 1941.

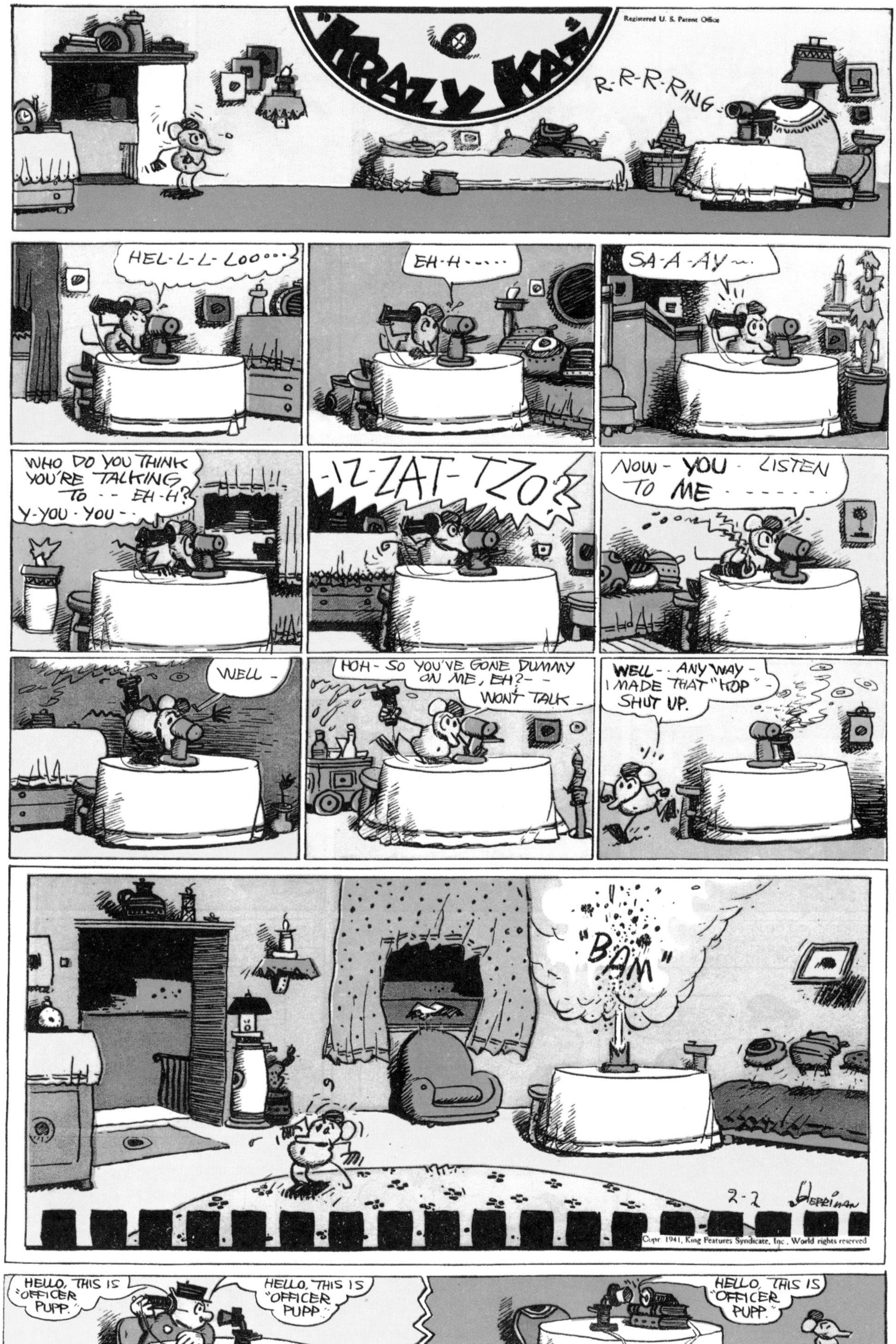
"KRAZY KAT"
Registered U. S. Patent Office
R-R-R-RING-
HEL-L-L-LOO···
EH-H-----
SA-A-AY—
WHO DO YOU THINK YOU'RE TALKING TO -- EH-H? Y-YOU - YOU --
-IZ-ZAT-TZO?
NOW - YOU - LISTEN TO ME ------
WELL -
HOH- SO YOU'VE GONE DUMMY ON ME, EH?- -
WON'T TALK -
WELL-- ANY WAY- I MADE THAT "HOP" SHUT UP.
"BAM"
2-2
Herriman
Copr. 1941, King Features Syndicate, Inc., World rights reserved
HELLO, THIS IS "OFFICER PUPP."
HELLO, THIS IS "OFFICER PUPP."
HELLO, THIS IS "OFFICER PUPP."

February 2nd, 1941.

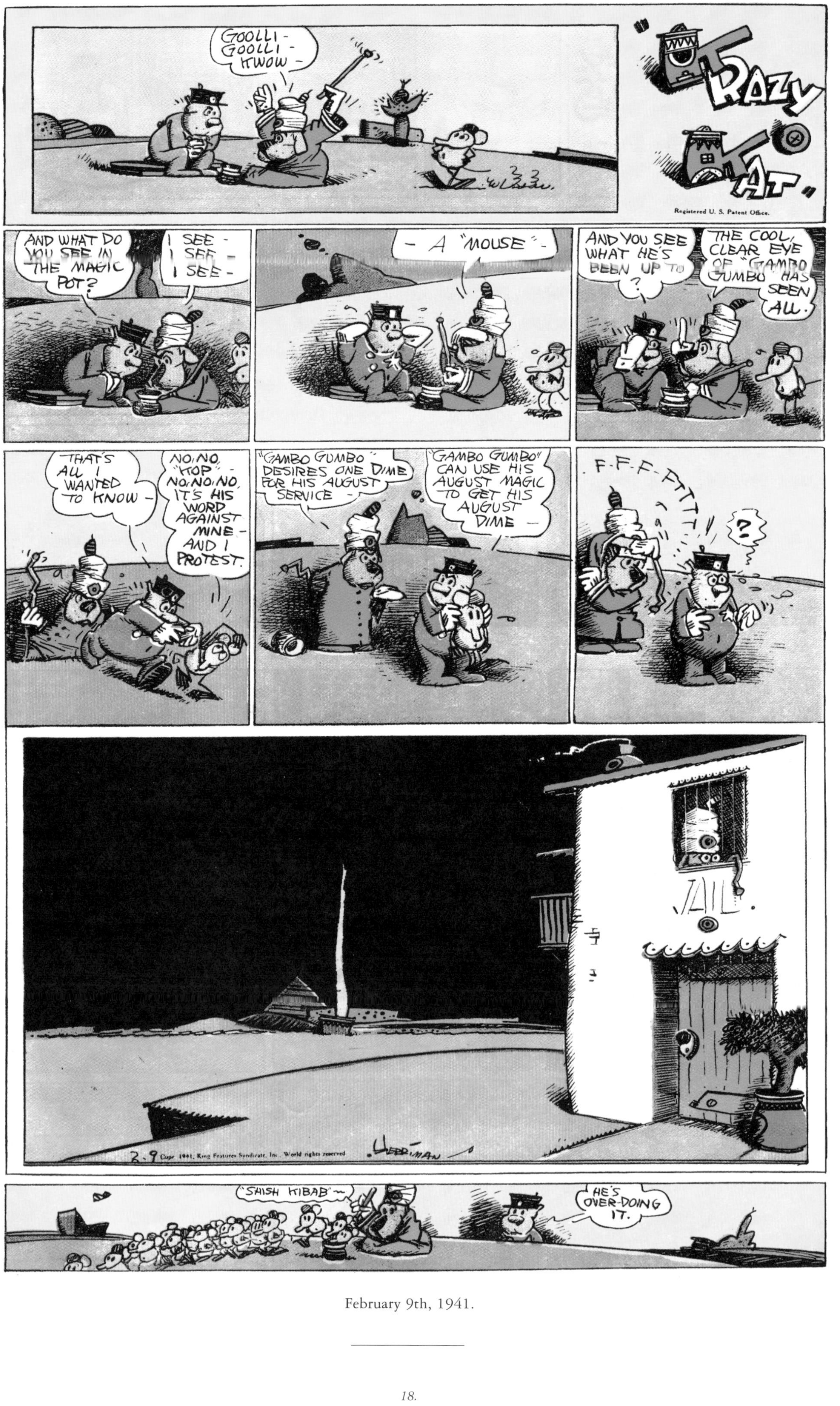
"KRAZY KAT"
Registered U. S. Patent Office.
GOOLLI - GOOLLI - KNOW -
AND WHAT DO YOU SEE IN THE MAGIC POT?
I SEE - I SEE - I SEE -
- A "MOUSE" -
AND YOU SEE WHAT HE'S BEEN UP TO ?
THE COOL, CLEAR EYE OF "GAMBO GUMBO" HAS SEEN ALL.
THAT'S ALL I WANTED TO KNOW -
NO, NO, "KOP" - NO, NO, NO, NO, IT'S HIS WORD AGAINST MINE - AND I PROTEST.
"GAMBO GUMBO" DESIRES ONE DIME FOR HIS AUGUST SERVICE -
"GAMBO GUMBO" CAN USE HIS AUGUST MAGIC TO GET HIS AUGUST DIME -
F-F-F-FTTTTT
?
JAIL.
2-9 Copr 1941, King Features Syndicate, Inc., World rights reserved
HERRIMAN
"SHISH KIBAB" ~
HE'S OVER-DOING IT.

February 9th, 1941.

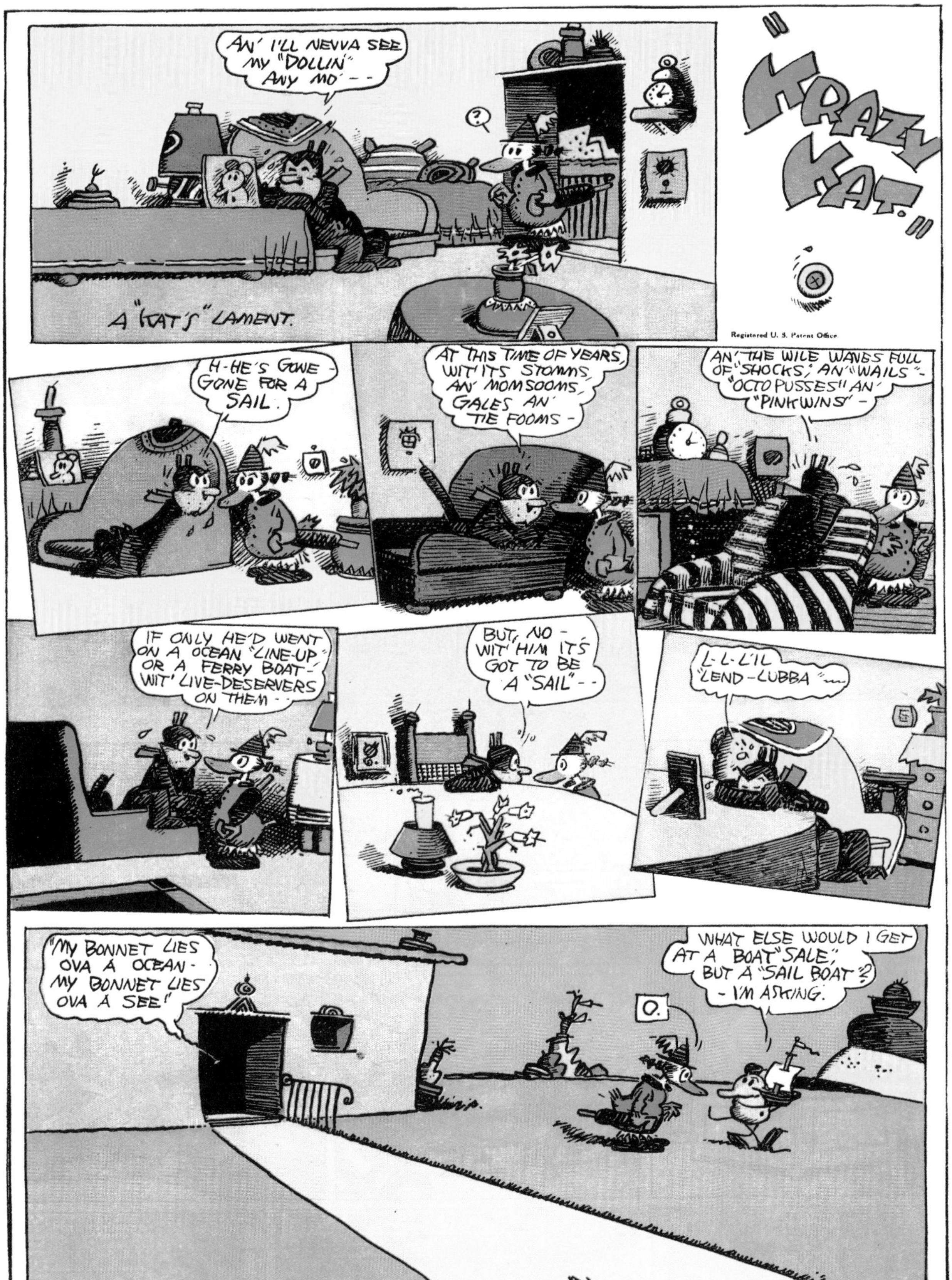
"KRAZY KAT."
Registered U. S. Patent Office.
AN' I'LL NEVVA SEE MY "DOLLIN" ANY MO' - -
?
A "KAT'S" LAMENT.
H-HE'S GONE - GONE FOR A SAIL.
AT THIS TIME OF YEARS, WIT ITS STOMMS, AN' MOMSOOMS, GALES AN' TIE FOOMS -
AN' THE WILE WAVES FULL OF "SHOCKS," AN' "WAILS" - "OCTOPUSSES" AN' "PINKWINS" -
IF ONLY HE'D WENT ON A OCEAN "LINE-UP" OR A FERRY BOAT - WIT' LIVE-DESERVERS ON THEM - -
BUT, NO - WIT' HIM IT'S GOT TO BE A "SAIL" - -
L-L-L'IL "LEND-LUBBA" ....
"MY BONNET LIES OVA A OCEAN - MY BONNET LIES OVA A SEE!"
O.
WHAT ELSE WOULD I GET AT A "BOAT SALE," BUT A "SAIL BOAT"? - I'M ASKING.
Copr. 1941, King Features Syndicate, Inc., World rights reserved.
2-16
HERRIMAN

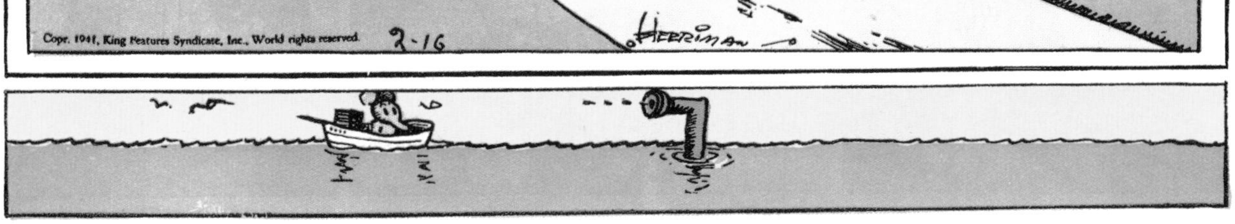

February 16th, 1941.

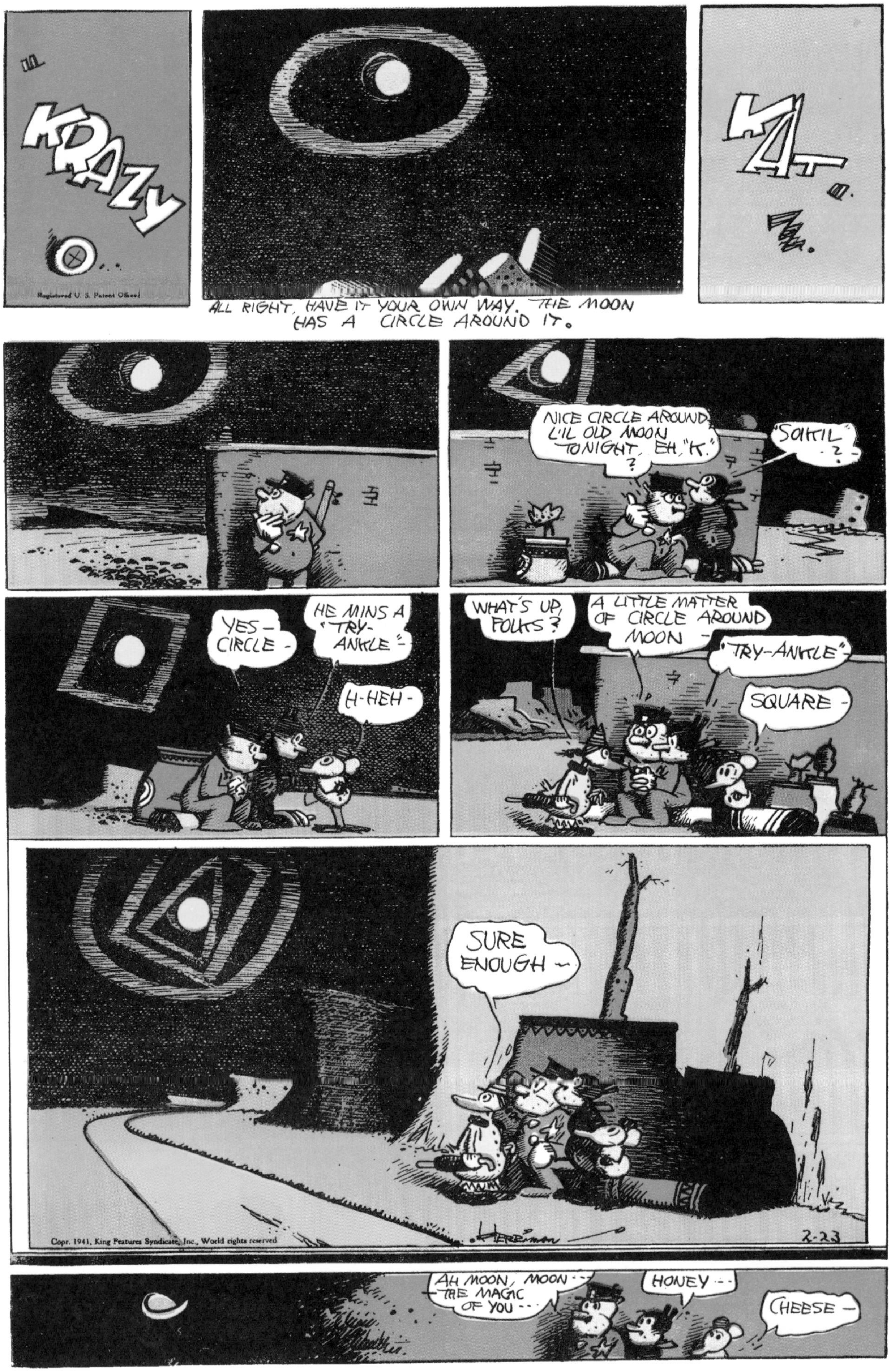
KRAZY
KAT
Registered U. S. Patent Office
ALL RIGHT, HAVE IT YOUR OWN WAY. THE MOON HAS A CIRCLE AROUND IT.
NICE CIRCLE AROUND L'IL OLD MOON TONIGHT, EH, "K."?
"SOIRTIL"
YES—CIRCLE—
HE MINS A "TRY-ANKLE"
H-HEH-
WHAT'S UP, FOLKS?
A LITTLE MATTER OF CIRCLE AROUND MOON—
"TRY-ANKLE"
SQUARE—
SURE ENOUGH—
Copr. 1941, King Features Syndicate, Inc., World rights reserved
Herriman
2-23
AH MOON, MOON— THE MAGIC OF YOU—
HONEY—
CHEESE—

February 23rd, 1941.

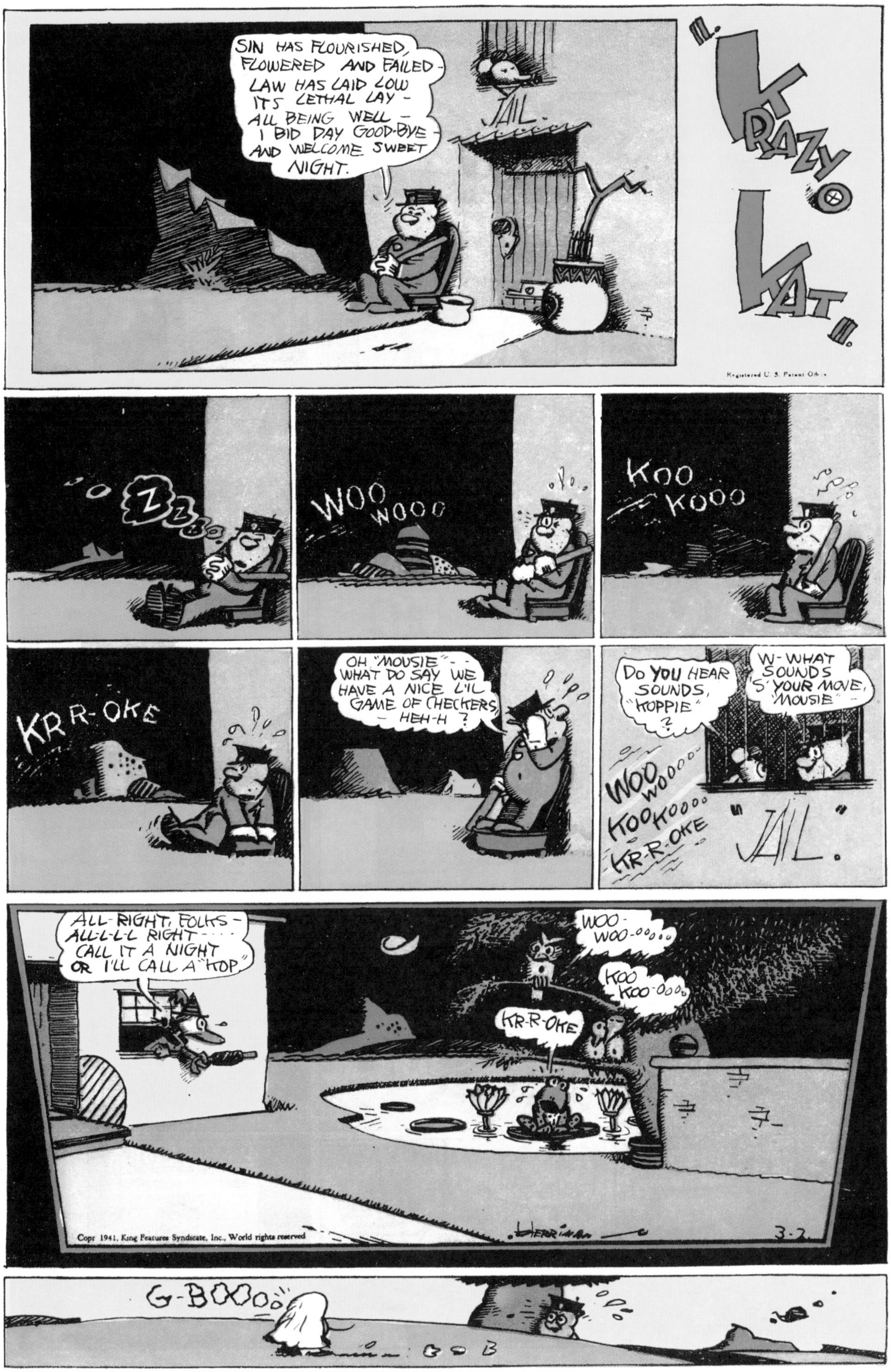
SIN HAS FLOURISHED, FLOWERED AND FAILED - LAW HAS LAID LOW ITS LETHAL LAY - ALL BEING WELL - I BID DAY GOOD-BYE AND WELCOME SWEET NIGHT.
JAIL.
"KRAZY KAT"
Registered U. S. Patent Office
WOO WOOO
KOO KOOO
KR R-OKE
OH "MOUSIE" - WHAT DO SAY WE HAVE A NICE L'IL GAME OF CHECKERS, - HEH-H ?
DO YOU HEAR SOUNDS, "KOPPIE" ?
W-WHAT SOUNDS S' YOUR MOVE, "MOUSIE"
WOO WOOOO KOO KOOOO KR-R-OKE
"JAIL."
ALL-RIGHT, FOLKS - ALL-L-L-L RIGHT - - - CALL IT A NIGHT OR I'LL CALL A "KOP"
WOO-WOO-OOOOO
KOO KOO-OOOO
KR-R-OKE
Copr 1941, King Features Syndicate, Inc., World rights reserved
Herriman
3-2.
G-BOOOO
G O B

March 2nd, 1941.

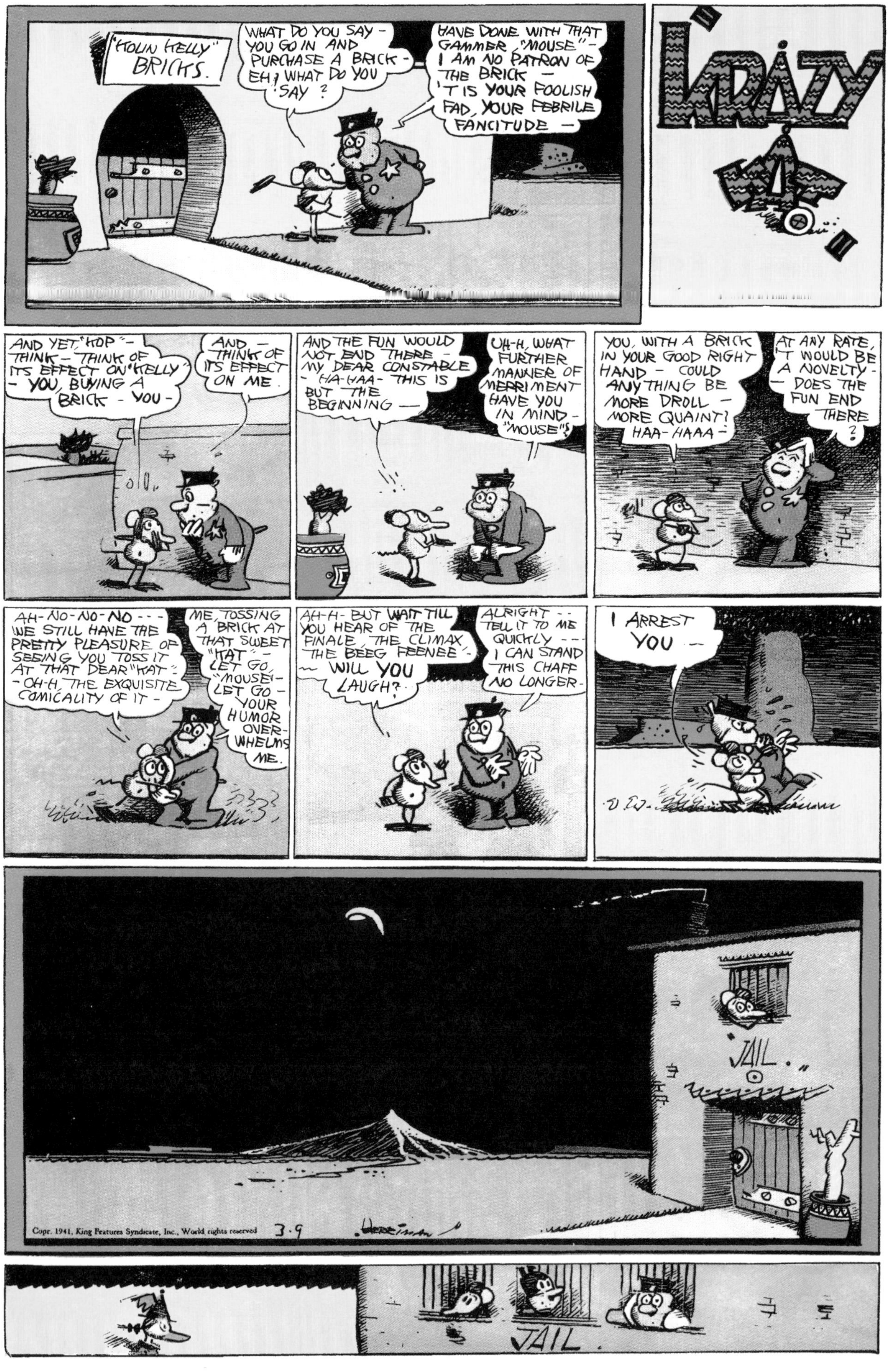
"KOLIN KELLY" BRICKS.
WHAT DO YOU SAY - YOU GO IN AND PURCHASE A BRICK - EH; WHAT DO YOU SAY ?
HAVE DONE WITH THAT GAMMER, "MOUSE" - I AM NO PATRON OF THE BRICK - 'T IS YOUR FOOLISH FAD, YOUR FEBRILE FANCITUDE -
KRAZY
KAT
AND YET, "KOP" - THINK - THINK OF ITS EFFECT ON "KELLY" - YOU, BUYING A BRICK - YOU -
AND - THINK OF ITS EFFECT ON ME.
AND THE FUN WOULD NOT END THERE - MY DEAR CONSTABLE - HA-HAA - THIS IS BUT THE BEGINNING —
UH-H, WHAT FURTHER MANNER OF MERRIMENT HAVE YOU IN MIND - "MOUSE"?
YOU, WITH A BRICK IN YOUR GOOD RIGHT HAND - COULD ANYTHING BE MORE DROLL - MORE QUAINT? HAA-HAAA -
AT ANY RATE, 'T WOULD BE A NOVELTY - DOES THE FUN END THERE ?
AH-NO-NO-NO - - - WE STILL HAVE THE PRETTY PLEASURE OF SEEING YOU TOSS IT AT THAT DEAR "KAT" - - OH-H, THE EXQUISITE COMICALITY OF IT -
ME, TOSSING A BRICK AT THAT SWEET "KAT" - LET GO, "MOUSE" - LET GO - YOUR HUMOR OVER-WHELMS ME.
AH-H- BUT WAIT TILL YOU HEAR OF THE FINALE, THE CLIMAX, THE BEEG FEENEE - WILL YOU LAUGH?
ALRIGHT - - TELL IT TO ME QUICKLY - - - I CAN STAND THIS CHAFF NO LONGER -
I ARREST YOU -
JAIL
Copr. 1941, King Features Syndicate, Inc., World rights reserved
3-9
Herriman
JAIL

March 9th, 1941.

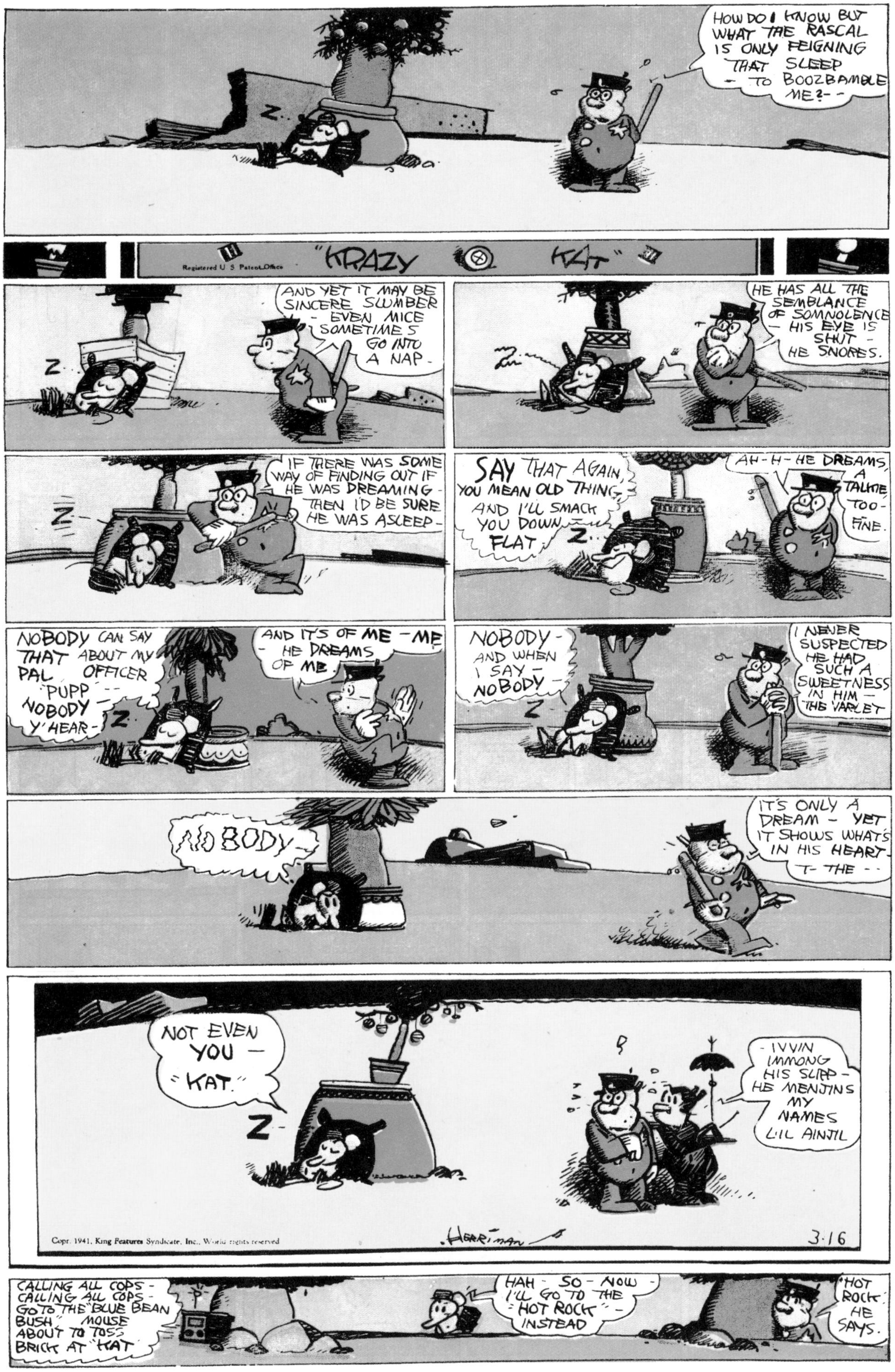
HOW DO I KNOW BUT WHAT THE RASCAL IS ONLY FEIGNING THAT SLEEP - TO BOOZBAMBLE ME?--
"KRAZY KAT"
Registered U.S. Patent Office
Z
AND YET IT MAY BE SINCERE SLUMBER - EVEN MICE SOMETIMES GO INTO A NAP-
HE HAS ALL THE SEMBLANCE OF SOMNOLENCE - HIS EYE IS SHUT - HE SNORES.
Z
IF THERE WAS SOME WAY OF FINDING OUT IF HE WAS DREAMING - THEN I'D BE SURE HE WAS ASLEEP-
SAY THAT AGAIN, YOU MEAN OLD THING, AND I'LL SMACK YOU DOWN FLAT
Z
AH-H- HE DREAMS, A TALKIE TOO- FINE.
NOBODY CAN SAY THAT ABOUT MY PAL OFFICER "PUPP"-- NOBODY - Y'HEAR-
Z
AND IT'S OF ME - ME HE DREAMS OF ME.
NOBODY - AND WHEN I SAY - NOBODY -
Z
I NEVER SUSPECTED HE HAD SUCH A SWEETNESS IN HIM - THE VARLET
NOBODY-
IT'S ONLY A DREAM - YET IT SHOWS WHAT'S IN HIS HEART - T- THE --
NOT EVEN YOU - "KAT."
Z
- IVVIN IMMONG HIS SLIPP - HE MENJINS MY NAMES LIL AINJIL
Copr. 1941, King Features Syndicate, Inc., World rights reserved
HERRIMAN
3·16
CALLING ALL COPS - CALLING ALL COPS - GO TO THE "BLUE BEAN BUSH" MOUSE ABOUT TO TOSS BRICK AT "KAT"
HAH - SO - NOW I'LL GO TO THE "HOT ROCK" - INSTEAD
"HOT ROCK" HE SAYS.

March 16th, 1941.

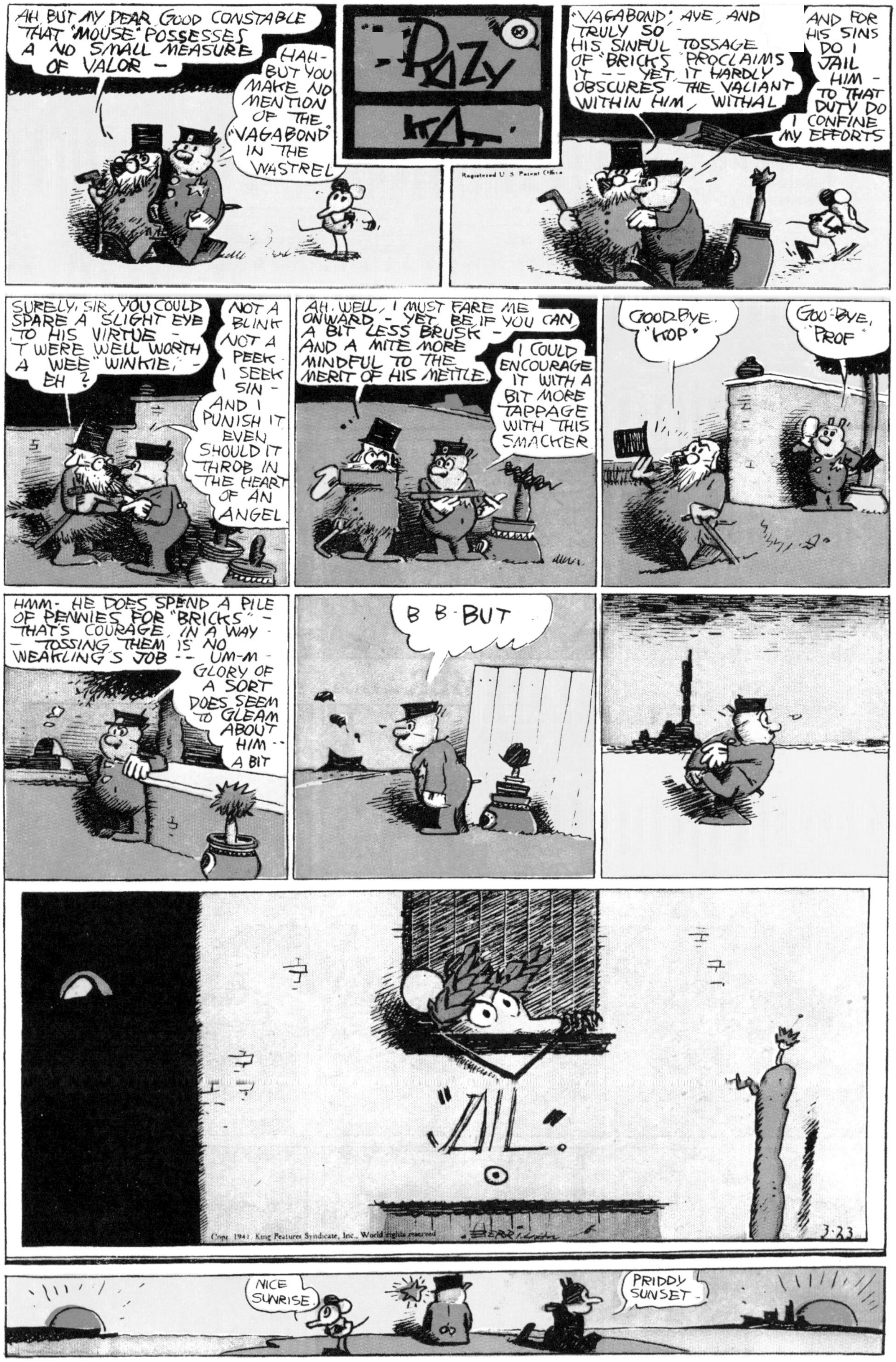
AH BUT MY DEAR GOOD CONSTABLE THAT "MOUSE" POSSESSES A NO SMALL MEASURE OF VALOR -
HAH - BUT YOU MAKE NO MENTION OF THE "VAGABOND" IN THE WASTREL
Registered U.S. Patent Office
"VAGABOND", AYE, AND TRULY SO - HIS SINFUL TOSSAGE OF "BRICKS" PROCLAIMS IT -- YET, IT HARDLY OBSCURES THE VALIANT WITHIN HIM, WITHAL
AND FOR HIS SINS DO I JAIL HIM - TO THAT DUTY DO I CONFINE MY EFFORTS
SURELY, SIR, YOU COULD SPARE A SLIGHT EYE TO HIS VIRTUE - 'T WERE WELL WORTH A WEE "WINKIE," - EH?
NOT A BLINK NOT A PEEK - I SEEK SIN - AND I PUNISH IT EVEN SHOULD IT THROB IN THE HEART OF AN ANGEL
AH, WELL, I MUST FARE ME ONWARD - YET, BE, IF YOU CAN, A BIT LESS BRUSK - AND A MITE MORE MINDFUL TO THE MERIT OF HIS METTLE
I COULD ENCOURAGE IT WITH A BIT MORE TAPPAGE WITH THIS SMACKER
GOOD-BYE "KOP"
GOO-BYE, "PROF"
HMM - HE DOES SPEND A PILE OF PENNIES FOR "BRICKS" - THAT'S COURAGE, IN A WAY - - TOSSING THEM IS NO WEAKLING'S JOB -- UM-M - GLORY OF A SORT DOES SEEM TO GLEAM ABOUT HIM -- A BIT
B B - BUT
"JAIL"
Copr. 1941 King Features Syndicate, Inc., World rights reserved
HERRIMAN
3·23
NICE SUNRISE
PRIDDY SUNSET

March 23rd, 1941.

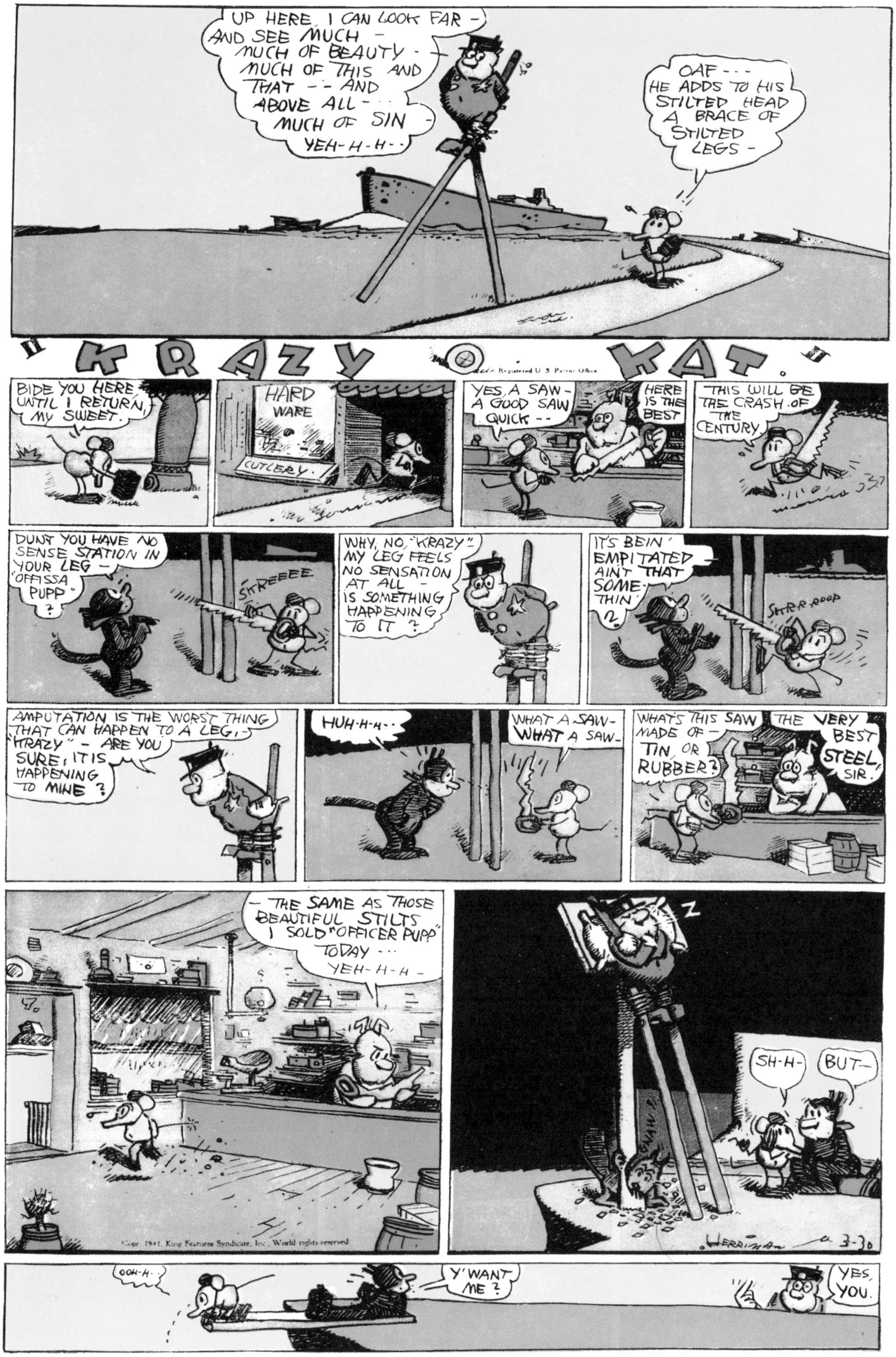
UP HERE, I CAN LOOK FAR - AND SEE MUCH - MUCH OF BEAUTY - MUCH OF THIS AND THAT -- AND ABOVE ALL - MUCH OF SIN - YEH-H-H--
OAF --- HE ADDS TO HIS STILTED HEAD A BRACE OF STILTED LEGS -
KRAZY KAT
Registered U. S. Patent Office
BIDE YOU HERE, UNTIL I RETURN, MY SWEET.
HARD WARE
CUTLERY
YES, A SAW - A GOOD SAW QUICK --
HERE IS THE BEST
THIS WILL BE THE CRASH OF THE CENTURY.
DUNT YOU HAVE NO SENSE STATION IN YOUR LEG - "OFFISSA PUPP" ?
STREEEEE
WHY, NO, "KRAZY" MY LEG FEELS NO SENSATION AT ALL - IS SOMETHING HAPPENING TO IT ?
IT'S BEIN' EMPITATED - AINT THAT SOME-THIN' ?
SHRR-ROOP
AMPUTATION IS THE WORST THING THAT CAN HAPPEN TO A LEG, - "KRAZY" - ARE YOU SURE, IT IS HAPPENING TO MINE ?
HUH-H-H--
WHAT A SAW - WHAT A SAW -
WHAT'S THIS SAW MADE OF - TIN OR RUBBER?
THE VERY BEST STEEL, SIR.
- THE SAME AS THOSE BEAUTIFUL STILTS I SOLD "OFFICER PUPP" TODAY --- YEH-H-H -
Copr. 1941, King Features Syndicate, Inc., World rights reserved
Z
SH-H-
BUT-
HERRIMAN 3-30
OOH-H-
Y' WANT ME ?
YES, YOU.

March 30th, 1941.

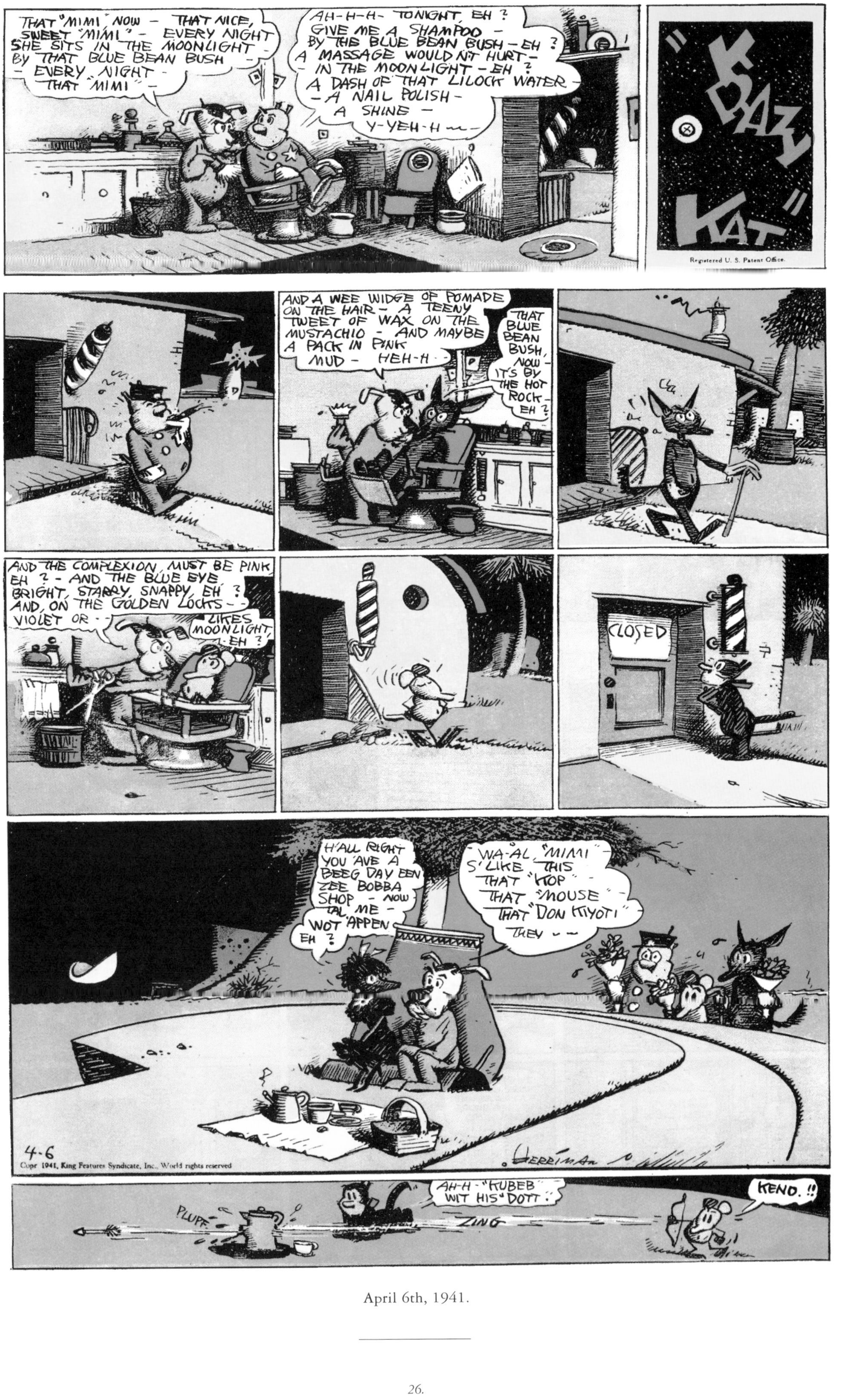
THAT "MIMI" NOW - THAT NICE, SWEET "MIMI" - EVERY NIGHT SHE SITS IN THE MOONLIGHT - BY THAT BLUE BEAN BUSH - - EVERY NIGHT - THAT "MIMI" -
AH-H-H- TONIGHT, EH? GIVE ME A SHAMPOO - BY THE BLUE BEAN BUSH - EH? A MASSAGE WOULD N'T HURT - IN THE MOON LIGHT - EH? A DASH OF THAT LILOCK WATER - - A NAIL POLISH - A SHINE - Y-YEH-H
"KRAZY KAT"
Registered U. S. Patent Office.
AND A WEE WIDGE OF POMADE ON THE HAIR - A TEENY TWEET OF WAX ON THE MUSTACHIO - AND MAYBE A PACK IN PINK MUD - HEH-H
THAT BLUE BEAN BUSH, NOW - IT'S BY THE HOT ROCK - EH?
AND THE COMPLEXION, MUST BE PINK EH? - AND THE BLUE EYE BRIGHT, STARRY, SNAPPY, EH? AND, ON THE GOLDEN LOCKS - VIOLET OR - -
LIKES MOONLIGHT, EH?
CLOSED
H'ALL RIGHT YOU 'AVE A BEEG DAY EEN ZEE BOBBA SHOP - NOW TAL ME - WOT 'APPEN EH?
WA-AL "MIMI" - S'LIKE THIS THAT "KOP" - THAT "MOUSE" - THAT "DON KIYOTI" THEY - -
4-6
Copr 1941, King Features Syndicate, Inc., World rights reserved
HERRIMAN
PLUFF
AH-H "KUBEB" WIT HIS "DOTT"
ZING
KENO.!!

April 6th, 1941.

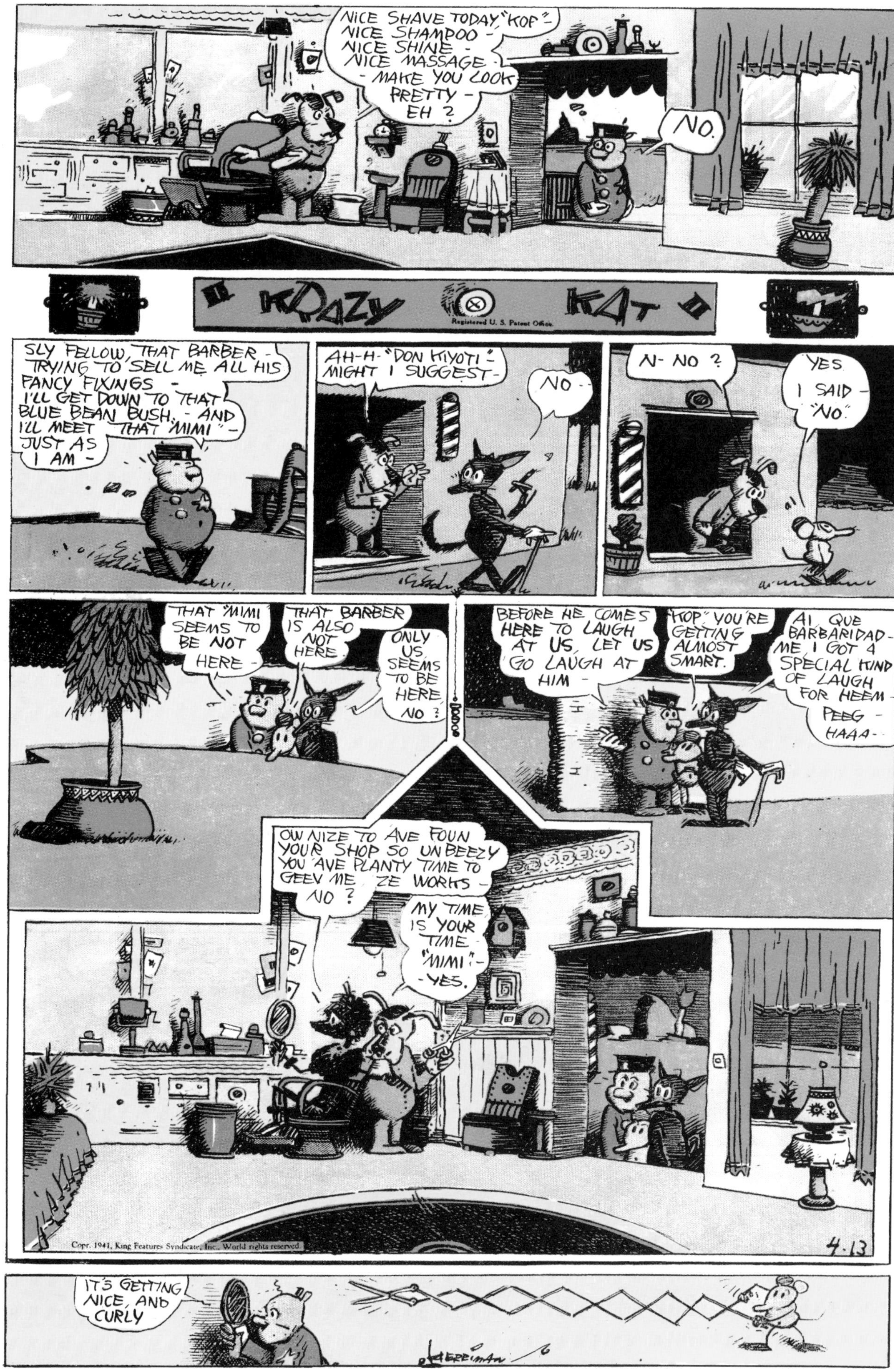
NICE SHAVE TODAY, "KOP" - NICE SHAMPOO - NICE SHINE - NICE MASSAGE - MAKE YOU LOOK PRETTY - EH ?
NO.
KRAZY KAT
Registered U. S. Patent Office.
SLY FELLOW, THAT BARBER - TRYING TO SELL ME ALL HIS FANCY FIXINGS - I'LL GET DOWN TO THAT BLUE BEAN BUSH, - AND I'LL MEET "THAT MIMI" - JUST AS I AM -
AH-H- "DON KIYOTI" - MIGHT I SUGGEST -
NO -
N- NO ?
YES I SAID - "NO".
THAT "MIMI" SEEMS TO BE NOT HERE -
THAT BARBER IS ALSO NOT HERE.
ONLY US SEEMS TO BE HERE, NO ?
BEFORE HE COMES HERE TO LAUGH AT US, LET US GO LAUGH AT HIM -
"KOP" YOU'RE GETTING ALMOST SMART.
AI, QUE BARBARIDAD - ME, I GOT A SPECIAL KIND OF LAUGH FOR HEEM - PEEG - HAAA -
OW NIZE TO AVE FOUN YOUR SHOP SO UNBEEZY YOU AVE PLANTY TIME TO GEEV ME ZE WORKS - NO ?
MY TIME IS YOUR TIME "MIMI" - YES.
Copr. 1941, King Features Syndicate, Inc., World rights reserved.
4.13
IT'S GETTING NICE, AND CURLY
HERRIMAN

April 13th, 1941.

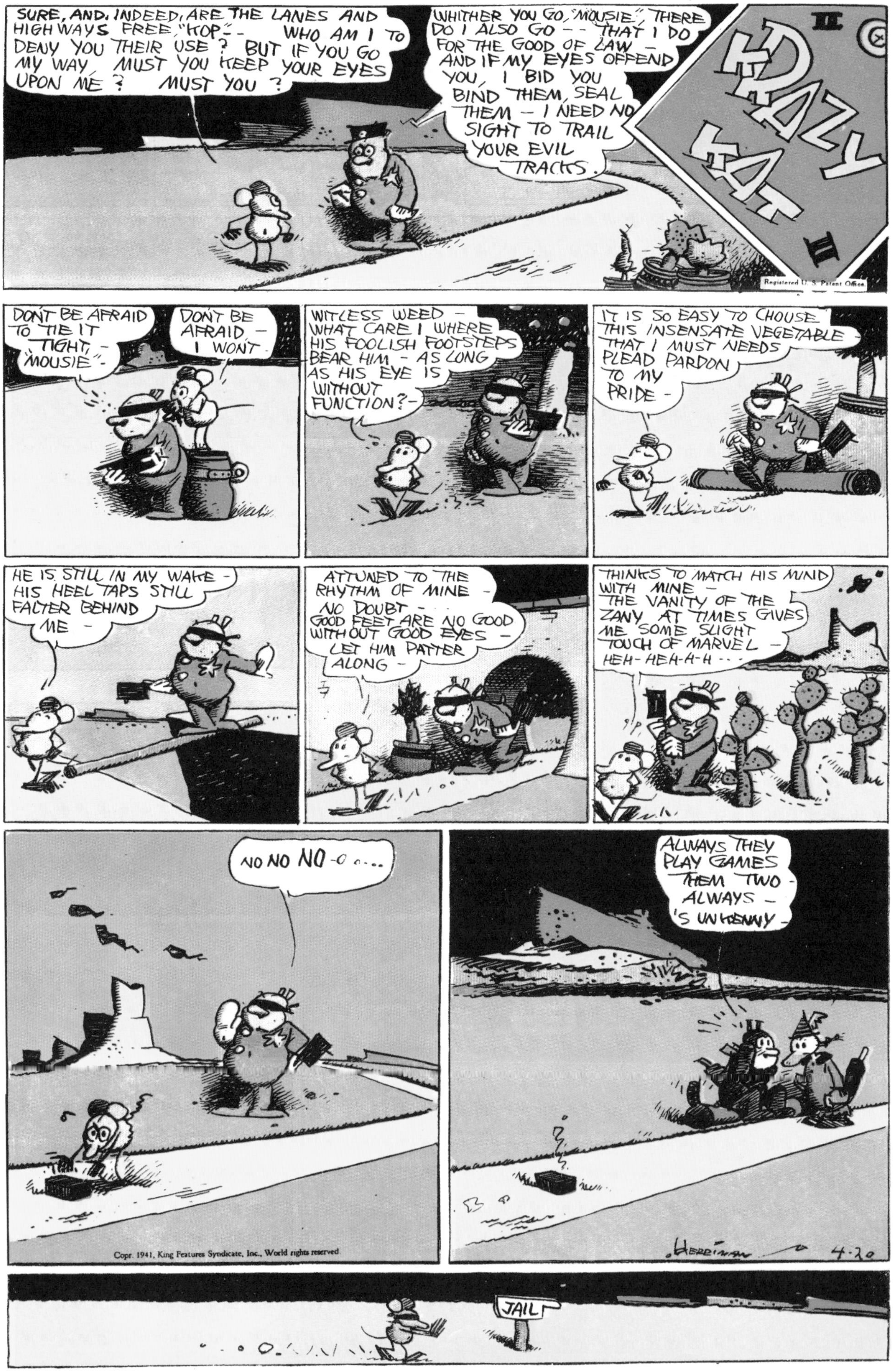
SURE, AND, INDEED, ARE THE LANES AND HIGHWAYS FREE, "KOP" -- WHO AM I TO DENY YOU THEIR USE? BUT IF YOU GO MY WAY, MUST YOU KEEP YOUR EYES UPON ME? MUST YOU?
WHITHER YOU GO, "MOUSIE", THERE DO I ALSO GO -- THAT I DO FOR THE GOOD OF LAW - AND IF MY EYES OFFEND YOU, I BID YOU BIND THEM, SEAL THEM - I NEED NO SIGHT TO TRAIL YOUR EVIL TRACKS.
KRAZY KAT
Registered U. S. Patent Office
DON'T BE AFRAID TO TIE IT TIGHT, "MOUSIE" -
DON'T BE AFRAID - I WON'T -
WITLESS WEED - WHAT CARE I WHERE HIS FOOLISH FOOTSTEPS BEAR HIM - AS LONG AS HIS EYE IS WITHOUT FUNCTION? -
IT IS SO EASY TO CHOUSE THIS INSENSATE VEGETABLE - THAT I MUST NEEDS PLEAD PARDON TO MY PRIDE -
HE IS STILL IN MY WAKE - HIS HEEL TAPS STILL FALTER BEHIND ME -
ATTUNED TO THE RHYTHM OF MINE - NO DOUBT - GOOD FEET ARE NO GOOD WITHOUT GOOD EYES - LET HIM PATTER ALONG -
THINKS TO MATCH HIS MIND WITH MINE - THE VANITY OF THE ZANY AT TIMES GIVES ME SOME SLIGHT TOUCH OF MARVEL - HEH-HEH-H-H ---
NO NO NO-o o...
ALWAYS THEY PLAY GAMES THEM TWO - ALWAYS - 'S UNKENNY -
Copr. 1941, King Features Syndicate, Inc., World rights reserved.
HERRIMAN 4-20
JAIL

April 20th, 1941.

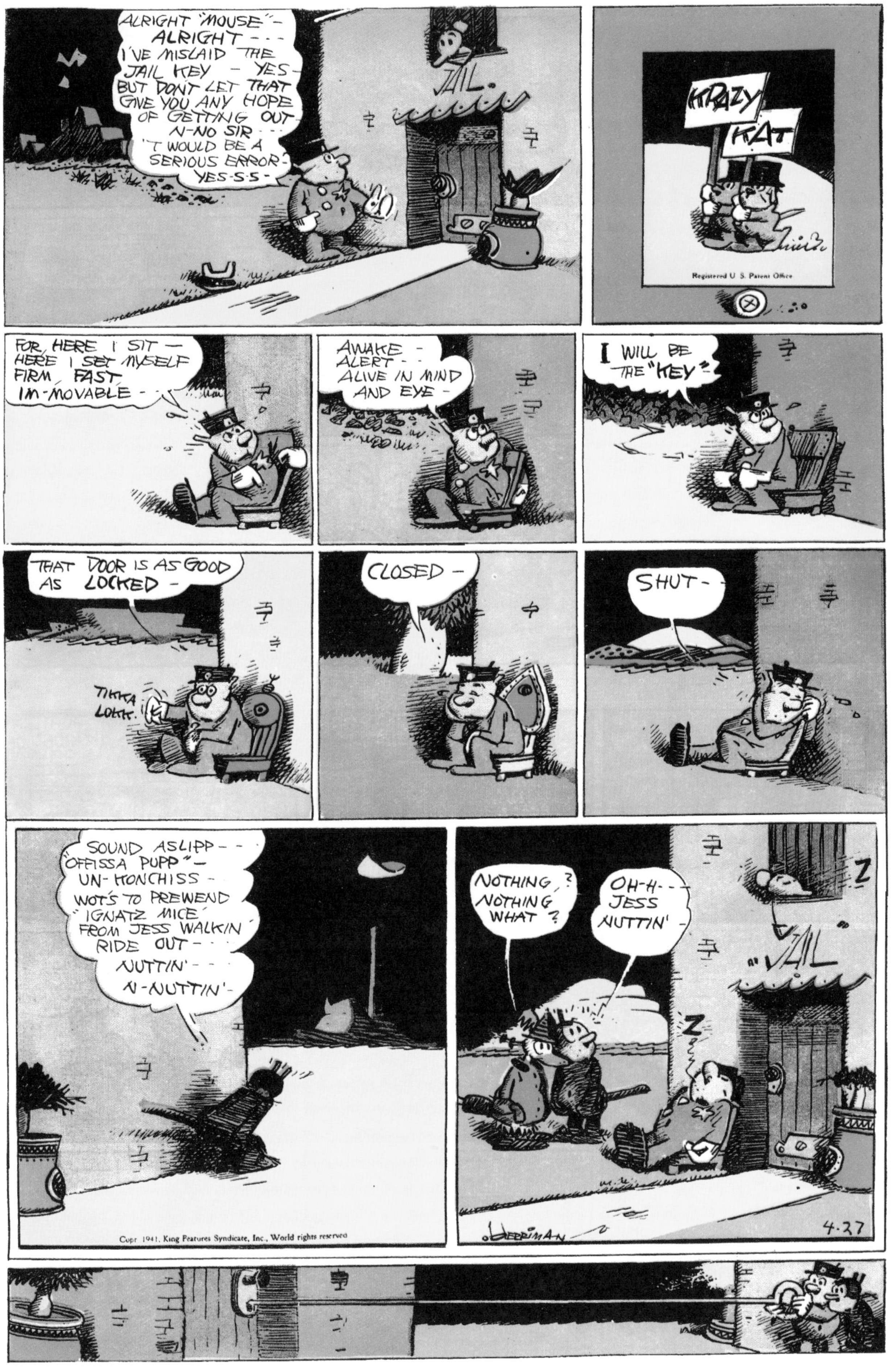
ALRIGHT "MOUSE" - ALRIGHT - - - I'VE MISLAID THE JAIL KEY - YES - BUT DON'T LET THAT GIVE YOU ANY HOPE OF GETTING OUT - N-NO SIR - - 'T WOULD BE A SERIOUS ERROR - YES-S-S -
JAIL
KRAZY
KAT
Registered U. S. Patent Office
FOR, HERE I SIT - HERE I SET MYSELF FIRM, FAST, IM-MOVABLE - -
AWAKE - ALERT - - ALIVE IN MIND AND EYE -
I WILL BE THE "KEY" -
THAT DOOR IS AS GOOD AS LOCKED -
TIKKA LOKK
CLOSED -
SHUT - -
SOUND ASLIPP - - - "OFFISSA PUPP" - UN-KONCHISS - WOT'S TO PREWEND "IGNATZ MICE" FROM JESS WALKIN' RIDE OUT - - NUTTIN' - - N-NUTTIN' -
Copr 1941, King Features Syndicate, Inc., World rights reserved
NOTHING ? NOTHING WHAT ?
OH-H - - JESS NUTTIN' -
Z
JAIL
Z
HERRIMAN
4.27

April 27th, 1941.

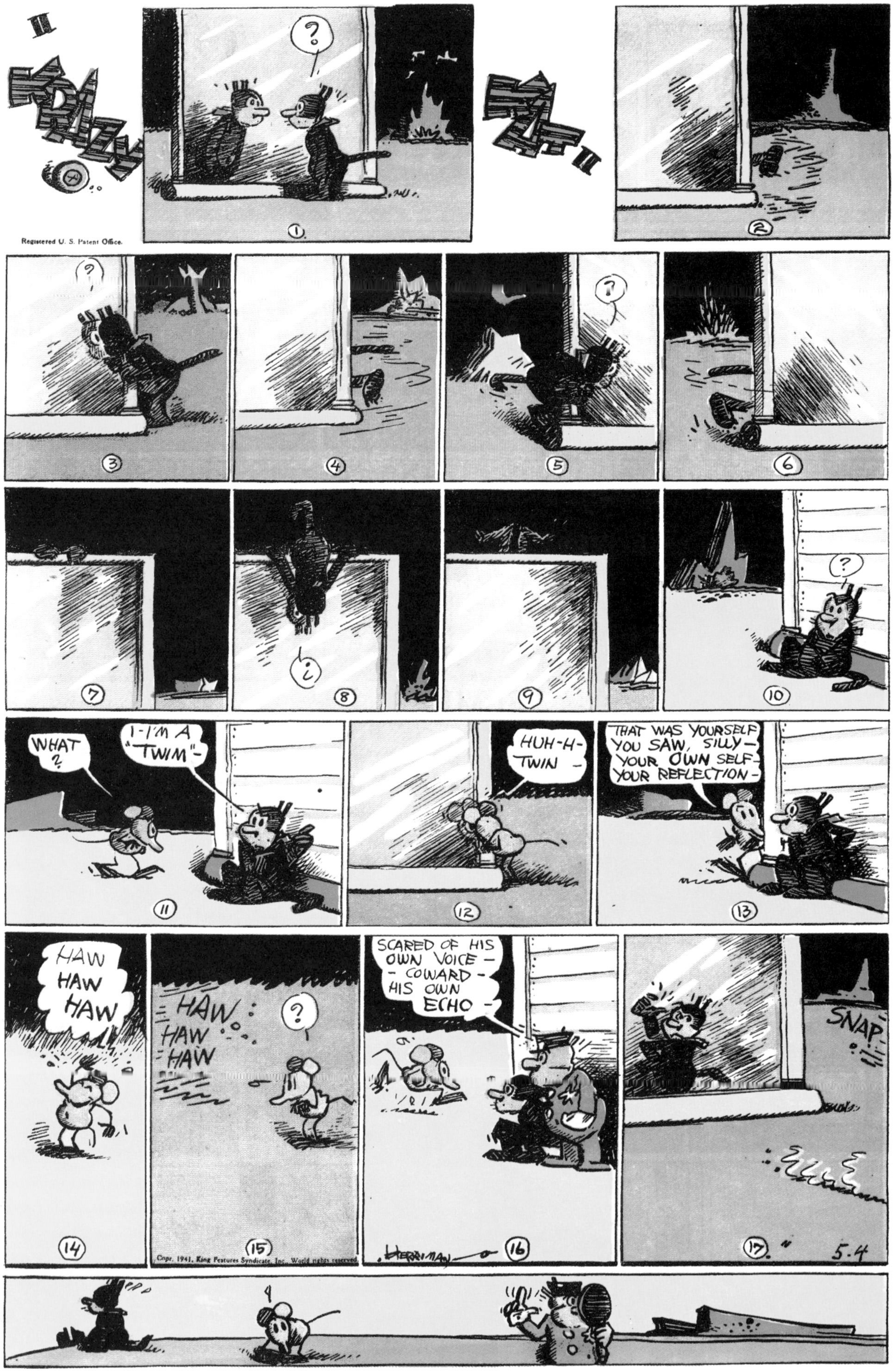
KRAZY KAT
Registered U. S. Patent Office.
?
?
?
¿
?
WHAT ?
I-I'M A "TWIN"-
HUH-H-TWIN -
THAT WAS YOURSELF YOU SAW, SILLY - YOUR OWN SELF - YOUR REFLECTION -
HAW HAW HAW
HAW HAW HAW
?
SCARED OF HIS OWN VOICE - - COWARD - HIS OWN ECHO -
SNAP
Copr. 1941, King Features Syndicate, Inc., World rights reserved.
HERRIMAN
5.4

May 4th, 1941.

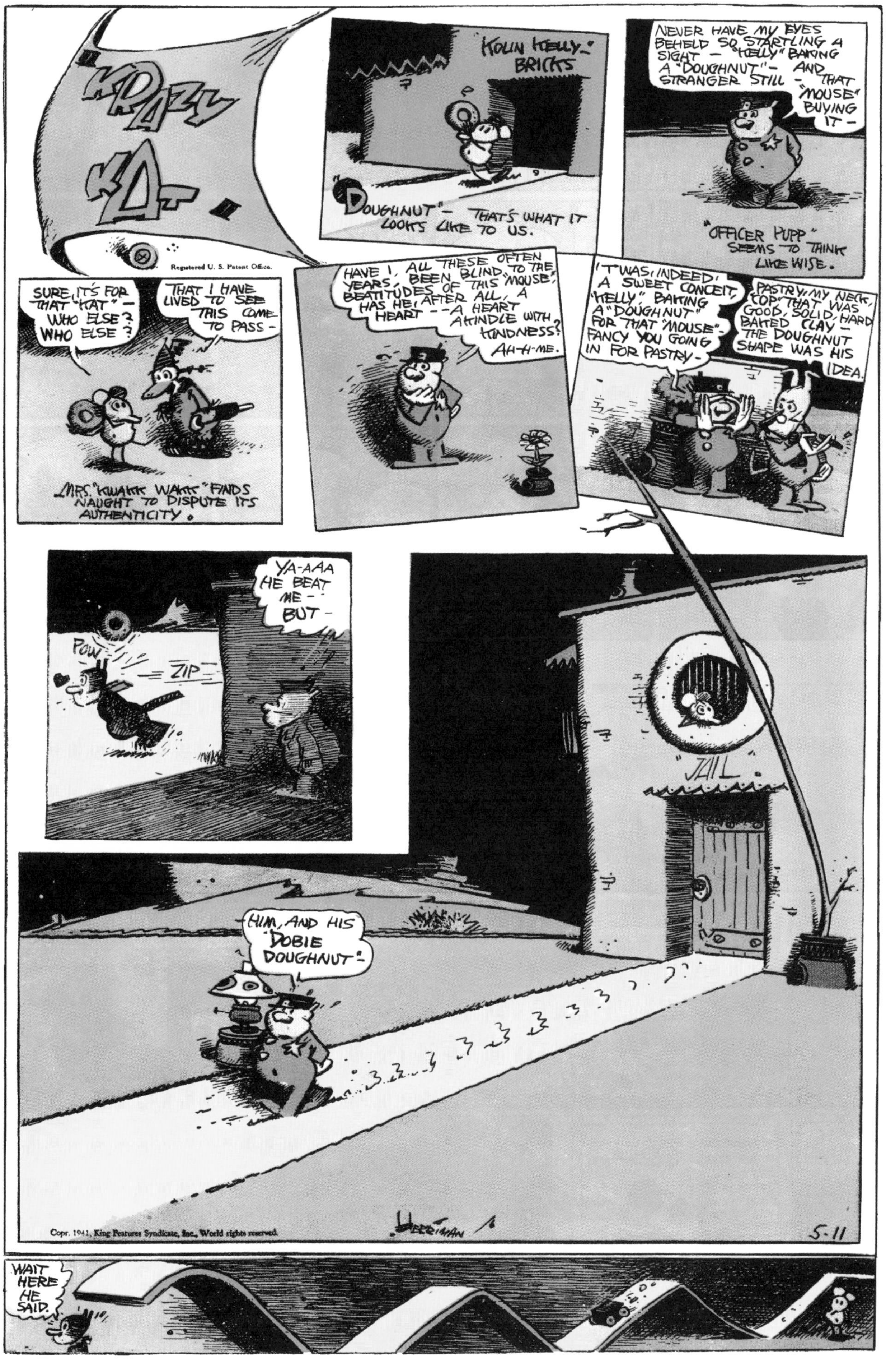
"KRAZY KAT"
Registered U. S. Patent Office.
"KOLIN KELLY" BRICKS
"DOUGHNUT" — THAT'S WHAT IT LOOKS LIKE TO US.
NEVER HAVE MY EYES BEHELD SO STARTLING A SIGHT — "KELLY" BAKING A "DOUGHNUT" — AND STRANGER STILL — THAT "MOUSE" BUYING IT —
"OFFICER PUPP" SEEMS TO THINK LIKE WISE.
SURE, IT'S FOR THAT "KAT" — WHO ELSE? WHO ELSE?
THAT I HAVE LIVED TO SEE THIS COME TO PASS —
MRS. "KWAKK WAKK" FINDS NAUGHT TO DISPUTE ITS AUTHENTICITY.
HAVE I, ALL THESE OFTEN YEARS, BEEN BLIND TO THE BEATITUDES OF THIS "MOUSE", HAS HE, AFTER ALL, A HEART — A HEART AKINDLE WITH KINDNESS? AH-H-ME.
"T'WAS, INDEED, A SWEET CONCEIT, "KELLY" BAKING A "DOUGHNUT" FOR THAT "MOUSE" — FANCY YOU GOING IN FOR PASTRY —
PASTRY, MY NECK, "COP" THAT WAS GOOD, SOLID, HARD BAKED CLAY — THE DOUGHNUT SHAPE WAS HIS IDEA.
YA-AAA HE BEAT ME — BUT —
POW
ZIP
"JAIL"
HIM, AND HIS "DOBIE DOUGHNUT" —
Copr. 1941, King Features Syndicate, Inc., World rights reserved.
HERRIMAN
5-11
WAIT HERE HE SAID.

May 11th, 1941.

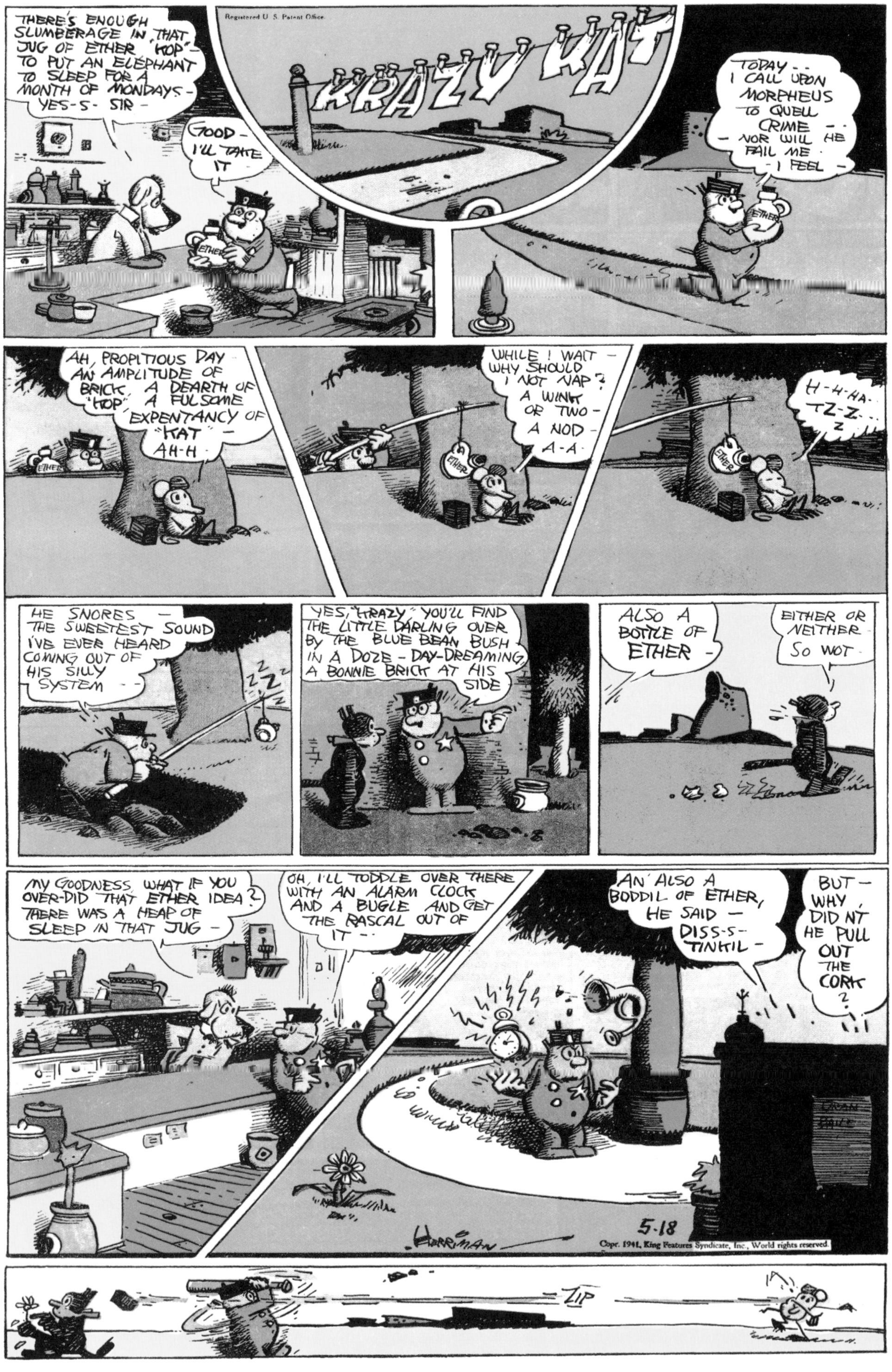
THERE'S ENOUGH SLUMBERAGE IN THAT JUG OF ETHER "KOP" - TO PUT AN ELEPHANT TO SLEEP FOR A MONTH OF MONDAYS - YES-S- SIR -
GOOD - I'LL TAKE IT
ETHER
Registered U. S. Patent Office.
KRAZY KAT
TODAY - - I CALL UPON MORPHEUS TO QUELL CRIME - - - NOR WILL HE FAIL ME - I FEEL -
ETHER
AH, PROPITIOUS DAY AN AMPLITUDE OF BRICK, A DEARTH OF "KOP" A FULSOME EXPENTANCY OF "KAT" - AH-H
WHILE I WAIT - WHY SHOULD I NOT NAP? A WINK OR TWO - A NOD - A-A
H-H-HA - TZ-Z- - Z
HE SNORES - THE SWEETEST SOUND I'VE EVER HEARD COMING OUT OF HIS SILLY SYSTEM - -
ZZZ
YES, "KRAZY" YOU'LL FIND THE LITTLE DARLING OVER BY THE BLUE BEAN BUSH IN A DOZE - DAY-DREAMING, A BONNIE BRICK AT HIS SIDE
ALSO A BOTTLE OF ETHER -
EITHER OR NEITHER - SO WOT -
MY GOODNESS, WHAT IF YOU OVER-DID THAT ETHER IDEA? THERE WAS A HEAP OF SLEEP IN THAT JUG -
OH, I'LL TODDLE OVER THERE WITH AN ALARM CLOCK AND A BUGLE AND GET THE RASCAL OUT OF IT - -
AN' ALSO A BODDIL OF ETHER, HE SAID - DISS-S-TINKIL -
BUT - WHY, DID N'T HE PULL OUT THE CORK ?
5-18
HARRIMAN
Copr. 1941, King Features Syndicate, Inc., World rights reserved.
ZIP

May 18th, 1941.

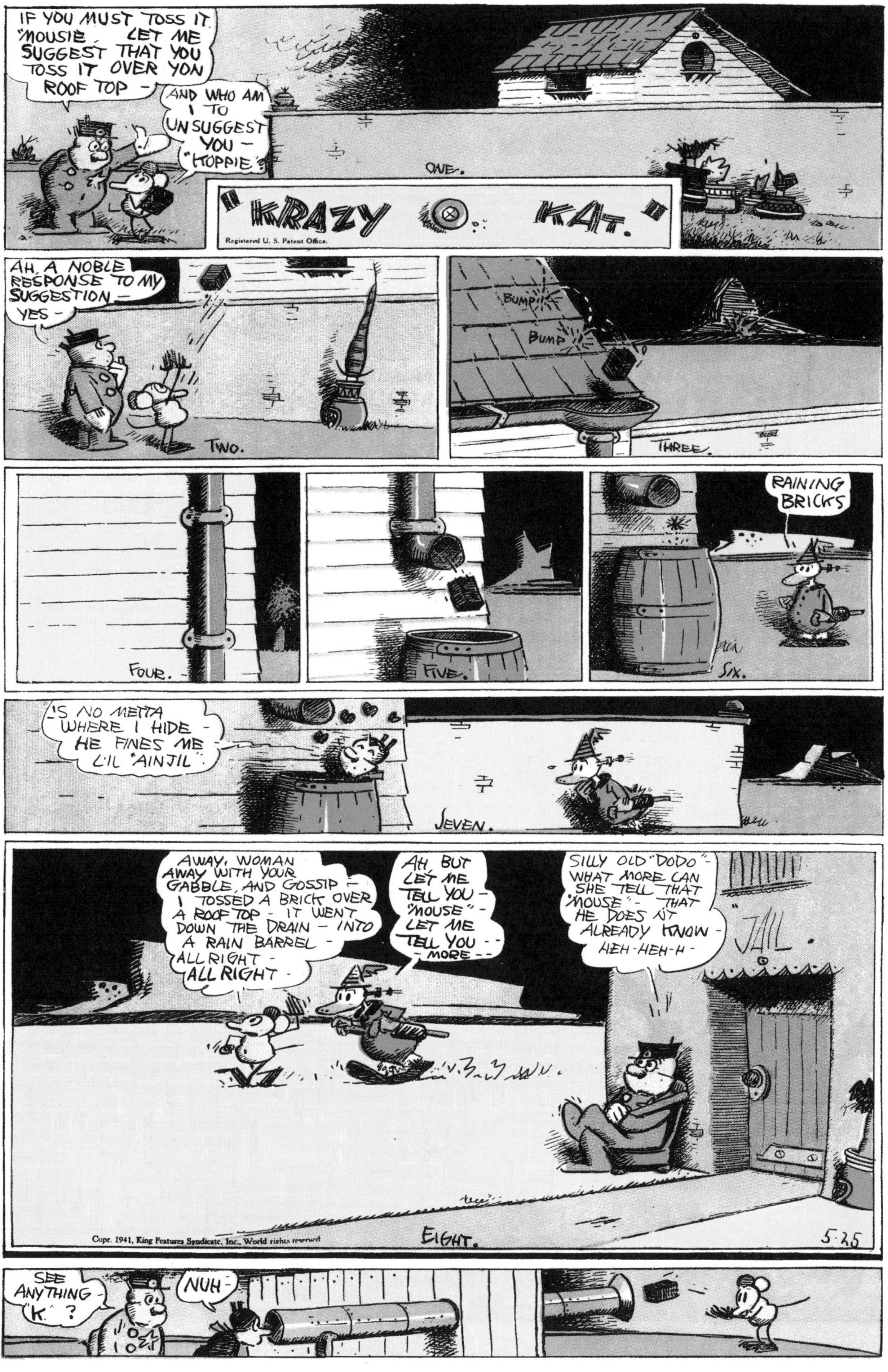
IF YOU MUST TOSS IT "MOUSIE", LET ME SUGGEST THAT YOU TOSS IT OVER YON ROOF TOP -
AND WHO AM I TO UNSUGGEST YOU - "KOPPIE"
ONE.
"KRAZY KAT."
Registered U. S. Patent Office.
AH, A NOBLE RESPONSE TO MY SUGGESTION - YES -
TWO.
BUMP
BUMP
THREE.
FOUR.
FIVE.
RAINING BRICKS
SIX.
IS NO METTA WHERE I HIDE - HE FINES ME L'IL "AINJIL".
SEVEN.
AWAY, WOMAN AWAY WITH YOUR GABBLE, AND GOSSIP - I TOSSED A BRICK OVER A ROOF TOP - IT WENT DOWN THE DRAIN - INTO A RAIN BARREL - ALL RIGHT - ALL RIGHT -
AH, BUT LET ME TELL YOU "MOUSE" - LET ME TELL YOU - - MORE - -
SILLY OLD "DODO" - WHAT MORE CAN SHE TELL THAT "MOUSE" - THAT HE DOES N'T ALREADY KNOW - HEH-HEH-H -
JAIL.
Copr. 1941, King Features Syndicate, Inc., World rights reserved
EIGHT.
5-25
SEE ANYTHING "K." ?
NUH

May 25th, 1941.

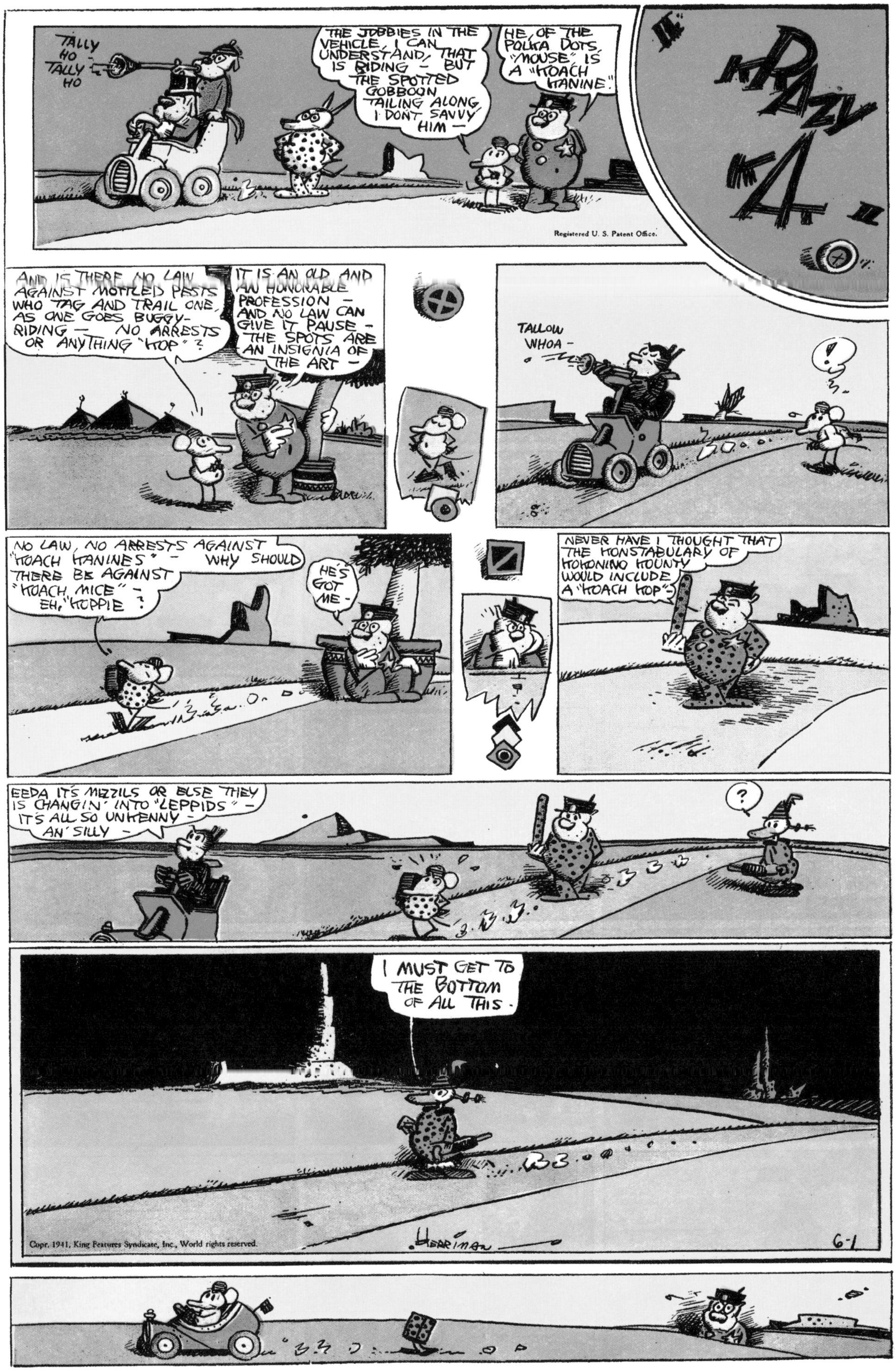
TALLY HO - TALLY HO
THE JOBBIES IN THE VEHICLE, I CAN UNDERSTAND, THAT IS RIDING - BUT THE SPOTTED GOBBOON TAILING ALONG, I DON'T SAVVY HIM -
HE, OF THE POLKA DOTS, "MOUSE" IS A "KOACH KANINE".
KRAZY KAT
Registered U. S. Patent Office.
AND IS THERE NO LAW AGAINST MOTTLED PESTS WHO TAG AND TRAIL ONE, AS ONE GOES BUGGY-RIDING - NO ARRESTS OR ANYTHING "KOP"?
IT IS AN OLD AND AN HONORABLE PROFESSION - AND NO LAW CAN GIVE IT PAUSE - THE SPOTS ARE AN INSIGNIA OF THE ART -
TALLOW WHOA -
!
NO LAW, NO ARRESTS AGAINST "KOACH KANINES" - WHY SHOULD THERE BE AGAINST "KOACH MICE" - EH, "KOPPIE"?
HE'S GOT ME -
NEVER HAVE I THOUGHT THAT THE KONSTABULARY OF KOKONINO KOUNTY WOULD INCLUDE A "KOACH KOP"
EEDA IT'S MEZZILS OR ELSE THEY IS CHANGIN' INTO "LEPPIDS" - IT'S ALL SO UNKENNY - AN' SILLY -
?
I MUST GET TO THE BOTTOM OF ALL THIS -
Copr. 1941, King Features Syndicate, Inc., World rights reserved.
HERRIMAN
6-1

June 1st, 1941.

GIDDIL OPP -
A "KAT" AMBULANT - ENCOACHED - A KWAINT KONCEPT - I APPROVE.
KRAZY KAT
YES "KOP" WE FOLLOW -
UHM-M- A "MOUSE" BESPOTTED, FOLLOWING - EMULATING THE "KOACH KANINE" -
Registered U. S. Patent Office.
BY WE, I MEAN, ME, AND YOU CAN WELL SEE WHOM -
SPOTTERY RAMPANT -
COME, COME - ANDA-LAY.
EVERY DOT A DELIGHT - EVERY SPOT A JOY - THIS DAY PROMISES MUCH.
SIN IS AFOOT - THE MOTTLED MENACE MARCHES ON - AND I CAN DO NOTHING ABOUT IT.
M-MY SPOTS, KOP ?
YES, "MOUSIE", YOUR "SPOTS".
APPEASEMENT, "KOP" ?
JAILMENT, NEVER-THE-LESS MADAME -
JAIL
Copr. 1941, King Features Syndicate, Inc., World rights reserved.
HERRIMAN
6-8

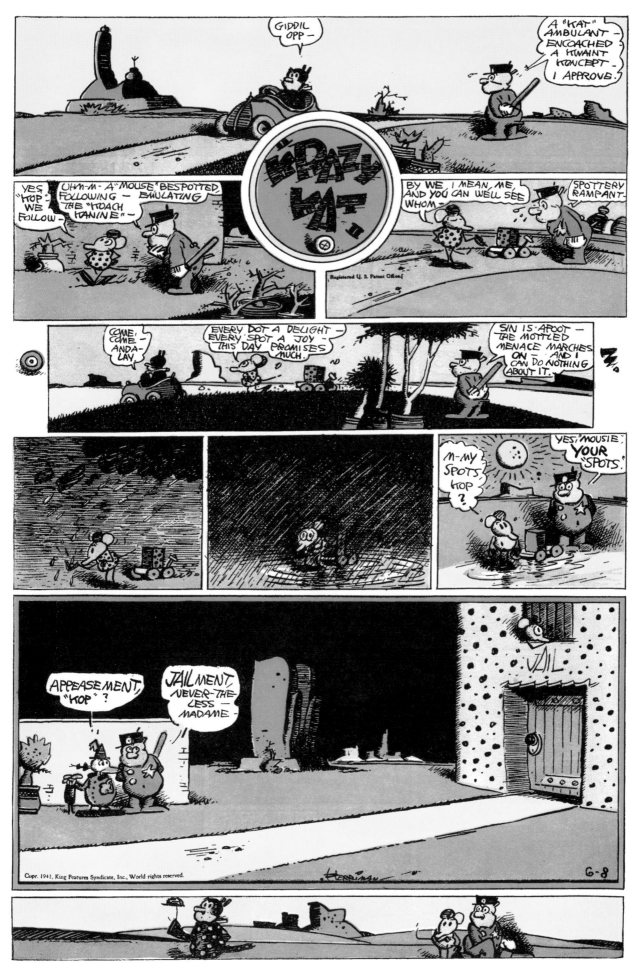

June 8th, 1941.

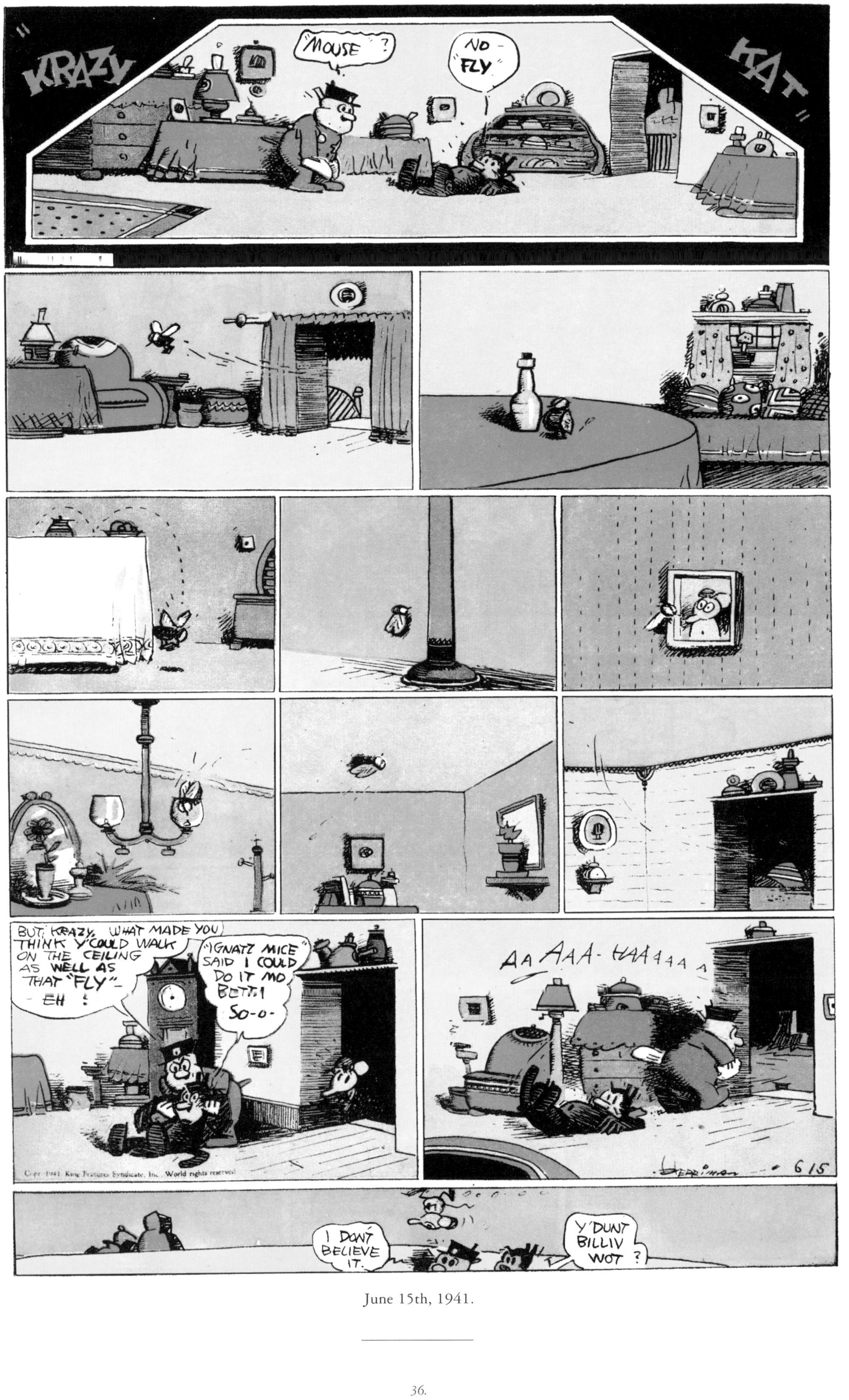
"KRAZY KAT"
"MOUSE"?
NO — FLY
BUT, KRAZY, WHAT MADE YOU THINK Y'COULD WALK ON THE CEILING AS WELL AS THAT "FLY" — EH !
"IGNATZ MICE" SAID I COULD DO IT MO BETTI SO-O-
AA AAA- HAAAAAA
I DON'T BELIEVE IT.
Y'DUNT BILLIV WOT ?
Copr. 1941, King Features Syndicate, Inc., World rights reserved
HERRIMAN 6 15

June 15th, 1941.

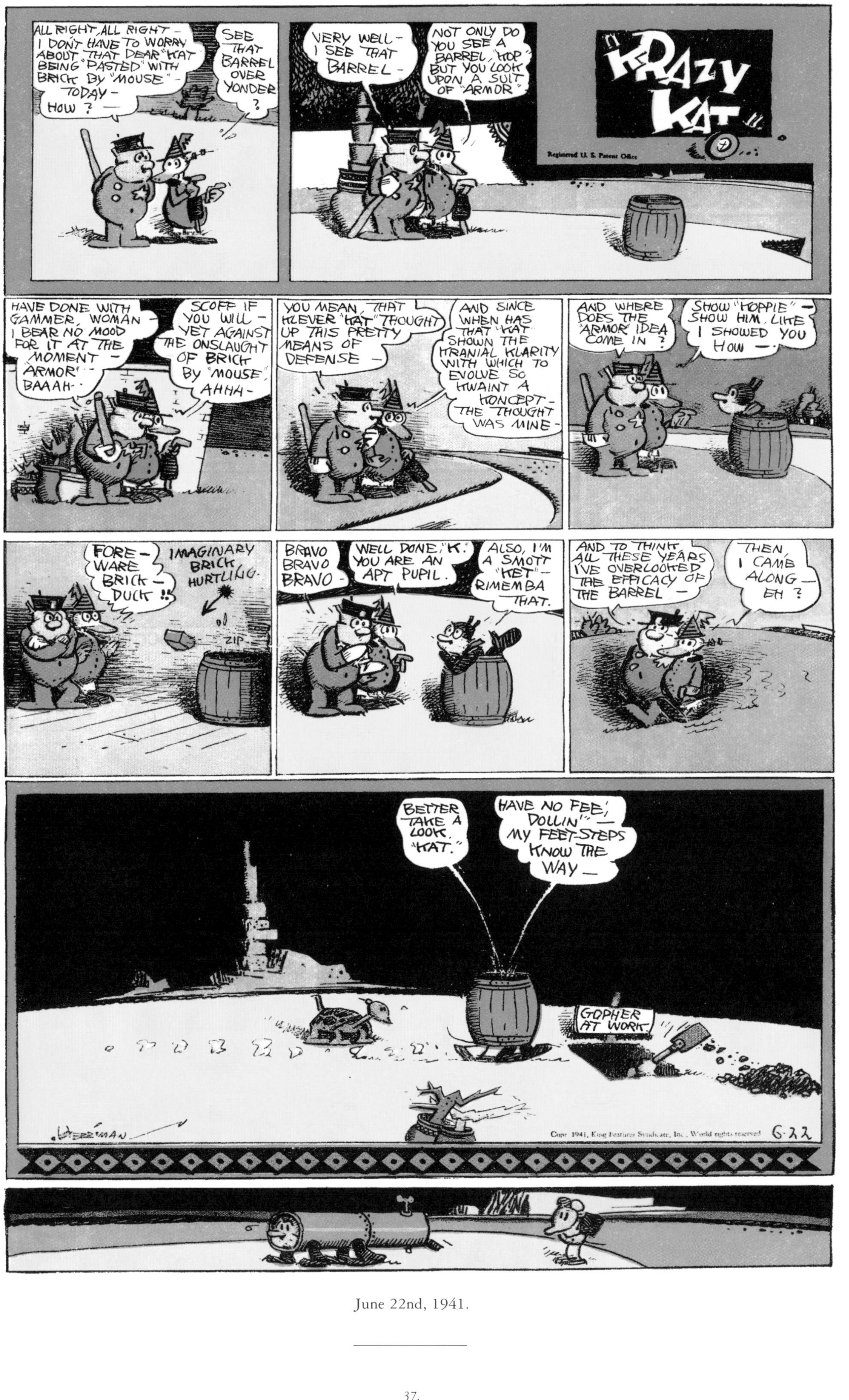
ALL RIGHT, ALL RIGHT – I DON'T HAVE TO WORRY ABOUT THAT DEAR "KAT" BEING "PASTED" WITH BRICK BY "MOUSE" – TODAY – HOW ? –
SEE THAT BARREL OVER YONDER ?
VERY WELL – I SEE THAT BARREL –
NOT ONLY DO YOU SEE A BARREL, "KOP" BUT YOU LOOK UPON A SUIT OF "ARMOR"
"KRAZY KAT"
Registered U. S. Patent Office
HAVE DONE WITH GAMMER, WOMAN I BEAR NO MOOD FOR IT AT THE MOMENT – "ARMOR" BAAAH –
SCOFF IF YOU WILL – YET AGAINST THE ONSLAUGHT OF BRICK BY "MOUSE", AHHA –
YOU MEAN, THAT KLEVER "KAT" THOUGHT UP THIS PRETTY MEANS OF DEFENSE –
AND SINCE WHEN HAS THAT "KAT" SHOWN THE KRANIAL KLARITY WITH WHICH TO EVOLVE SO KWAINT A KONCEPT – THE THOUGHT WAS MINE –
AND WHERE DOES THE "ARMOR" IDEA COME IN ?
SHOW "KOPPIE" – SHOW HIM, LIKE I SHOWED YOU HOW –.
FORE-WARE BRICK – DUCK !!
IMAGINARY BRICK HURTLING.
ZIP
BRAVO BRAVO BRAVO –
WELL DONE, "K." YOU ARE AN APT PUPIL.
ALSO, I'M A SMOTT "KET" – RIMEMBA THAT.
AND TO THINK ALL THESE YEARS I'VE OVERLOOKED THE EFFICACY OF THE BARREL –
THEN, I CAME ALONG – EH ?
BETTER TAKE A LOOK, "KAT."
HAVE NO FEE', DOLLIN'" – MY FEET-STEPS KNOW THE WAY –
GOPHER AT WORK.
HERRIMAN
Copr. 1941, King Features Syndicate, Inc., World rights reserved
6-22

June 22nd, 1941.

ADIOS, CHAPARRITA, CHULA - - -
A COVERED DISH, IN IT COULD BE A RAGGOO OF LAMB, OR A SAVORY STEW, A MESS OF FRIJOLES, OR A "CREEP SUSSETT" - YET ALL I CAN PICTURE IN MY MIND IS THE SINISTER SHAPE OF SIN -
Registered U. S. Patent Office
IF YOU HAVE AUGHT TO SAY TO ME, "KOP," I BEG THAT YOU SPEAK QUICKLY - I HAVE A NEED OF SPEED - -
GRANT ME A BIT OF A MOMENT "MOUSIE" THINK ME NOT TOO DISTASTEFUL, TOO BRASH THAT I PLEAD FOR THIS BOON - -
WERE THIS MOMENT MINE "KOPPIE" - I WOULD GIVE IT ALL TO YOU, EVERY TICK OF IT, EVER TOCK OF IT - - BUT
YOU DILUTE THE VIRILE TEA OF COURAGE WHICH FEEDS MY HEART, YOU SOFTEN THE STERN OF ME WITH THE SWEET SOOTHE OF YOUR GENEROSITY - - YET, STILL MUST I BID YOU, PAUSE -
ALL RIGHT, "KOP" ALL RIGHT - YOU'RE TRYING TO FIND OUT WHAT'S IN THIS DISH - — EH ???
YES -
AND YOU WOULD ALSO LIKE TO KNOW TO WHOM I AM DELIVERING IT - - EH ?
UH-HUH -
WELL, IT IS A GIFT - A TOKEN FROM "KOLIN KELLY" TO "KRAZY KAT" -
AH-HAH-H-H - AND COULD THIS "GIFTIE" BE SQUARE RED, AND OFTEN TIMES CALLED "BRICK ?"
ALL RIGHT, "KOP," IT IS SQUARE, IT IS RED AND BY MANY, CALLED A "BRICK" -
ALL OF WHICH MAKES IT NO FIT GIFT FOR THAT DEAR "KAT" - COME WE GO BACK TO THE BRICK-YARD.
SHAME ON YOU, "KELLY" - HAVING THIS "MOUSE" BEAR YOUR GIFT OF BRICK TO THAT NICE "KAT" - SHAME, "KELLY" SHAME -
BUT, "KOP," IT IS A STRAW-BERRY ICE CREAM "BRICK" AND -
OOH-H-H - W- WHY DID NT YOU TELLLLLL ME'
S' PROBABLY ALL MELTED, BY NOW -
YEH -
WELL, WE EXPECTED THAT "MOUSE" WITH IT - AN HOUR AGO - HOW COME YOU FETCH IT, "KOP" ?
I-I-I FIGURED IT WOULD BE SAFER IN THE HANDS OF THE LAW - - - AND DELIVER IT TO THAT DEAR KAT, IN PERSON -
HE WENT DOWN TO "KELLY'S" - TO SEE ABOUT IT - - -
THERE IS A HEPPY LEND FUR FUR - A-WA-AY -
OOOYY
6-29

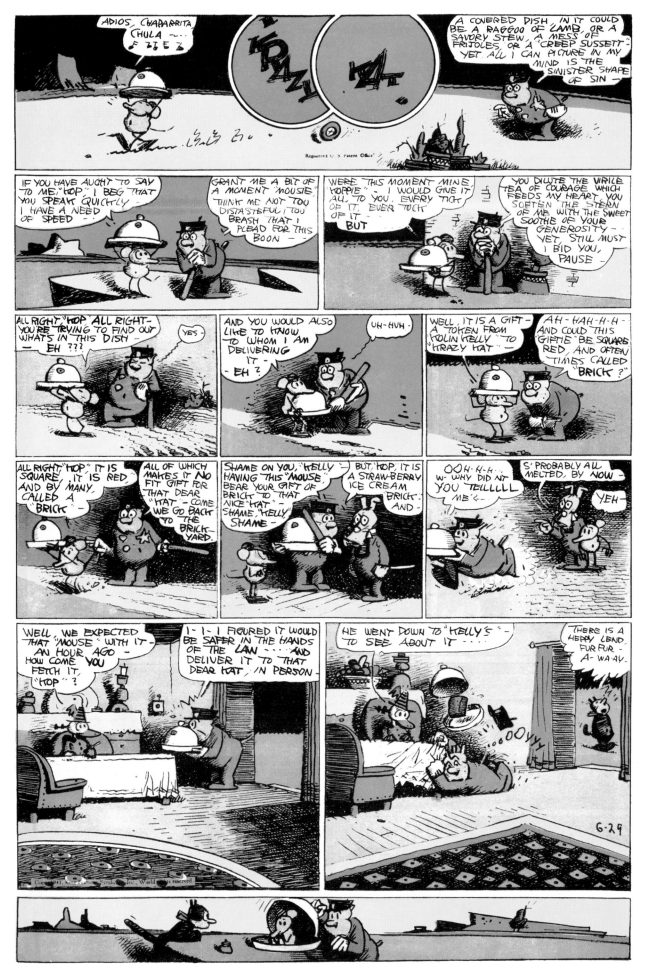

June 29th, 1941.

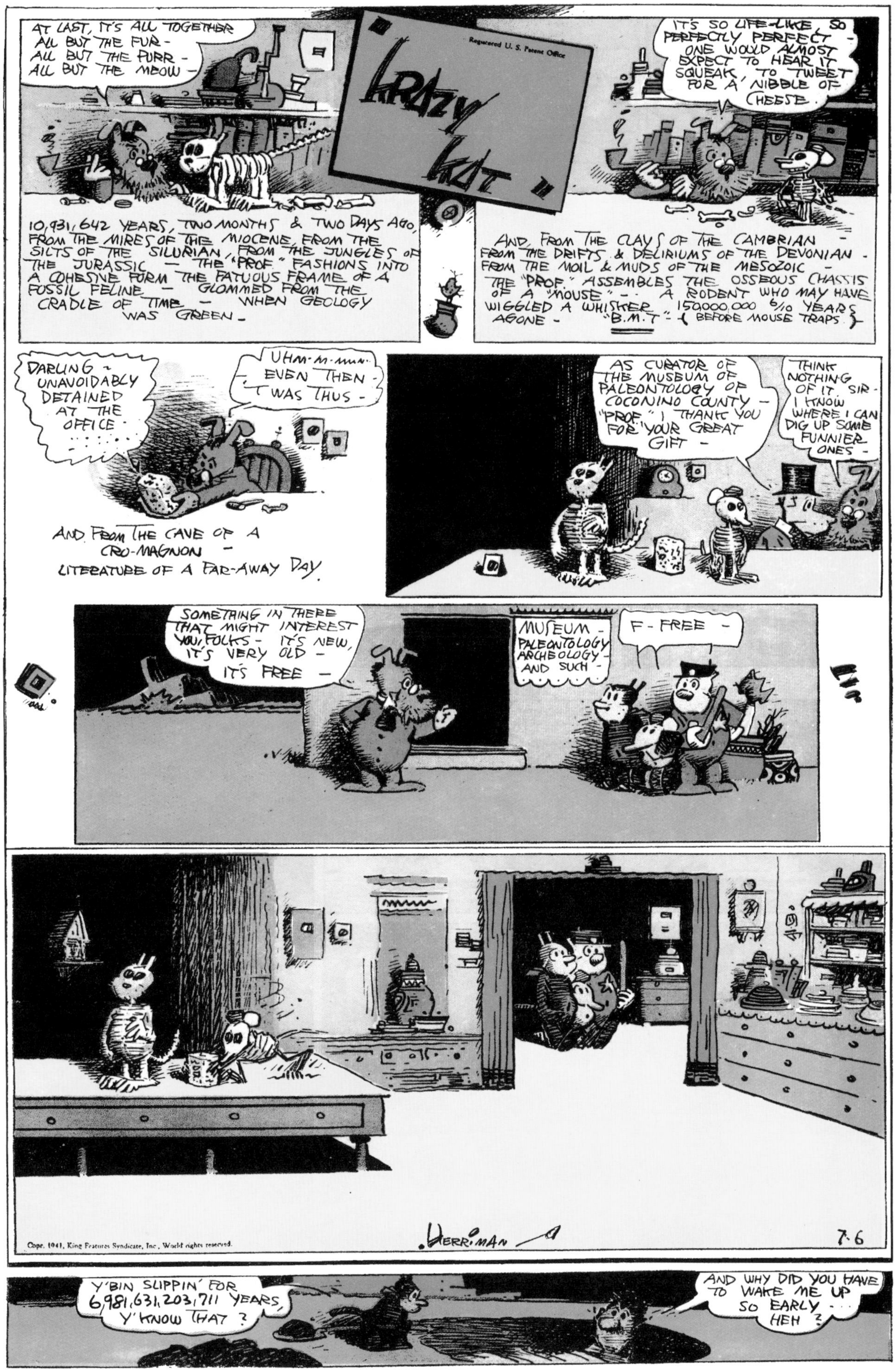
AT LAST, IT'S ALL TOGETHER ALL BUT THE FUR - ALL BUT THE PURR - ALL BUT THE MEOW -
Registered U. S. Patent Office
KRAZY KAT
10,931,642 YEARS, TWO MONTHS & TWO DAYS AGO, FROM THE MIRES OF THE MIOCENE, FROM THE SILTS OF THE SILURIAN, FROM THE JUNGLES OF THE JURASSIC - THE "PROF" FASHIONS INTO A COHESIVE FORM THE FATUOUS FRAME OF A FOSSIL FELINE - GLOMMED FROM THE CRADLE OF TIME - WHEN GEOLOGY WAS GREEN -
IT'S SO LIFE-LIKE, SO PERFECTLY PERFECT - ONE WOULD ALMOST EXPECT TO HEAR IT SQUEAK, TO TWEET FOR A NIBBLE OF CHEESE.
AND, FROM THE CLAYS OF THE CAMBRIAN - FROM THE DRIFTS & DELIRIUMS OF THE DEVONIAN - FROM THE MOIL & MUDS OF THE MESOZOIC - THE "PROF." ASSEMBLES THE OSSEOUS CHASSIS OF A "MOUSE" - A RODENT WHO MAY HAVE WIGGLED A WHISKER 150,000,000 6/10 YEARS AGONE - "B.M.T" - (BEFORE MOUSE TRAPS.)
DARLING - UNAVOIDABLY DETAINED AT THE OFFICE
UHM-M-MM - EVEN THEN - 'TWAS THUS -
AND FROM THE CAVE OF A CRO-MAGNON - LITERATURE OF A FAR-AWAY DAY.
AS CURATOR OF THE MUSEUM OF PALEONTOLOGY OF COCONINO COUNTY - "PROF," I THANK YOU FOR YOUR GREAT GIFT -
THINK NOTHING OF IT, SIR - I KNOW WHERE I CAN DIG UP SOME FUNNIER ONES -
SOMETHING IN THERE THAT MIGHT INTEREST YOU, FOLKS - IT'S NEW, IT'S VERY OLD - IT'S FREE -
MUSEUM - PALEONTOLOGY ARCHEOLOGY AND SUCH -
F - FREE -
Copr. 1941, King Features Syndicate, Inc., World rights reserved.
HERRIMAN
7-6
Y'BIN SLIPPIN' FOR 6,981,631,203,711 YEARS, Y'KNOW THAT ?
AND WHY DID YOU HAVE TO WAKE ME UP SO EARLY - - - HEH ?

July 6th, 1941.

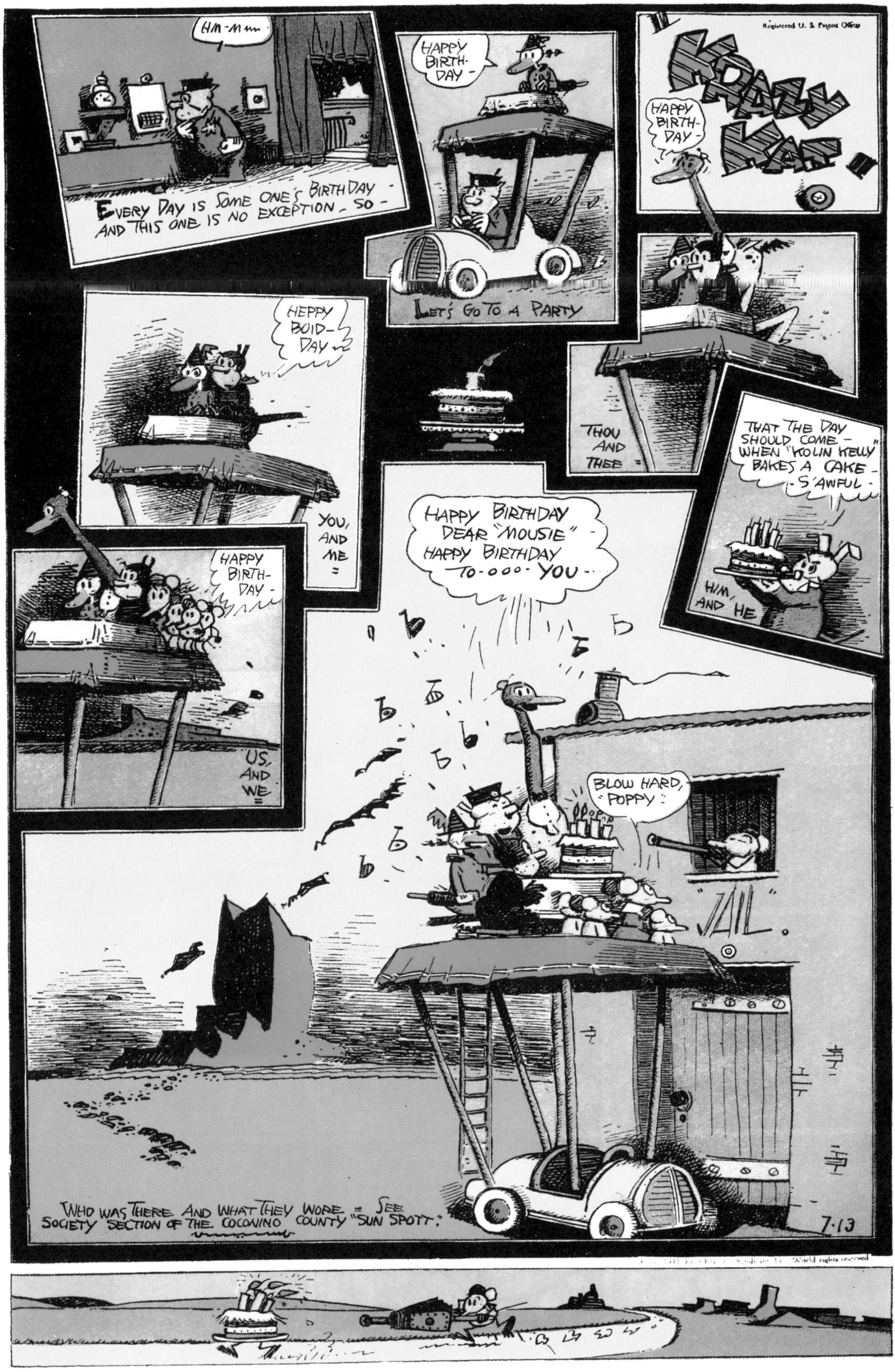
HM-MM
EVERY DAY IS SOME ONE'S BIRTH DAY - AND THIS ONE IS NO EXCEPTION - SO -
HAPPY BIRTH-DAY -
LET'S GO TO A PARTY
KRAZY KAT
HAPPY BIRTH-DAY -
THOU AND THEE =
HEPPY BOID-DAY
YOU, AND ME =
THAT THE DAY SHOULD COME - WHEN "KOLIN KELLY" BAKES A CAKE - S'AWFUL -
HIM, AND HE
HAPPY BIRTH-DAY -
US, AND WE =
HAPPY BIRTHDAY DEAR "MOUSIE" - HAPPY BIRTHDAY TO-OOO- YOU -
BLOW HARD, "POPPY"
JAIL
WHO WAS THERE AND WHAT THEY WORE = SEE SOCIETY SECTION OF THE COCONINO COUNTY "SUN SPOTT."
7-13

July 13th, 1941.

PASS - "KAT"
KRAZY KAT
PASS - "PELICAN"
PASS, "KANGAROO" - YOU AND THE "BAMBINO" IN THE BASKET -
MUST BE BIG PARTY OR A SWARRY GOING ON OVER THAT WAY - -
PASS ? MRS. KWAKK WAKK ?? EH ???
ME ? - NO - THIS IS AS FAR AS I GO - - WHY ?
OH, I JUST THOUGHT YOU MIGHT WANT TO - SO MANY FINE FOLKS HAVE PASSED BY, I HAD A IDEA YOU WOULD WISH TO PASS ALSO - - -
AND WAS "MOUSE" AND "BRICK" AMONG THE ELITES WHO PASSED ? - "MOUSE" AND "BRICK" ?
NO MA'M - NO - NEITHER "MOUSE" NOR NEITHER "BRICK" HAVE PASSED THIS WAY - "KAT" DID, "KANGAROO" DID "PELICAN" DID - BUT "MOUSE", NO - "BRICK" NO - NO NO NO -
N-N-N-NOOOO..
AND WHAT COULD A "PELICAN" PACK IN HIS CHIN BAG ?
I'D SAY A "FISH" WHAT ELSE ?
COULD BE A "BRICK" - - EH ?
AND WHAT COULD A "KANGAROO" HAVE AS A PASSENGER IN HIS PAUNCH POUCH ?
WHAT BUT A CHILD "KANGAROO" - EH - WHAT ?
WHAT ABOUT A "MOUSE" - EH, WHAT ?
LETTING THEM ALL PASS - "KOP" ?
7-20
Copr. 1941, King Features Syndicate, Inc., World rights reserved.
HERRIMAN

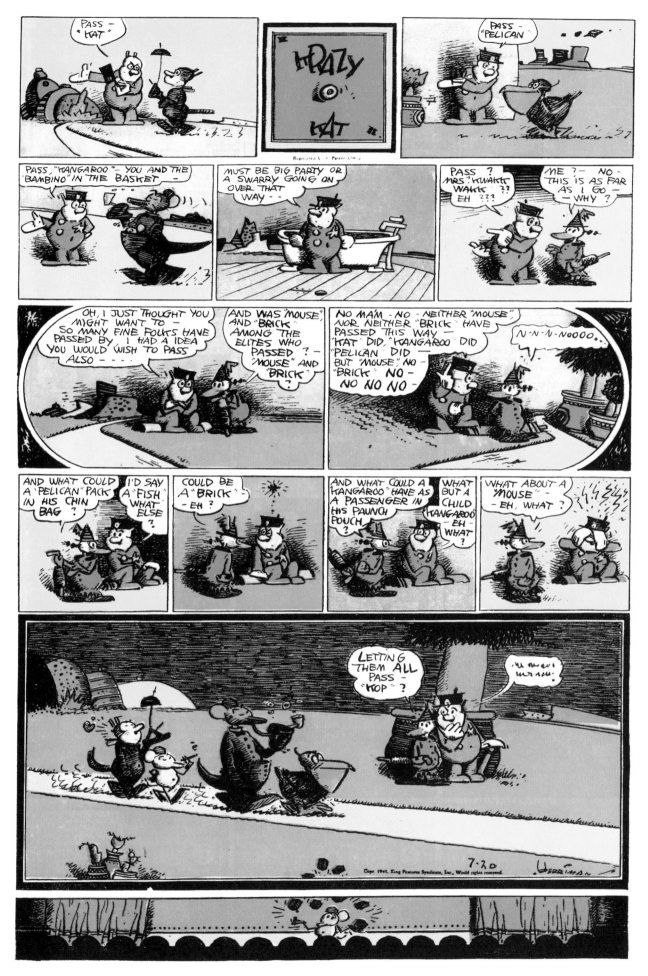

July 20th, 1941.

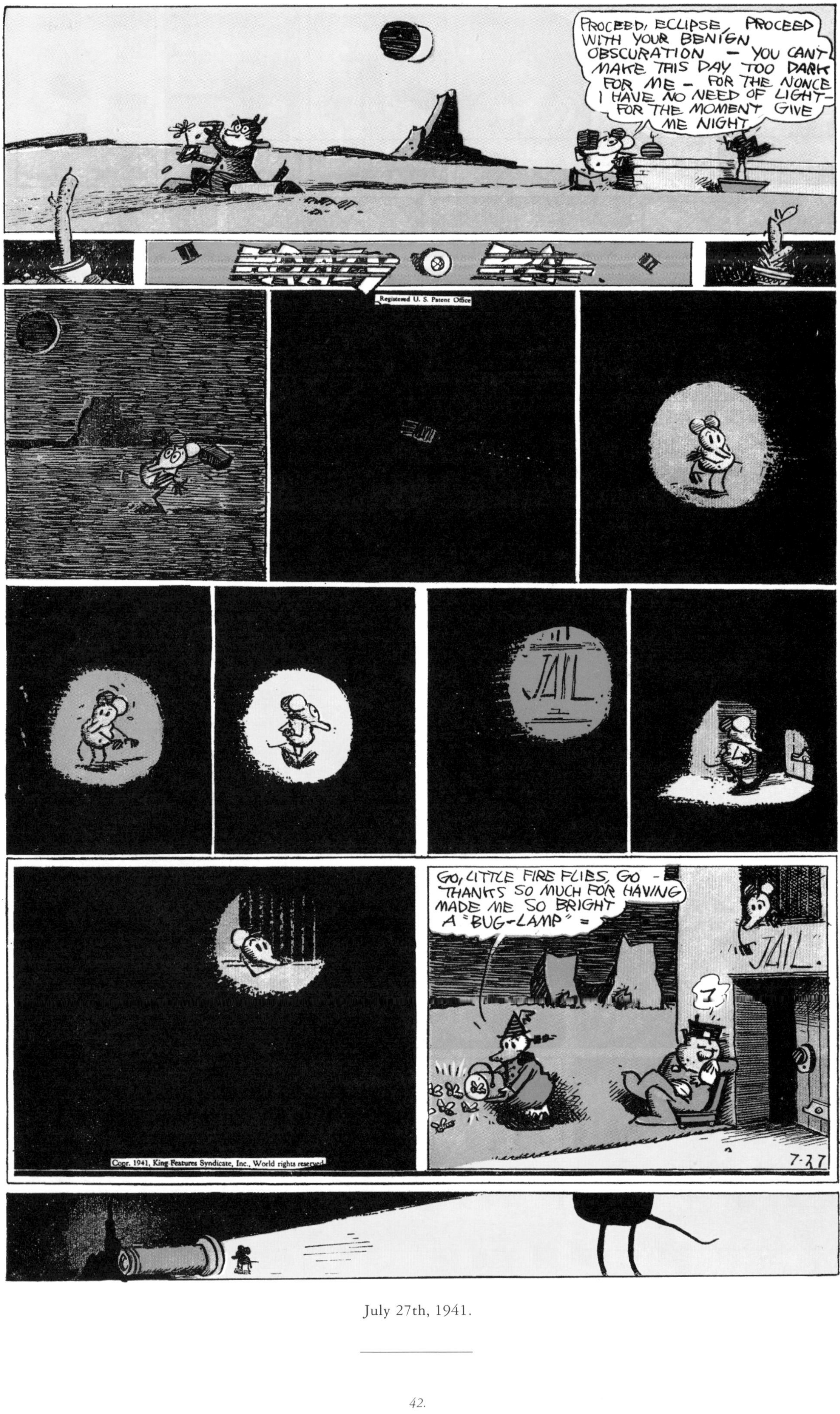
PROCEED, ECLIPSE, PROCEED WITH YOUR BENIGN OBSCURATION — YOU CANT MAKE THIS DAY TOO DARK FOR ME — FOR THE NONCE I HAVE NO NEED OF LIGHT — FOR THE MOMENT GIVE ME NIGHT
Registered U. S. Patent Office
JAIL
Copr. 1941, King Features Syndicate, Inc., World rights reserved
GO, LITTLE FIRE FLIES, GO — THANKS SO MUCH FOR HAVING MADE ME SO BRIGHT A "BUG-LAMP" =
JAIL
7-27

July 27th, 1941.

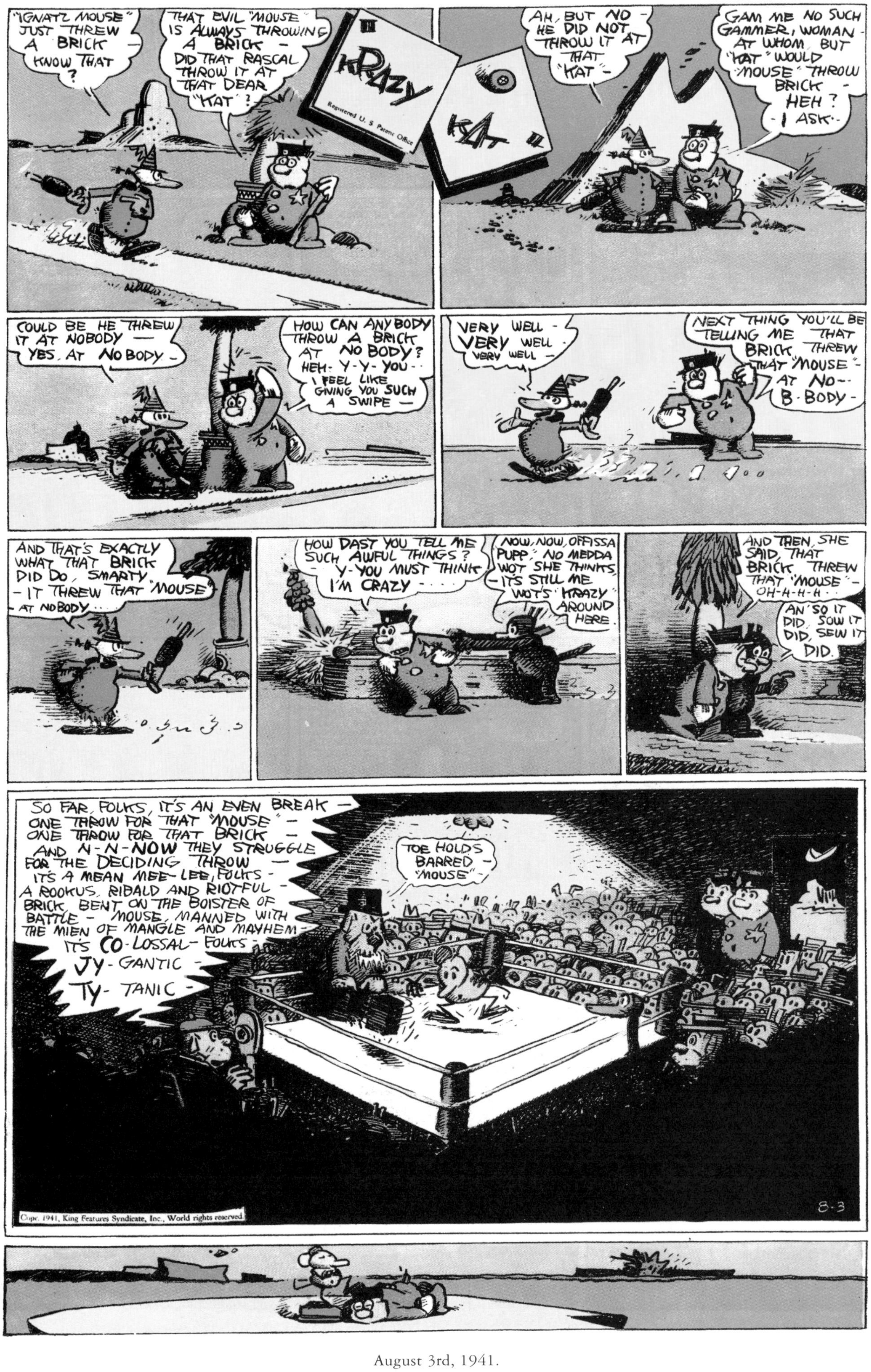
"IGNATZ MOUSE" JUST THREW A BRICK — KNOW THAT ?
THAT EVIL "MOUSE" IS ALWAYS THROWING A BRICK — DID THAT RASCAL THROW IT AT THAT DEAR "KAT" ?
KRAZY KAT
Registered U. S. Patent Office
AH, BUT NO — HE DID NOT THROW IT AT THAT "KAT" —
GAM ME NO SUCH GAMMER, WOMAN — AT WHOM BUT "KAT" WOULD "MOUSE" THROW BRICK — HEH ? — I ASK —
COULD BE HE THREW IT AT NOBODY — YES, AT NOBODY —
HOW CAN ANYBODY THROW A BRICK AT NOBODY? HEH-Y-Y-YOU — I FEEL LIKE GIVING YOU SUCH A SWIPE —
VERY WELL — VERY WELL — VERY WELL —
NEXT THING YOU'LL BE TELLING ME THAT BRICK THREW THAT "MOUSE" — AT NO — B-BODY —
AND THAT'S EXACTLY WHAT THAT BRICK DID DO, SMARTY — IT THREW THAT "MOUSE" — AT NOBODY . . .
HOW DAST YOU TELL ME SUCH AWFUL THINGS ? — Y-YOU MUST THINK I'M CRAZY . . .
NOW, NOW, OFFISSA PUPP, NO MEDDA WOT SHE THINKS, — IT'S STILL ME WOT'S "KRAZY" AROUND HERE.
AND THEN, SHE SAID, THAT BRICK THREW THAT "MOUSE" — OH-H-H-H —
AN' SO IT DID, SOW IT DID, SEW IT DID.
SO FAR, FOLKS, IT'S AN EVEN BREAK — ONE THROW FOR THAT "MOUSE" — ONE THROW FOR THAT "BRICK" — AND N-N-NOW THEY STRUGGLE FOR THE DECIDING THROW — IT'S A MEAN MEE-LEE, FOLKS — A ROOKUS, RIBALD AND RIOTFUL — BRICK, BENT ON THE BOISTER OF BATTLE — MOUSE, MANNED WITH THE MIEN OF MANGLE AND MAYHEM — IT'S CO-LOSSAL — FOLKS — JY-GANTIC — TY-TANIC —
TOE HOLDS BARRED — "MOUSE" —
Copr. 1941, King Features Syndicate, Inc., World rights reserved.
8-3

August 3rd, 1941.

"KRAZY KAT"
Registered U. S. Patent Office
I SEE A SAD SOUL, SORROWING IN A JAIL - LEAN WITH A LARGE LACK OF LIBERTY, - SCARRED WITH THE SCORN OF SECLUSION - TWITTED BY THE THUMB OF TYRANNY -
OMEEYO-MY - WHO COULD IT BE ?
WELL, HE LOOKS A BIT MOUSY - UPON GIVING ANOTHER LOOK, I SEE THAT IT IS A "MOUSE" - A BRAVE "MOUSE" -
UNWITTING OF HIS UNFED HUNGER - - LONGING ONLY FOR A SONG - A LILT, A LAY, A LULLABY - - -
AH & HA -
L'IL DOLLIN' MICE - I'LL GIVE HIM MUSIC - IVVIN DOUGH HE IS IN JAIL HE WILL HAVE HOMINY - AN' MELLIDY -
THAT SWEET "KAT" WILL WASTE NONE OF HIS PRETTY DITTIES ON THAT WORTHLESS "MOUSE" IF I CAN HELP IT.
"MUSICS"
I WILL ACT IN ADVANCE.
JAIL
AH-H - HONORABLE DISCHARGE.
SKUFF !!!
JAIL
NOW WILL I PUT EAR TO THAT DEAR "KAT'S" SWEET SONG - I, WHO AM REALLY WORTHY OF THAT GENTLE GESTURE
RAPTURE - RAPTURE - RA-A-A...
JAIL.
UR-R-RK JUPP
JAIL
I MUST FIND THAT "KOP" AND TELL HIM THE EVIL I JUST SEEN - IT IS MY DUTY TO REPORT IT - - THAT "MOUSE" WILL NEVER SUSPECT 'TWAS I WHO TOLD -
JAIL.
A-AH-H-- THE MOCKERY OF IT ALL -
Copr. 1941, King Features Syndicate, Inc., World rights reserved.
8-10
HERRIMAN

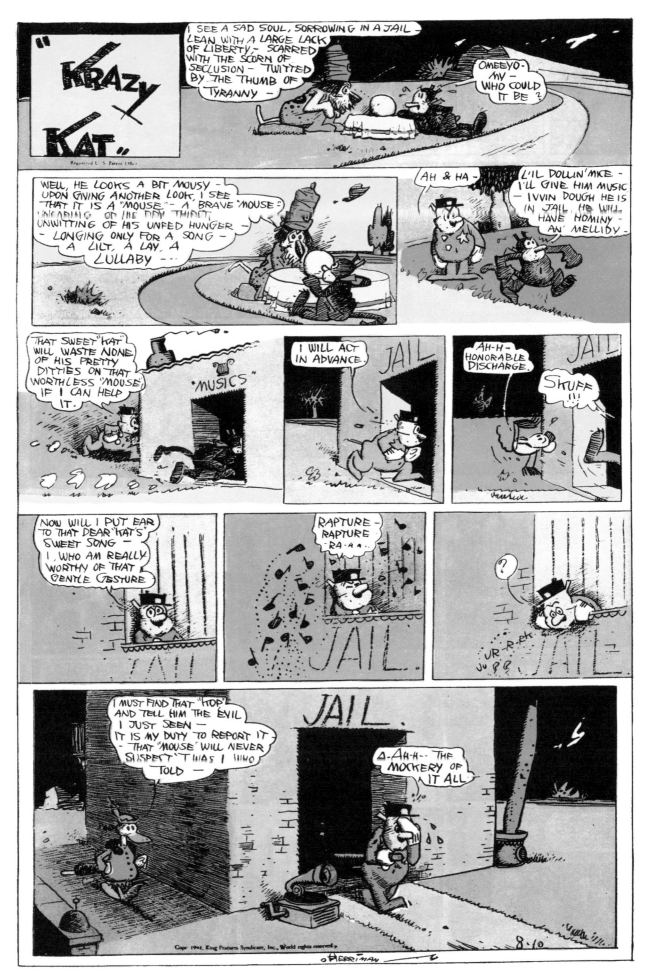

August 10th, 1941.

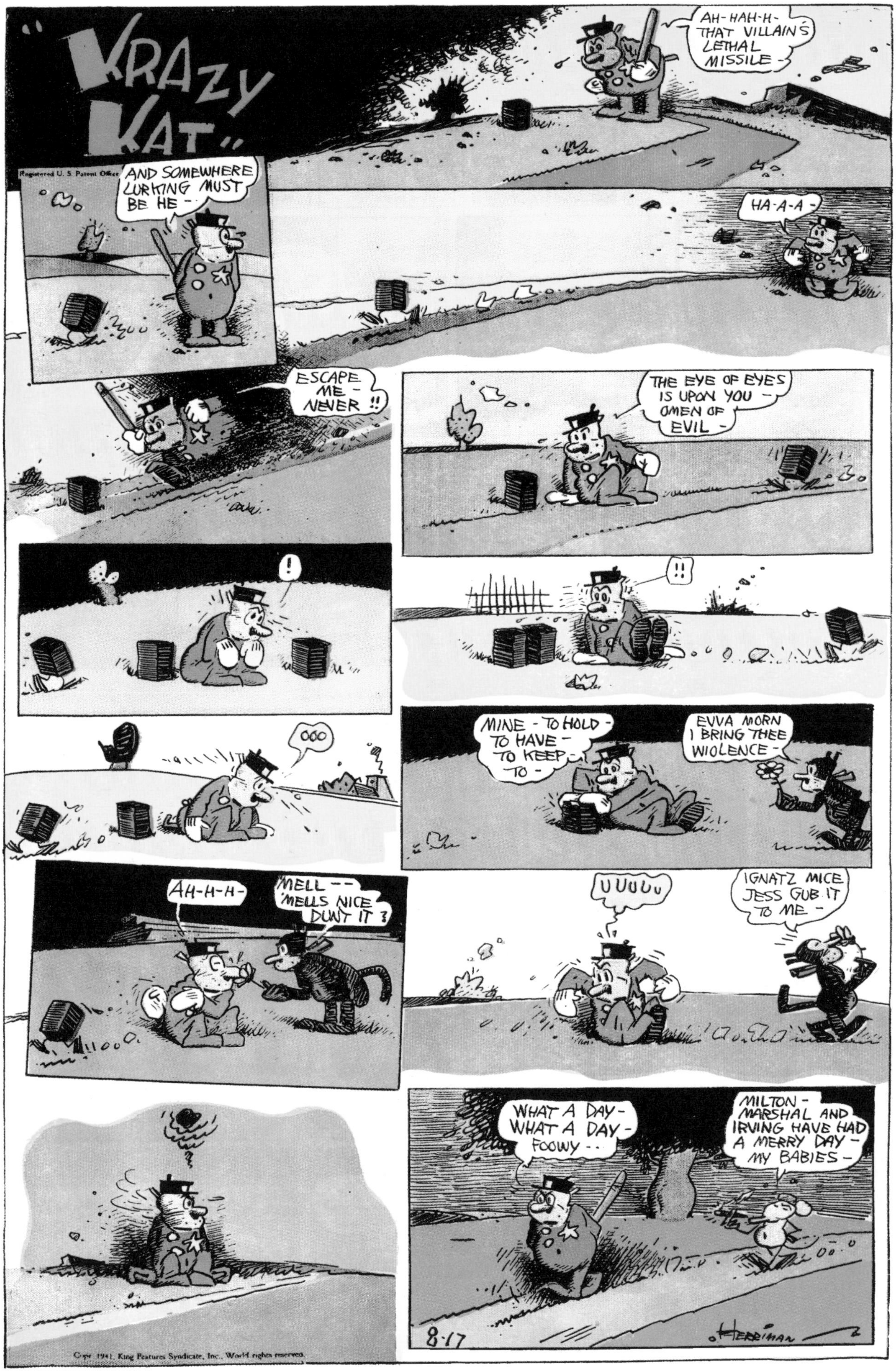
"KRAZY KAT"
Registered U. S. Patent Office
AH-HAH-H- THAT VILLAIN'S LETHAL MISSILE-
AND SOMEWHERE LURKING MUST BE HE-
HA-A-A-
ESCAPE ME NEVER !!
THE EYE OF EYES IS UPON YOU - OMEN OF EVIL-
!
!!
OOO
MINE - TO HOLD - TO HAVE - TO KEEP - TO -
EVVA MORN I BRING THEE WIOLENCE-
AH-H-H-
MELL -- MELLS NICE DUNT IT ?
UUUUU
IGNATZ MICE JESS GUB IT TO ME -
?
WHAT A DAY - WHAT A DAY - FOOWY --
MILTON - MARSHAL AND IRVING HAVE HAD A MERRY DAY - MY BABIES -
8-17
HERRIMAN
Copr 1941, King Features Syndicate, Inc., World rights reserved.

August 17th, 1941.

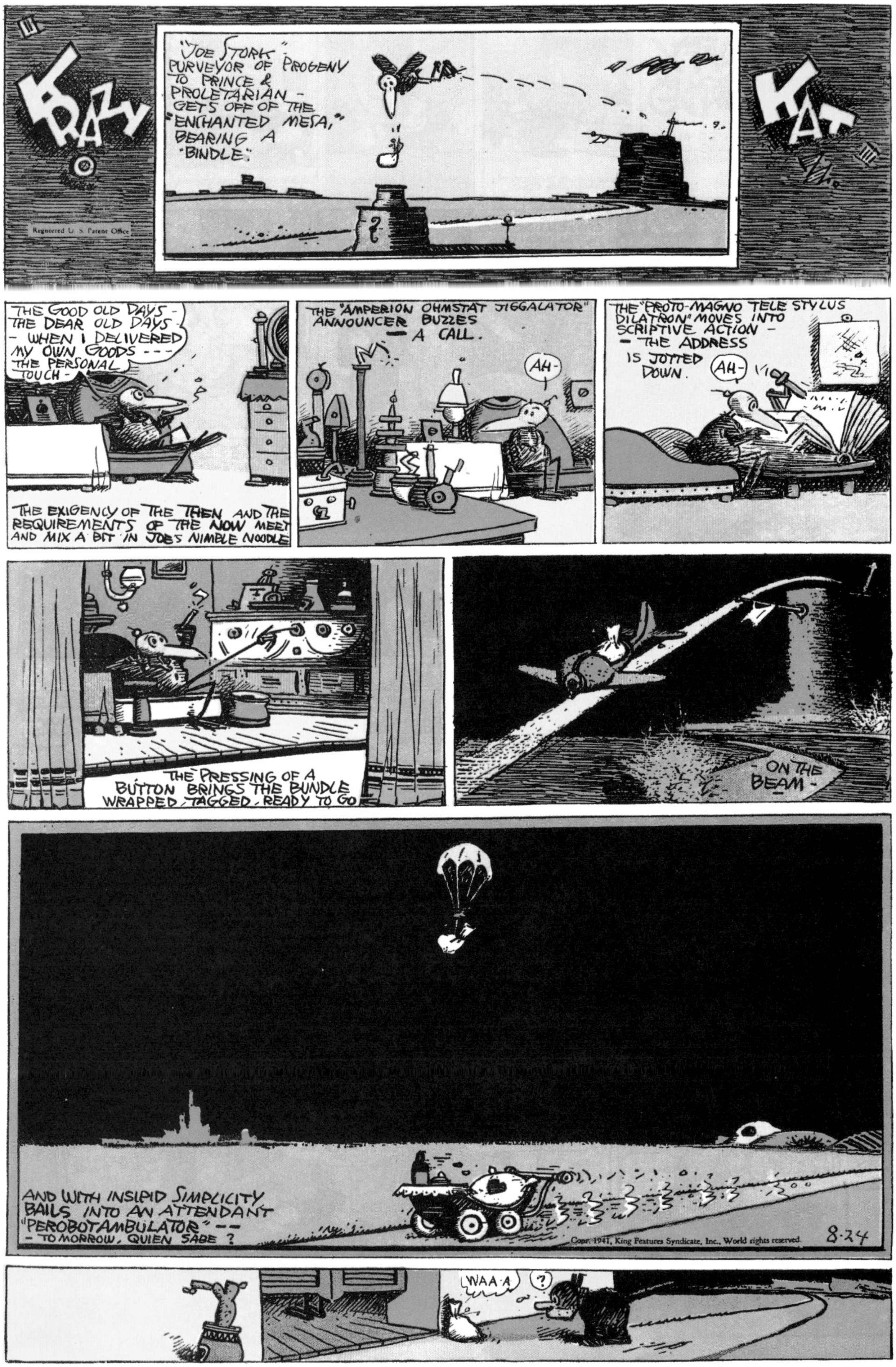
KRAZY KAT
Registered U. S. Patent Office
"JOE STORK" PURVEYOR OF PROGENY TO PRINCE & PROLETARIAN - GETS OFF OF THE "ENCHANTED MESA," BEARING A "BINDLE."
THE GOOD OLD DAYS - THE DEAR OLD DAYS - WHEN I DELIVERED MY OWN GOODS --- THE PERSONAL TOUCH -
THE EXIGENCY OF THE THEN AND THE REQUIREMENTS OF THE NOW MEET AND MIX A BIT IN JOE'S NIMBLE NOODLE
THE "AMPERION OHMSTAT JIGGALATOR" ANNOUNCER BUZZES — A CALL.
AH-
THE "PROTO-MAGNO TELE STYLUS DILATRON" MOVES INTO SCRIPTIVE ACTION - — THE ADDRESS IS JOTTED DOWN.
AH-
THE PRESSING OF A BUTTON BRINGS THE BUNDLE WRAPPED, TAGGED, READY TO GO
- ON THE BEAM -
AND WITH INSIPID SIMPLICITY BAILS INTO AN ATTENDANT "PEROBOTAMBULATOR" -- - TO MORROW, QUIEN SABE ?
Copr. 1941, King Features Syndicate, Inc., World rights reserved.
8·24
WAA-A
?

August 24th, 1941.

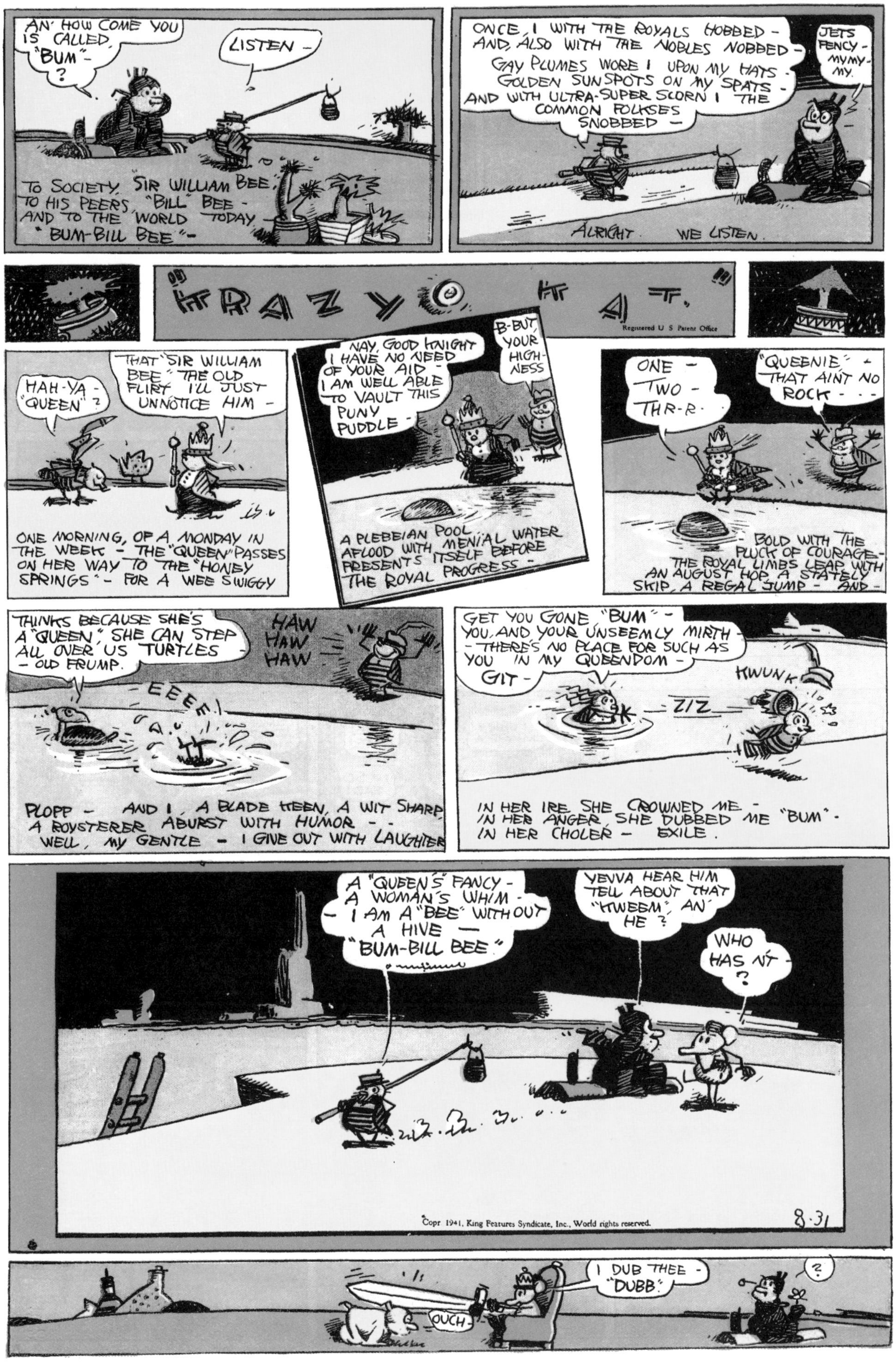
AN' HOW COME YOU IS CALLED "BUM"- ?
LISTEN -
TO SOCIETY, "SIR WILLIAM BEE" TO HIS PEERS, "BILL" BEE - AND TO THE WORLD TODAY "BUM-BILL BEE" -
ONCE, I WITH THE ROYALS HOBBED - AND, ALSO WITH THE NOBLES NOBBED -
GAY PLUMES WORE I UPON MY HATS - GOLDEN SUNSPOTS ON MY SPATS - AND WITH ULTRA-SUPER SCORN I THE COMMON FOLKSES SNOBBED -
JETS FENCY - MYMY - MY.
ALRIGHT. WE LISTEN.
KRAZY KAT
Registered U S Patent Office
HAH-YA "QUEEN"?
THAT "SIR WILLIAM BEE," THE OLD FLIRT. I'LL JUST UNNOTICE HIM -
ONE MORNING, OF A MONDAY IN THE WEEK - THE "QUEEN" PASSES ON HER WAY TO THE "HONEY SPRINGS" - FOR A WEE SWIGGY
NAY, GOOD KNIGHT I HAVE NO NEED OF YOUR AID - I AM WELL ABLE TO VAULT THIS PUNY PUDDLE -
B-BUT, YOUR HIGHNESS
A PLEBEIAN POOL, AFLOOD WITH MENIAL WATER PRESENTS ITSELF BEFORE THE ROYAL PROGRESS -
ONE - TWO - THR-R-
"QUEENIE" - THAT AIN'T NO ROCK - - -
BOLD WITH THE PLUCK OF COURAGE - THE ROYAL LIMBS LEAP WITH AN AUGUST HOP, A STATELY SKIP, A REGAL JUMP - AND -
THINKS BECAUSE SHE'S A "QUEEN," SHE CAN STEP ALL OVER US TURTLES - OLD FRUMP.
HAW HAW HAW
EEEE
PLOPP - AND I, A BLADE KEEN, A WIT SHARP A ROYSTERER ABURST WITH HUMOR - - WELL, MY GENTLE - I GIVE OUT WITH LAUGHTER
GET YOU GONE "BUM" - YOU, AND YOUR UNSEEMLY MIRTH - THERE'S NO PLACE FOR SUCH AS YOU IN MY QUEENDOM - GIT -
ZIZ
KWUNK
IN HER IRE SHE CROWNED ME - IN HER ANGER, SHE DUBBED ME "BUM" - IN HER CHOLER - EXILE.
A "QUEEN'S" FANCY - A WOMAN'S WHIM - I AM A "BEE" WITHOUT A HIVE - "BUM-BILL BEE"
YEVVA HEAR HIM TELL ABOUT THAT "KWEEM," AN' HE?
WHO HAS N'T ?
Copr 1941, King Features Syndicate, Inc., World rights reserved.
8-31
I DUB THEE - "DUBB"
OUCH
?

August 31st, 1941.

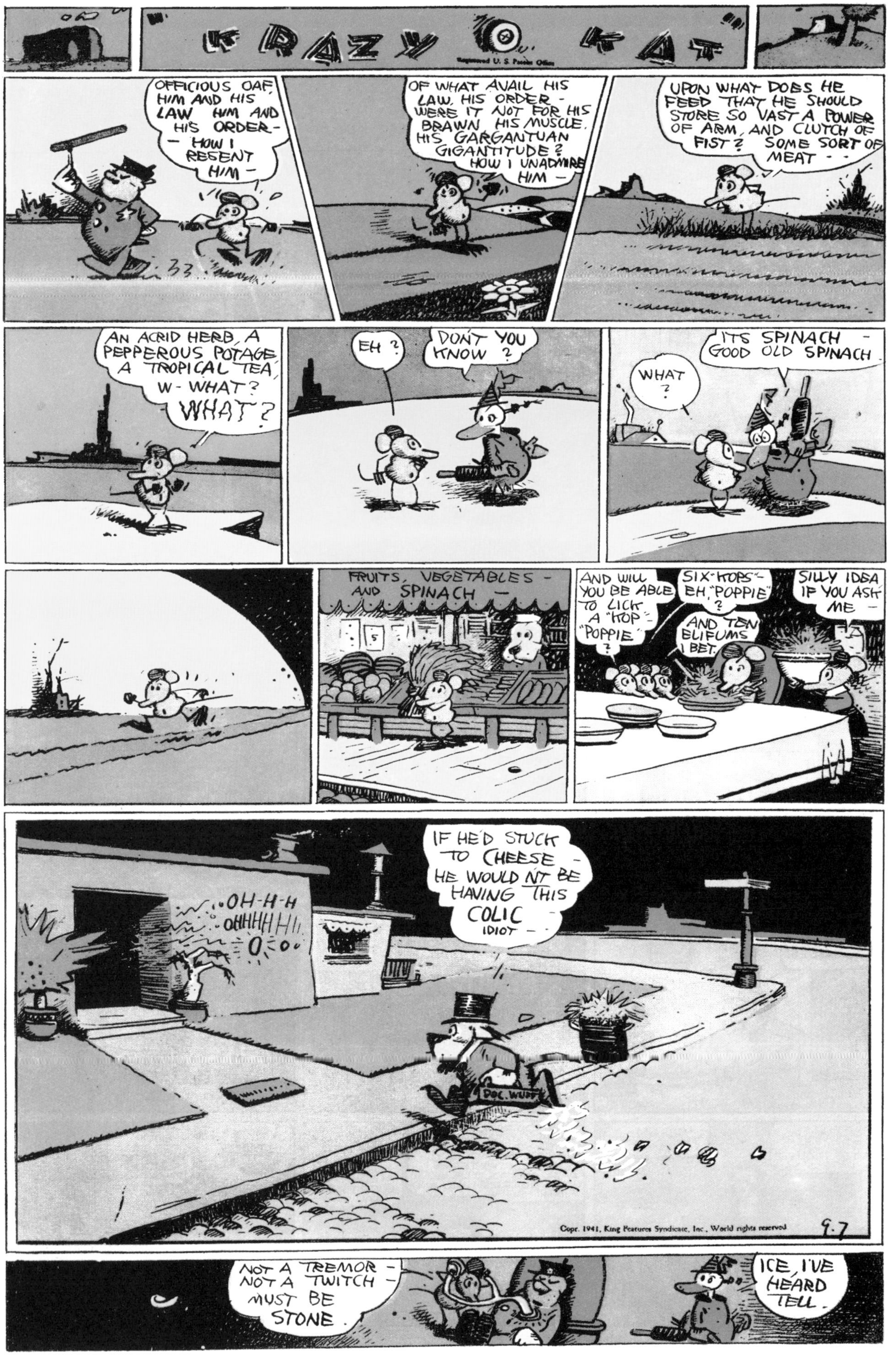
KRAZY KAT
Registered U. S. Patent Office
OFFICIOUS OAF, HIM AND HIS LAW HIM AND HIS ORDER - HOW I RESENT HIM -
OF WHAT AVAIL HIS LAW, HIS ORDER - WERE IT NOT FOR HIS BRAWN, HIS MUSCLE, HIS GARGANTUAN GIGANTITUDE? HOW I UNADMIRE HIM -
UPON WHAT DOES HE FEED THAT HE SHOULD STORE SO VAST A POWER OF ARM, AND CLUTCH OF FIST? SOME SORT OF MEAT - -
AN ACRID HERB, A PEPPEROUS POTAGE A TROPICAL TEA, W- WHAT? WHAT?
EH?
DON'T YOU KNOW?
WHAT?
ITS SPINACH - GOOD OLD SPINACH.
FRUITS, VEGETABLES - AND SPINACH -
AND WILL YOU BE ABLE TO LICK A "KOP" "POPPIE"?
SIX "KOPS" - EH, "POPPIE"?
AND TEN ELIFUMS I BET.
SILLY IDEA IF YOU ASK ME -
OH-H-H OHHHHH O-O
IF HE'D STUCK TO CHEESE - HE WOULD N'T BE HAVING THIS COLIC - IDIOT -
DOC. WUFF
Copr. 1941, King Features Syndicate, Inc., World rights reserved
9-7
NOT A TREMOR - NOT A TWITCH - MUST BE STONE.
ICE, I'VE HEARD TELL.

September 7th, 1941.

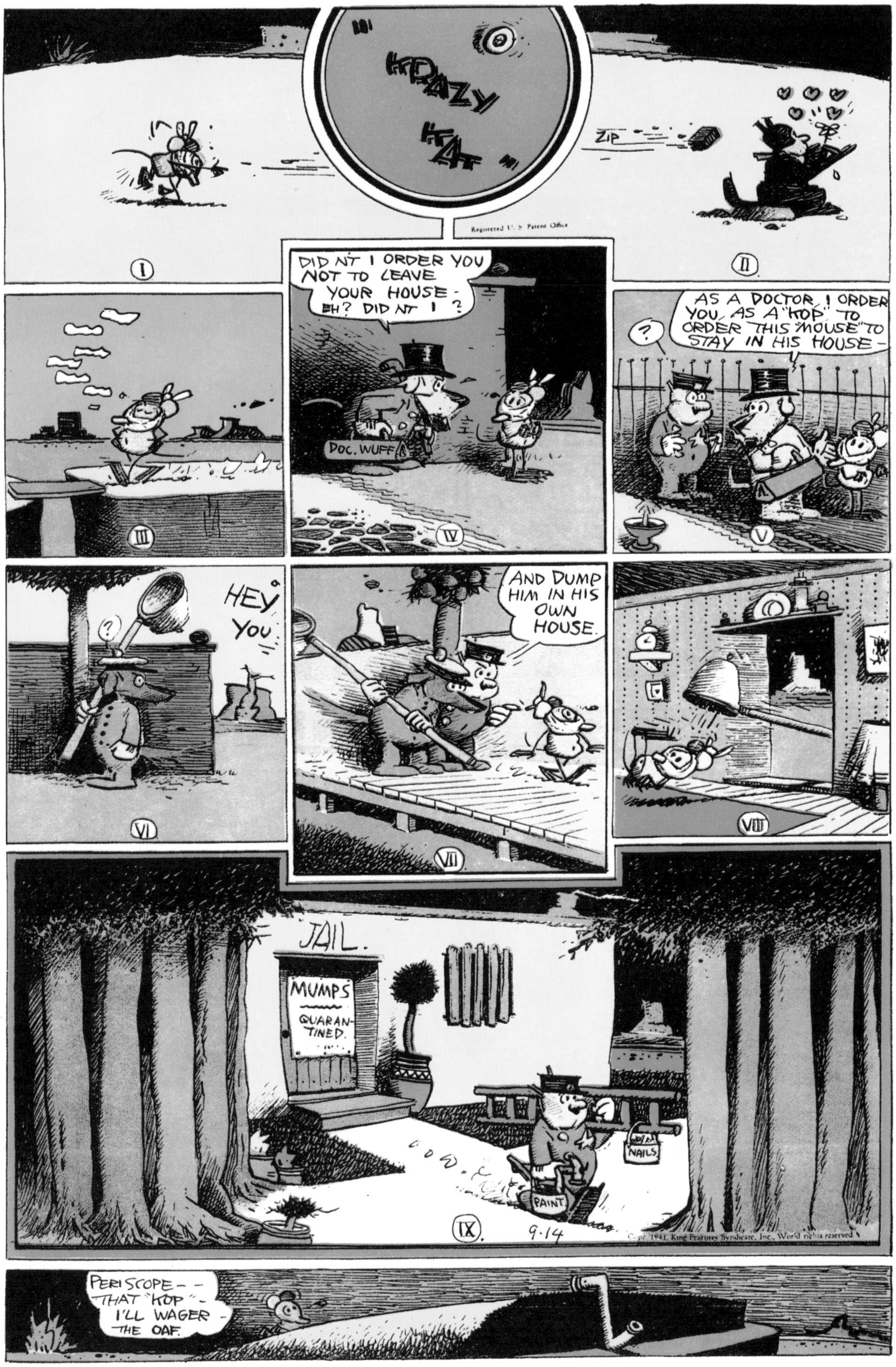
KRAZY KAT
Registered U. S. Patent Office
ZIP
I
II
DID NT I ORDER YOU NOT TO LEAVE YOUR HOUSE - EH? DID NT I ?
DOC. WUFF
?
AS A DOCTOR, I ORDER YOU, AS A "KOP" TO ORDER THIS "MOUSE" TO STAY IN HIS HOUSE -
III
IV
V
HEY YOU
?
AND DUMP HIM IN HIS OWN HOUSE.
VI
VII
VIII
JAIL.
MUMPS
QUARANTINED.
NAILS
PAINT
IX
9·14
Copr. 1941, King Features Syndicate, Inc., World rights reserved
PERISCOPE - - THAT "KOP" - I'LL WAGER - THE OAF.

September 14th, 1941.

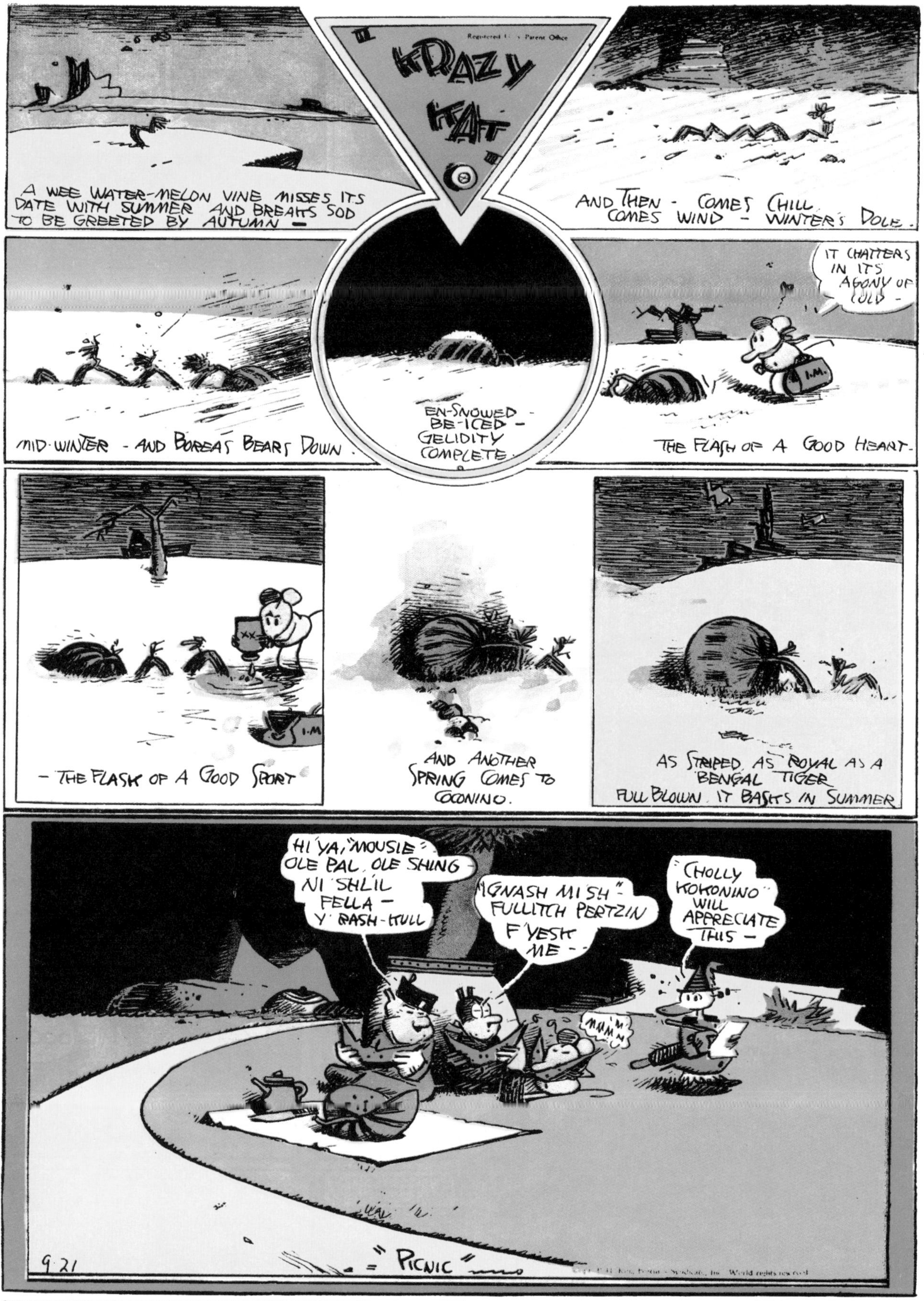
KRAZY KAT
A WEE WATER-MELON VINE MISSES ITS DATE WITH SUMMER AND BREAKS SOD TO BE GREETED BY AUTUMN —
AND THEN - COMES CHILL COMES WIND - WINTER'S DOLE.
MID-WINTER - AND BOREAS BEARS DOWN.
EN-SNOWED - BE-ICED - GELIDITY COMPLETE.
IT CHATTERS IN ITS AGONY OF COLD -
I.M.
THE FLASH OF A GOOD HEART -
XX
- THE FLASK OF A GOOD SPORT
AND ANOTHER SPRING COMES TO COCONINO.
AS STRIPED AS ROYAL AS A BENGAL TIGER FULL BLOWN IT BASKS IN SUMMER
HI YA, "MOUSIE" OLE PAL OLE SHING - NI SHLIL FELLA - Y' BASH-HULL
"GNASH MISH" - FULLITCH PERTZIN F'YESH ME - -
"CHOLLY KOKONINO" WILL APPRECIATE THIS -
MMMM
9.21
"PICNIC"

September 21st, 1941.

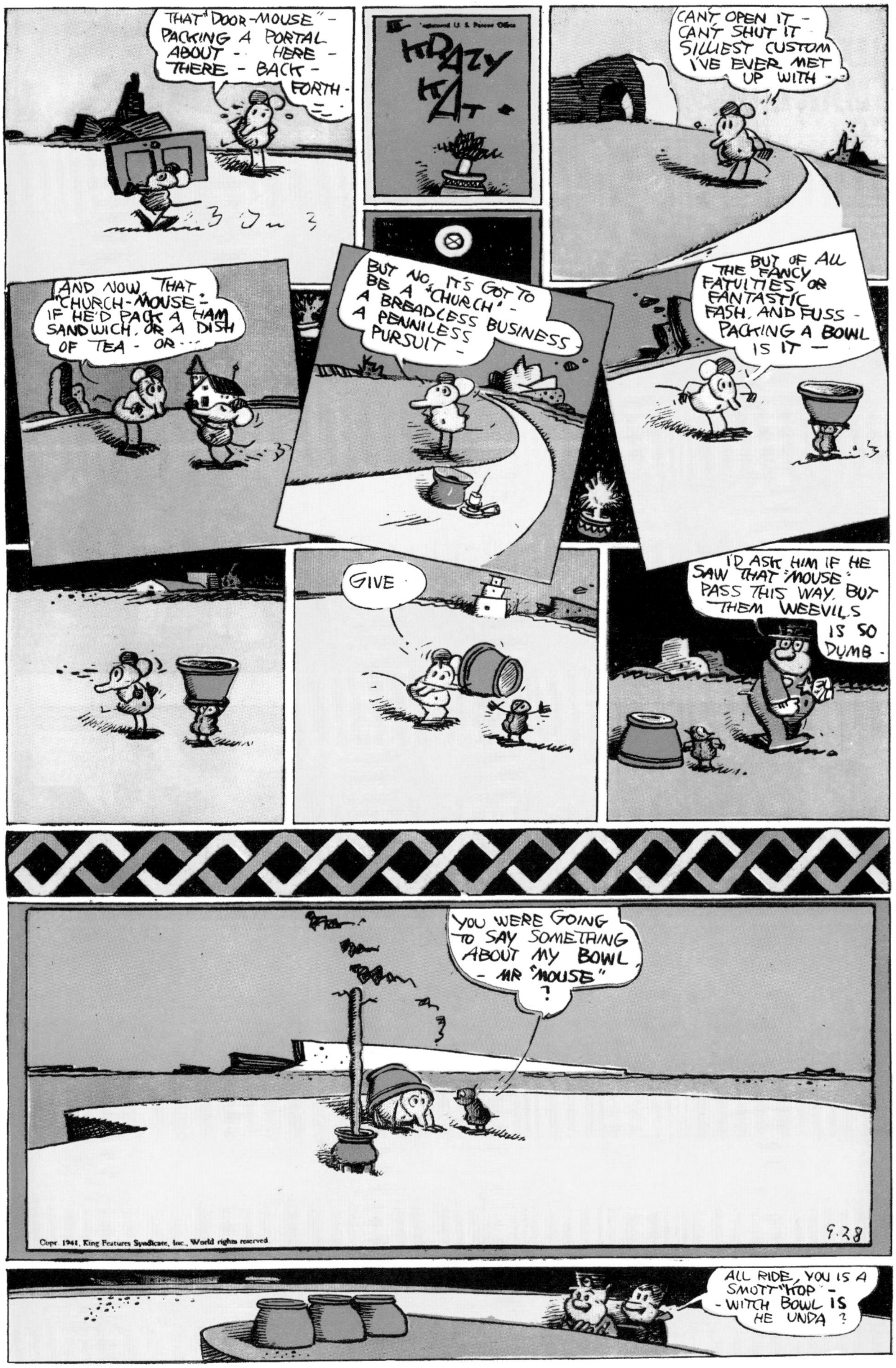
THAT "DOOR-MOUSE" - PACKING A PORTAL ABOUT - HERE - THERE - BACK - FORTH -
KRAZY KAT
CAN'T OPEN IT - CAN'T SHUT IT SILLIEST CUSTOM I'VE EVER MET UP WITH -
AND NOW, THAT "CHURCH-MOUSE" - IF HE'D PACK A HAM SANDWICH, OR A DISH OF TEA - OR - -
BUT NO, IT'S GOT TO BE A "CHURCH" - A BREADLESS BUSINESS A PENNILESS PURSUIT -
BUT OF ALL THE FANCY FATUITIES OR FANTASTIC FASH, AND FUSS - PACKING A BOWL IS IT -
GIVE
I'D ASK HIM IF HE SAW THAT "MOUSE" PASS THIS WAY, BUT THEM WEEVILS IS SO DUMB -
YOU WERE GOING TO SAY SOMETHING ABOUT MY BOWL - MR "MOUSE" ?
Copr. 1941, King Features Syndicate, Inc., World rights reserved.
9.28
ALL RIDE, YOU IS A SMOTT "KOP" - WITCH BOWL IS HE UNDA ?

September 28th, 1941.

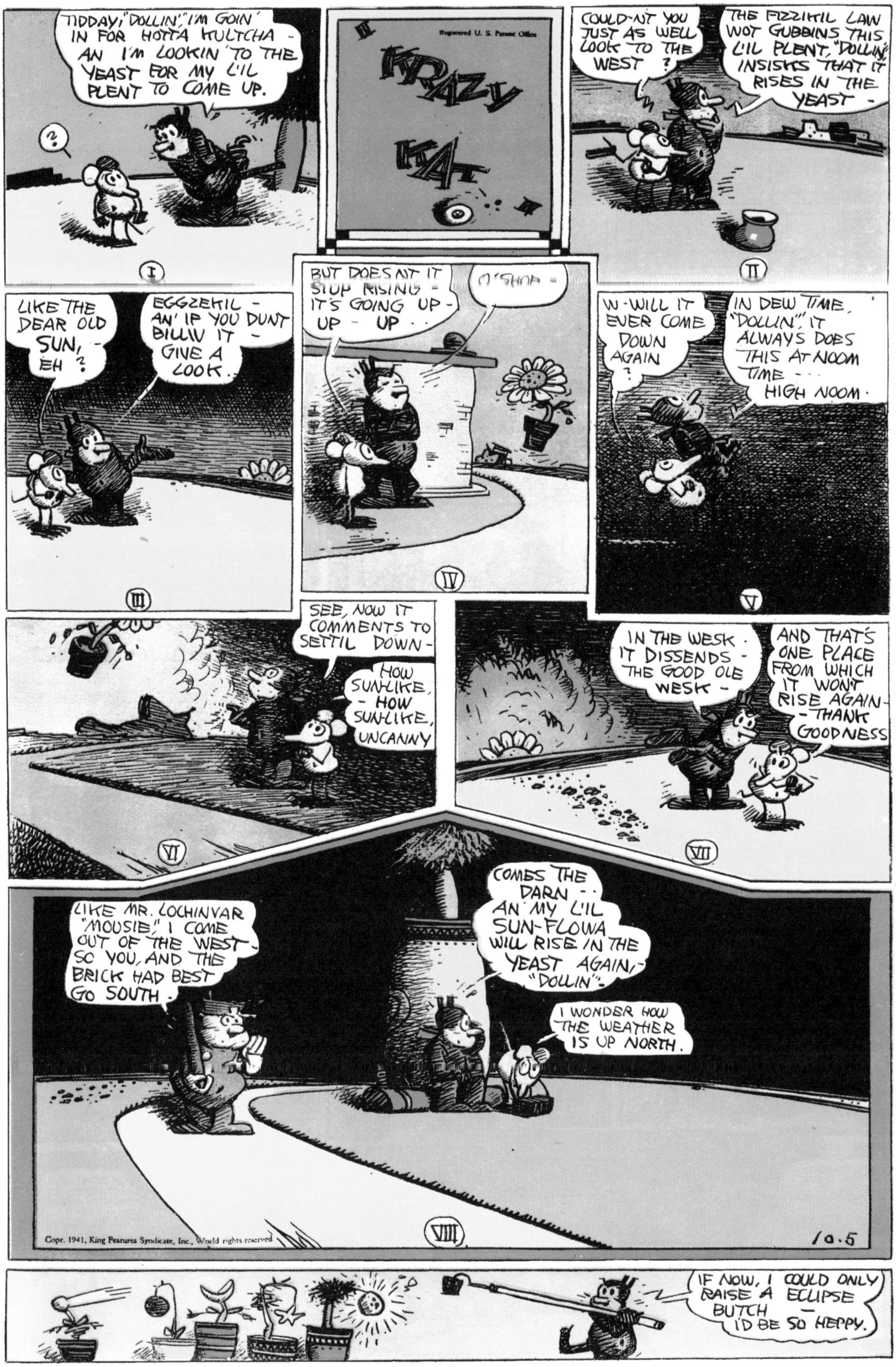
Registered U. S. Patent Office
KRAZY KAT
TIDDAY, "DOLLIN'," I'M GOIN' IN FOR HOTTA HULTCHA - AN I'M LOOKIN' TO THE YEAST FOR MY L'IL PLENT TO COME UP.
COULD-N'T YOU JUST AS WELL LOOK TO THE WEST ?
THE FIZZIKIL LAW WOT GUBBINS THIS L'IL PLENT, "DOLLIN" INSISKS THAT IT RISES IN THE YEAST -
LIKE THE DEAR OLD SUN, - EH ?
EGGZEKIL - AN' IF YOU DUNT BILLIV IT - GIVE A LOOK.
BUT DOES N'T IT STOP RISING - IT'S GOING UP - UP - UP - -
O'SHOO -
W-WILL IT EVER COME DOWN AGAIN ?
IN DEW TIME, "DOLLIN'," IT ALWAYS DOES THIS AT NOOM TIME - - HIGH NOOM.
SEE, NOW IT COMMENTS TO SETTIL DOWN -
HOW SUN-LIKE, - HOW SUN-LIKE, UNCANNY
IN THE WESK - IT DISSENDS - THE GOOD OLE WESK -
AND THAT'S ONE PLACE FROM WHICH IT WON'T RISE AGAIN - - THANK GOODNESS
LIKE MR. LOCHINVAR "MOUSIE," I COME OUT OF THE WEST - SO YOU, AND THE BRICK HAD BEST GO SOUTH -
COMES THE DARN - - AN' MY L'IL SUN-FLOWA WILL RISE IN THE YEAST AGAIN, - "DOLLIN" -
I WONDER HOW THE WEATHER IS UP NORTH.
Copr. 1941, King Features Syndicate, Inc., World rights reserved
10.5
IF NOW, I COULD ONLY RAISE A ECLIPSE BUTCH - I'D BE SO HEPPY.

October 5th, 1941.

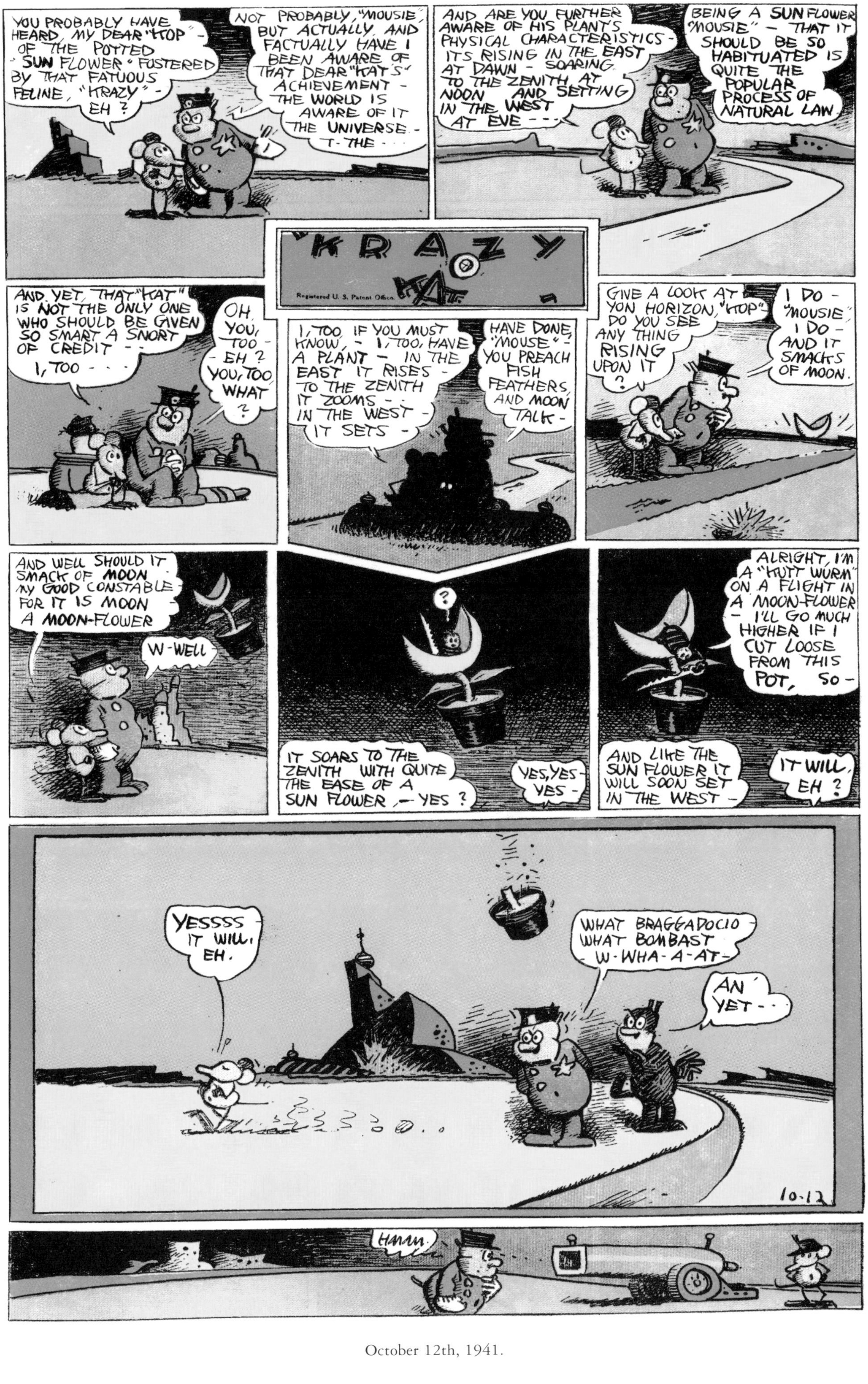

YOU PROBABLY HAVE HEARD, MY DEAR "KOP" - OF THE POTTED "SUN FLOWER" FOSTERED BY THAT FATUOUS FELINE, "KRAZY" - EH ?
NOT PROBABLY, "MOUSIE", BUT ACTUALLY, AND FACTUALLY HAVE I BEEN AWARE OF THAT DEAR "KAT'S" ACHIEVEMENT - THE WORLD IS AWARE OF IT THE UNIVERSE - T- THE - - -
AND ARE YOU FURTHER AWARE OF HIS PLANT'S PHYSICAL CHARACTERISTICS - ITS RISING IN THE EAST AT DAWN - SOARING TO THE ZENITH AT NOON AND SETTING IN THE WEST AT EVE - - -
BEING A SUN FLOWER "MOUSIE" - THAT IT SHOULD BE SO HABITUATED IS QUITE THE POPULAR PROCESS OF NATURAL LAW
"KRAZY KAT"
Registered U. S. Patent Office.
AND YET, THAT "KAT" IS NOT THE ONLY ONE WHO SHOULD BE GIVEN SO SMART A SNORT OF CREDIT - - I, TOO - - -
OH, YOU, TOO - EH ? YOU, TOO WHAT ?
I, TOO, IF YOU MUST KNOW, - I, TOO, HAVE A PLANT - IN THE EAST IT RISES - TO THE ZENITH IT ZOOMS - - IN THE WEST - IT SETS -
HAVE DONE, "MOUSE" - YOU PREACH FISH FEATHERS, AND MOON TALK -
GIVE A LOOK AT YON HORIZON, "KOP" DO YOU SEE ANY THING RISING UPON IT ?
I DO - "MOUSIE", I DO - AND IT SMACKS OF MOON.
AND WELL SHOULD IT SMACK OF MOON MY GOOD CONSTABLE FOR IT IS MOON - A MOON-FLOWER
W-WELL
?
IT SOARS TO THE ZENITH WITH QUITE THE EASE OF A SUN FLOWER, - YES ?
YES, YES - YES -
ALRIGHT, I'M A "KUTT WURM" ON A FLIGHT IN A MOON-FLOWER - I'LL GO MUCH HIGHER IF I CUT LOOSE FROM THIS POT, SO -
AND LIKE THE SUN FLOWER IT WILL SOON SET IN THE WEST -
IT WILL, EH ?
YESSSS - IT WILL, EH.
WHAT BRAGGADOCIO - WHAT BOMBAST - W-WHA-A-AT -
AN' YET - -
10-12
HAAAH.

October 12th, 1941.

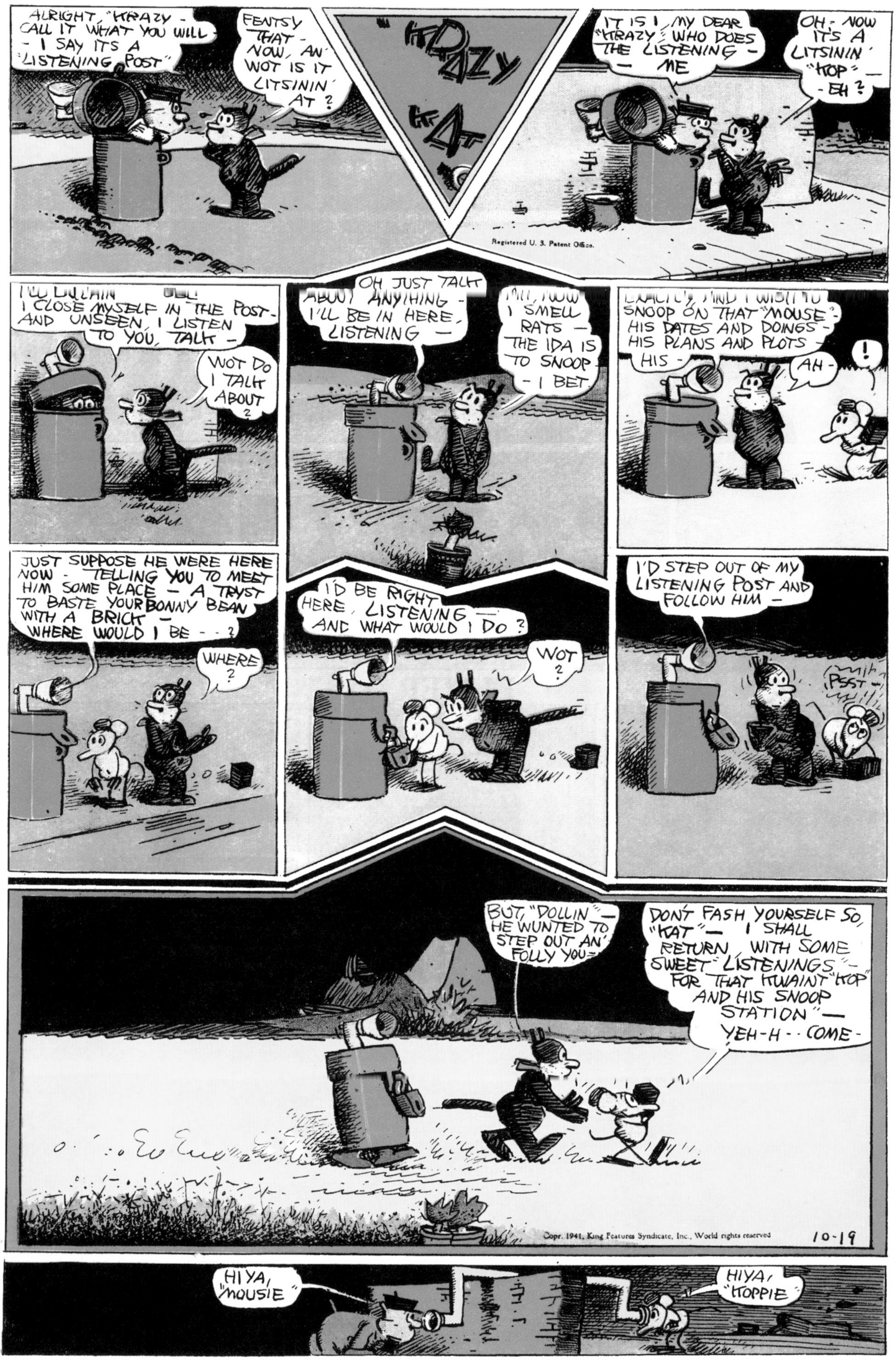
ALRIGHT, "KRAZY" - CALL IT WHAT YOU WILL - I SAY ITS A "LISTENING POST"
FENTSY THAT - NOW, AN' WOT IS IT LITSININ' AT ?
"KRAZY KAT"
Registered U. S. Patent Office.
IT IS I, MY DEAR "KRAZY" WHO DOES THE LISTENING - - ME
OH - NOW IT'S A LITSININ' "KOP" - - EH ?
I CLOSE MYSELF IN THE POST - AND UNSEEN, I LISTEN TO YOU, TALK -
WOT DO I TALK ABOUT ?
OH JUST TALK ABOUT ANYTHING - I'LL BE IN HERE, LISTENING -
I SMELL RATS - THE IDA IS TO SNOOP - I BET.
SNOOP ON THAT "MOUSE" - HIS DATES AND DOINGS - HIS PLANS AND PLOTS - HIS -
AH -
!
JUST SUPPOSE HE WERE HERE NOW - TELLING YOU TO MEET HIM SOME PLACE - A TRYST TO BASTE YOUR BONNY BEAN WITH A BRICK - WHERE WOULD I BE - - ?
WHERE ?
I'D BE RIGHT HERE, LISTENING - AND WHAT WOULD I DO ?
WOT ?
I'D STEP OUT OF MY LISTENING POST AND FOLLOW HIM -
PSST -
BUT, "DOLLIN'" - HE WUNTED TO STEP OUT AN' FOLLY YOU -
DON'T FASH YOURSELF SO, "KAT" - I SHALL RETURN, WITH SOME SWEET LISTENINGS, - FOR THAT KWAINT "KOP" AND HIS SNOOP STATION" - YEH-H - - COME -
Copr. 1941, King Features Syndicate, Inc., World rights reserved
10-19
HI YA, "MOUSIE"
HIYA, "KOPPIE"

October 19th, 1941.

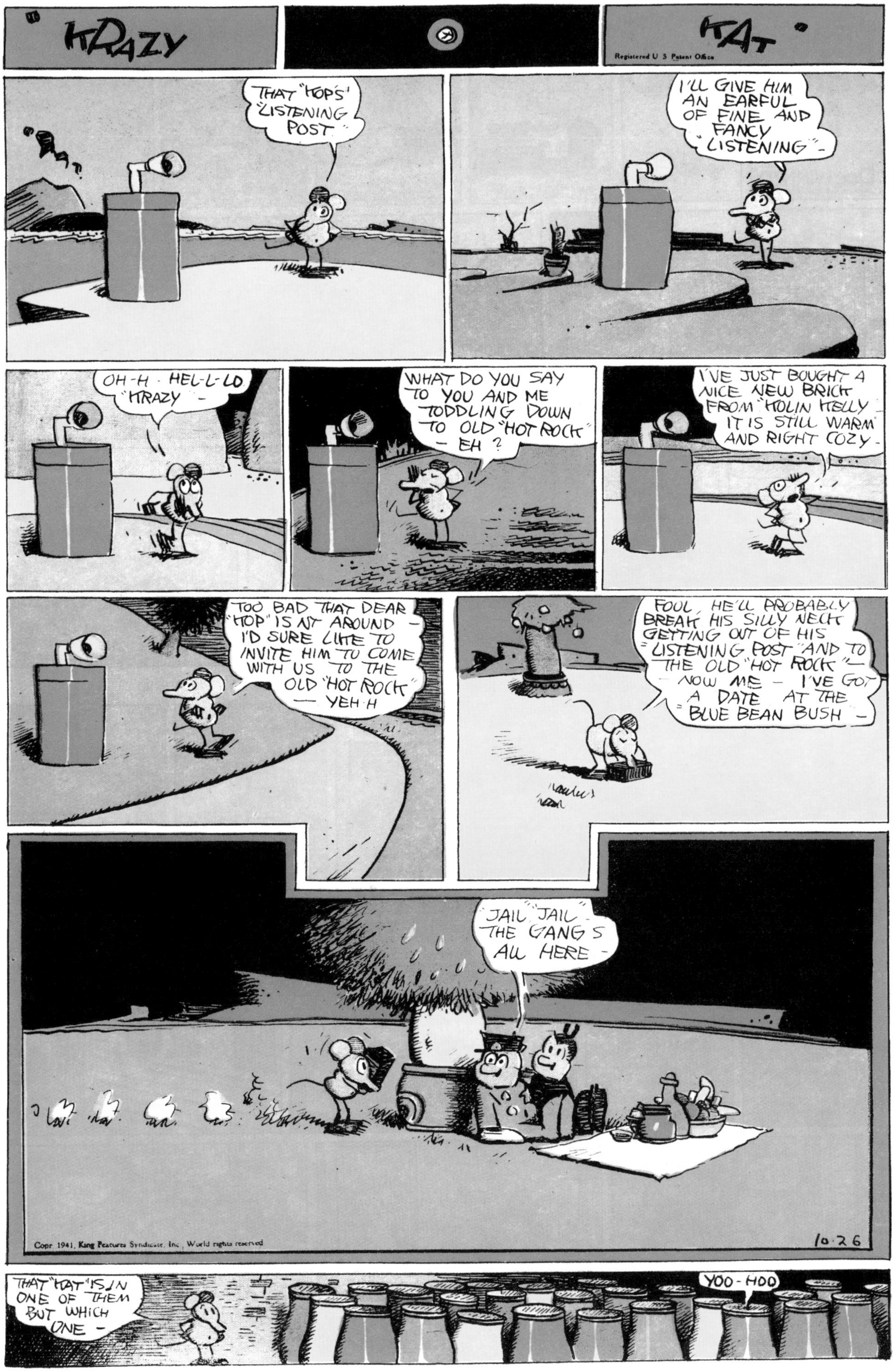
"KRAZY KAT"
Registered U S Patent Office
THAT "KOPS' "LISTENING POST"
I'LL GIVE HIM AN EARFUL OF FINE AND FANCY "LISTENING" -
OH-H HEL-L-LO "KRAZY" -
WHAT DO YOU SAY TO YOU AND ME TODDLING DOWN TO OLD "HOT ROCK" - EH ?
I'VE JUST BOUGHT A NICE NEW BRICK FROM "KOLIN KELLY" - IT IS STILL WARM AND RIGHT COZY -
TOO BAD THAT DEAR "KOP" IS N'T AROUND - I'D SURE LIKE TO INVITE HIM TO COME WITH US TO THE OLD "HOT ROCK" — YEH-H
FOOL, HE'LL PROBABLY BREAK HIS SILLY NECK GETTING OUT OF HIS "LISTENING POST" AND TO THE OLD "HOT ROCK" — - NOW ME - I'VE GOT A DATE AT THE "BLUE BEAN BUSH" -
"JAIL" "JAIL" - THE GANG'S ALL HERE -
Copr. 1941, King Features Syndicate, Inc., World rights reserved
10-26
THAT "KAT" IS IN ONE OF THEM BUT WHICH ONE -
YOO-HOO

October 26th, 1941.

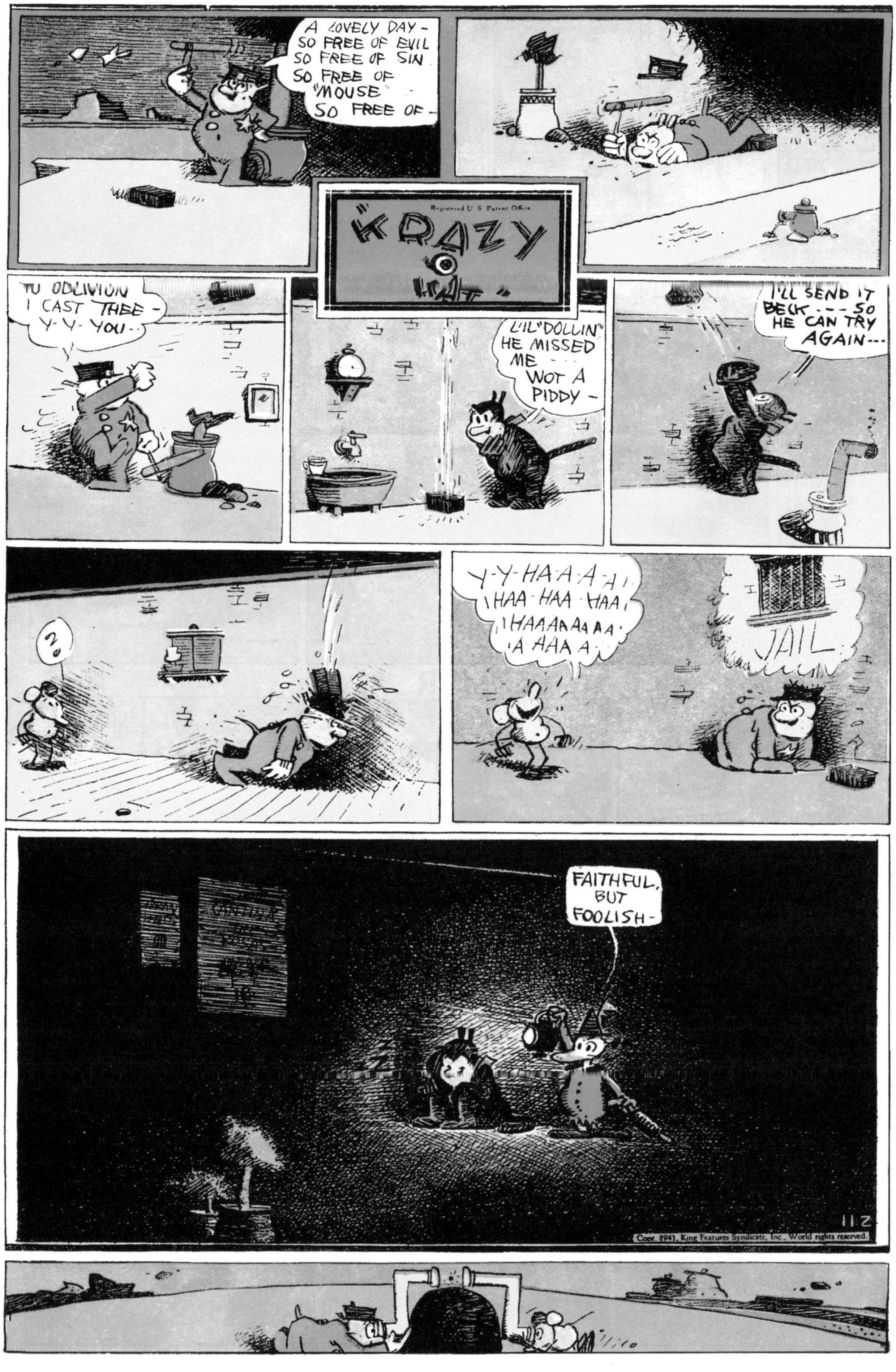
A LOVELY DAY - SO FREE OF EVIL SO FREE OF SIN SO FREE OF "MOUSE" - SO FREE OF -
Registered U.S. Patent Office
KRAZY KAT
TO OBLIVION I CAST THEE - Y-Y-YOU..
L'IL "DOLLIN" HE MISSED ME --- WOT A PIDDY -
I'LL SEND IT BECK --- SO HE CAN TRY AGAIN---
?
Y-Y-HA-A-A-A! HAA-HAA-HAA! HAAAAAAAA! A-AAA-A-
JAIL
FAITHFUL, BUT FOOLISH -
11-2
Copr. 1941, King Features Syndicate, Inc., World rights reserved.

November 2nd, 1941.

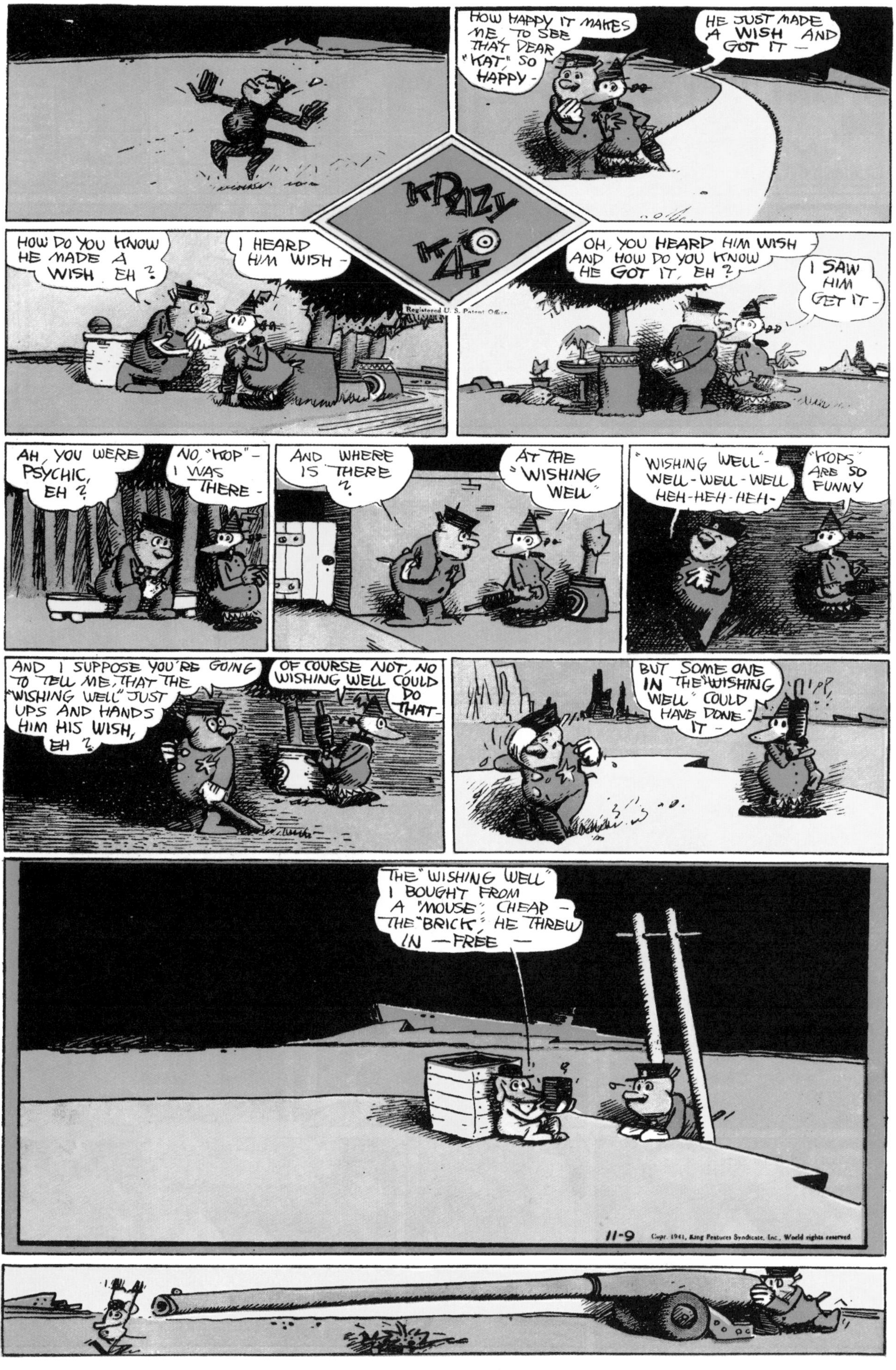

HOW HAPPY IT MAKES ME TO SEE THAT DEAR "KAT" SO HAPPY -
HE JUST MADE A WISH AND GOT IT -
KRAZY KAT
Registered U. S. Patent Office
HOW DO YOU KNOW HE MADE A WISH EH ?
I HEARD HIM WISH -
OH, YOU HEARD HIM WISH - AND HOW DO YOU KNOW HE GOT IT, EH ?
I SAW HIM GET IT -
AH, YOU WERE PSYCHIC, EH ?
NO, "KOP" - I WAS THERE -
AND WHERE IS THERE ?
AT THE "WISHING WELL"
"WISHING WELL" - WELL - WELL - WELL HEH-HEH-HEH -
"KOPS" ARE SO FUNNY
AND I SUPPOSE YOU'RE GOING TO TELL ME, THAT THE "WISHING WELL" JUST UPS AND HANDS HIM HIS WISH, EH ?
OF COURSE NOT, NO WISHING WELL COULD DO THAT -
BUT SOME ONE IN THE "WISHING WELL" COULD HAVE DONE IT -
THE "WISHING WELL" I BOUGHT FROM A "MOUSE", CHEAP - THE "BRICK", HE THREW IN - FREE -
11-9
Copr. 1941, King Features Syndicate, Inc., World rights reserved

November 9th, 1941.

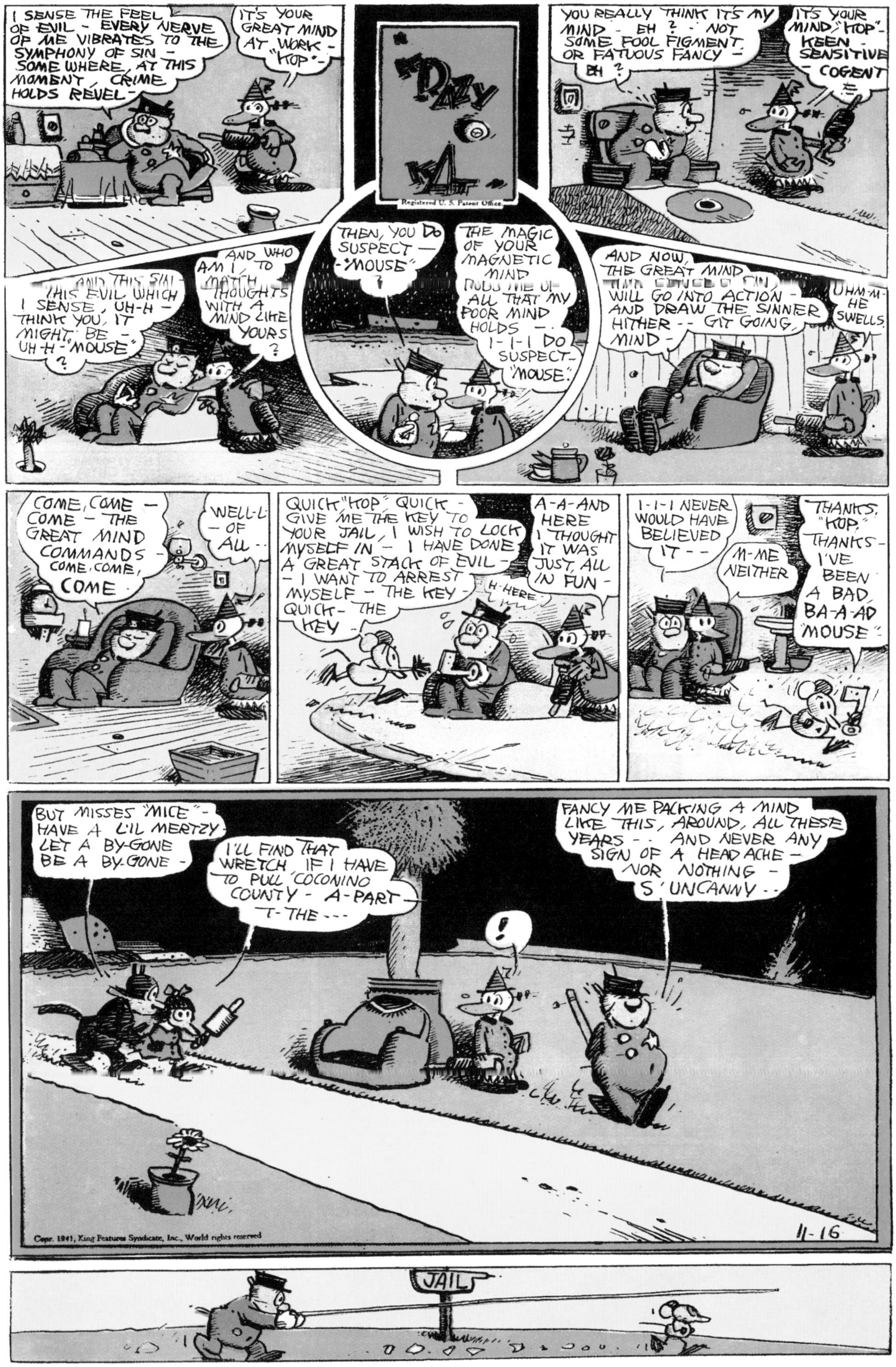
I SENSE THE FEEL OF EVIL - EVERY NERVE OF ME VIBRATES TO THE SYMPHONY OF SIN - SOME WHERE, AT THIS MOMENT, CRIME HOLDS REVEL -
IT'S YOUR GREAT MIND AT WORK - "KOP" -
Registered U. S. Patent Office.
YOU REALLY THINK IT'S MY MIND - EH ? - NOT SOME FOOL FIGMENT, OR FATUOUS FANCY - EH ?
IT'S YOUR MIND, "KOP" - KEEN - SENSITIVE - COGENT
AND THIS SIN - THIS EVIL WHICH I SENSE, UH-H - THINK YOU, IT MIGHT BE - UH-H - "MOUSE" ?
AND WHO AM I, TO MATCH THOUGHTS WITH A MIND LIKE YOURS ?
THEN, YOU DO SUSPECT - - "MOUSE" ?
THE MAGIC OF YOUR MAGNETIC MIND ALL THAT MY POOR MIND HOLDS - I-I-I DO SUSPECT - "MOUSE".
AND NOW, THE GREAT MIND WILL GO INTO ACTION - AND DRAW THE SINNER HITHER - - GIT GOING, MIND -
UHM-M - HE SWELLS.
COME, COME - COME - THE GREAT MIND COMMANDS - COME, COME, COME
WELL-L - OF ALL - -
QUICK "KOP" QUICK - GIVE ME THE KEY TO YOUR JAIL, I WISH TO LOCK MYSELF IN - I HAVE DONE A GREAT STACK OF EVIL - - I WANT TO ARREST MYSELF - THE KEY - QUICK - THE KEY -
H-HERE
A-A-AND HERE I THOUGHT IT WAS JUST, ALL IN FUN -
I-I-I NEVER WOULD HAVE BELIEVED IT - -
M-ME NEITHER
THANKS, "KOP", THANKS - I'VE BEEN A BAD, BA-A-AD "MOUSE" -
BUT MISSES "MICE" - HAVE A LI'L MERTZY - LET A BY-GONE BE A BY-GONE -
I'LL FIND THAT WRETCH IF I HAVE TO PULL COCONINO COUNTY - A-PART - T-THE - - -
FANCY ME PACKING A MIND LIKE THIS, AROUND, ALL THESE YEARS - - AND NEVER ANY SIGN OF A HEADACHE - NOR NOTHING - S'UNCANNY - -
!
Copr. 1941, King Features Syndicate, Inc., World rights reserved
11-16
JAIL

November 16th, 1941.

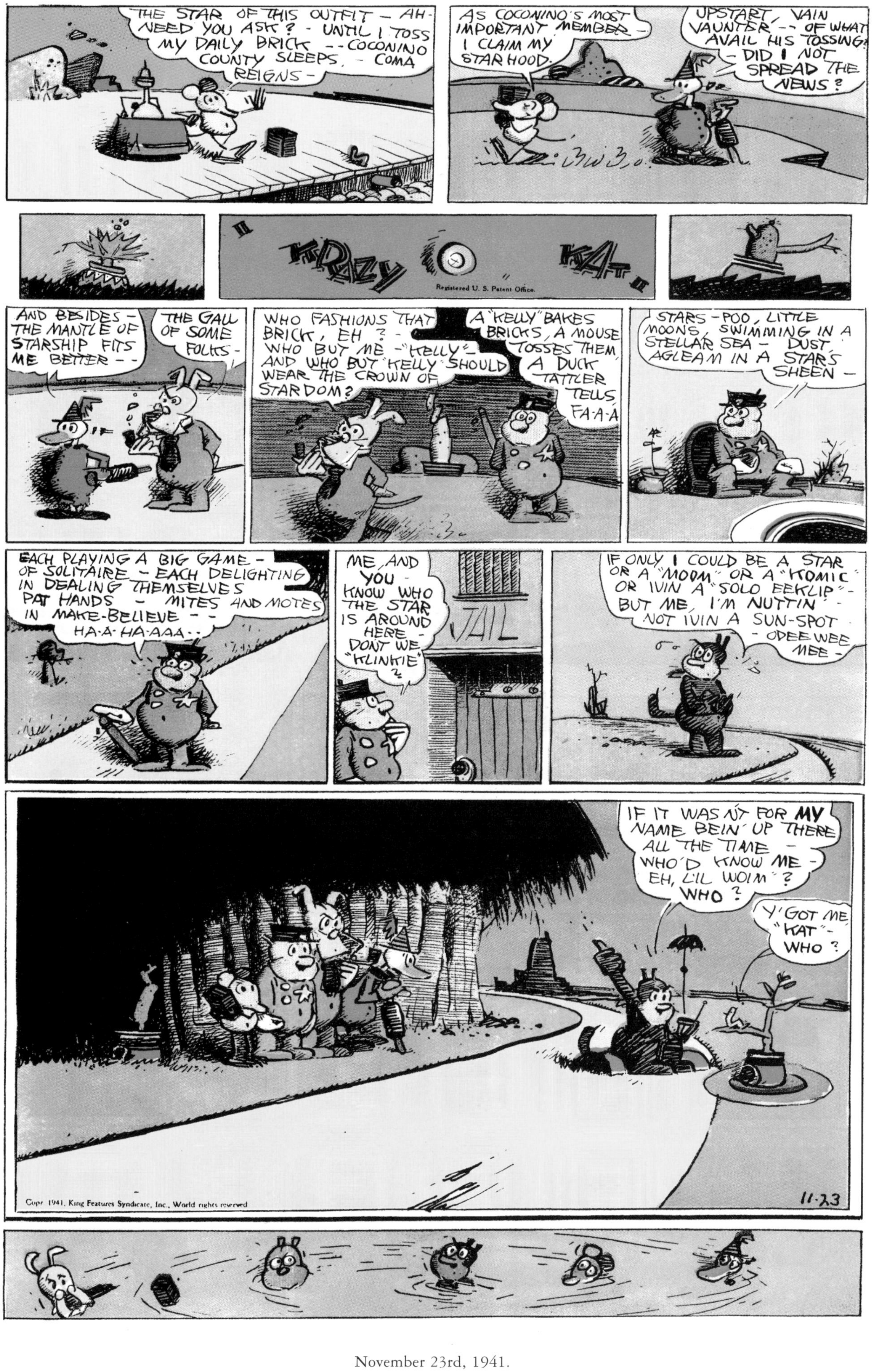
THE STAR OF THIS OUTFIT - AH - NEED YOU ASK? - UNTIL I TOSS MY DAILY BRICK -- COCONINO COUNTY SLEEPS, - COMA REIGNS -
AS COCONINO'S MOST IMPORTANT MEMBER - I CLAIM MY STAR HOOD.
UPSTART, VAIN VAUNTER -- OF WHAT AVAIL HIS TOSSING? - DID I NOT SPREAD THE NEWS?
KRAZY KAT
Registered U. S. Patent Office.
AND BESIDES - THE MANTLE OF STARSHIP FITS ME BETTER --
THE GALL OF SOME FOLKS -
WHO FASHIONS THAT BRICK, EH? - WHO BUT ME - "KELLY" - AND WHO BUT KELLY SHOULD WEAR THE CROWN OF STARDOM?
A "KELLY" BAKES BRICKS, A MOUSE TOSSES THEM, A DUCK TATTLER TELLS FA-A-A
STARS - POO, LITTLE MOONS, SWIMMING IN A STELLAR SEA - DUST, AGLEAM IN A STAR'S SHEEN -
EACH PLAYING A BIG GAME - OF SOLITAIRE - EACH DELIGHTING IN DEALING THEMSELVES PAT HANDS - MITES AND MOTES IN MAKE-BELIEVE -- HA-A-HA-AAA --
ME, AND YOU - KNOW WHO THE STAR IS AROUND HERE - DONT WE, "KLINKIE"?
JAIL
IF ONLY I COULD BE A STAR OR A "MOOM" OR A "KOMIC" OR IVIN A "SOLO EEKLIP" - BUT ME, I'M NUTTIN' - NOT IVIN A SUN-SPOT - ODEE WEE MEE -
IF IT WAS N'T FOR MY NAME BEIN' UP THERE ALL THE TIME - WHO'D KNOW ME - EH, LIL WOIM? WHO?
Y' GOT ME "KAT" - WHO?
Copr. 1941, King Features Syndicate, Inc., World rights reserved
11-23

November 23rd, 1941.

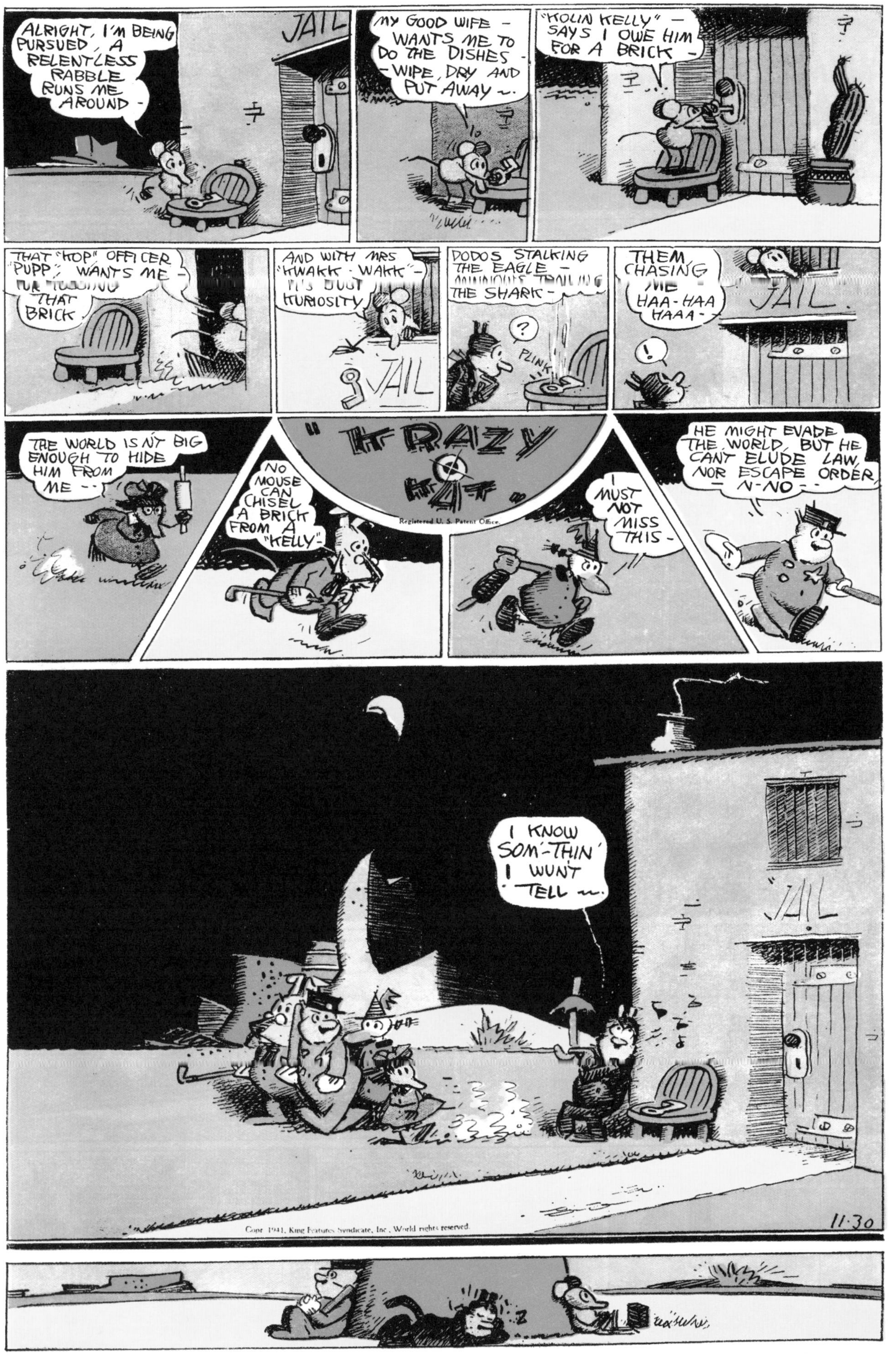
ALRIGHT, I'M BEING PURSUED, A RELENTLESS RABBLE RUNS ME AROUND -
JAIL
MY GOOD WIFE - WANTS ME TO DO THE DISHES - WIPE, DRY AND PUT AWAY ~.
"KOLIN KELLY" - SAYS I OWE HIM FOR A BRICK -
THAT "KOP" OFFICER "PUPP," WANTS ME -
THAT BRICK
AND WITH MRS "KWAKK-WAKK" - IT'S JUST KURIOSITY
JAIL
DODOS STALKING THE EAGLE -
THE SHARK -
?
PLINK
THEM CHASING ME
HAA-HAA HAAA -
!
JAIL
THE WORLD IS N'T BIG ENOUGH TO HIDE HIM FROM ME --
NO MOUSE CAN CHISEL A BRICK FROM A "KELLY"
"KRAZY KAT"
Registered U. S. Patent Office.
I MUST NOT MISS THIS -
HE MIGHT EVADE THE WORLD, BUT HE CANT ELUDE LAW, NOR ESCAPE ORDER, - N-NO --
I KNOW SOM'-THIN' I WUN'T TELL ~.
JAIL
Copr. 1941, King Features Syndicate, Inc., World rights reserved.
11·30
Z

November 30th, 1941.

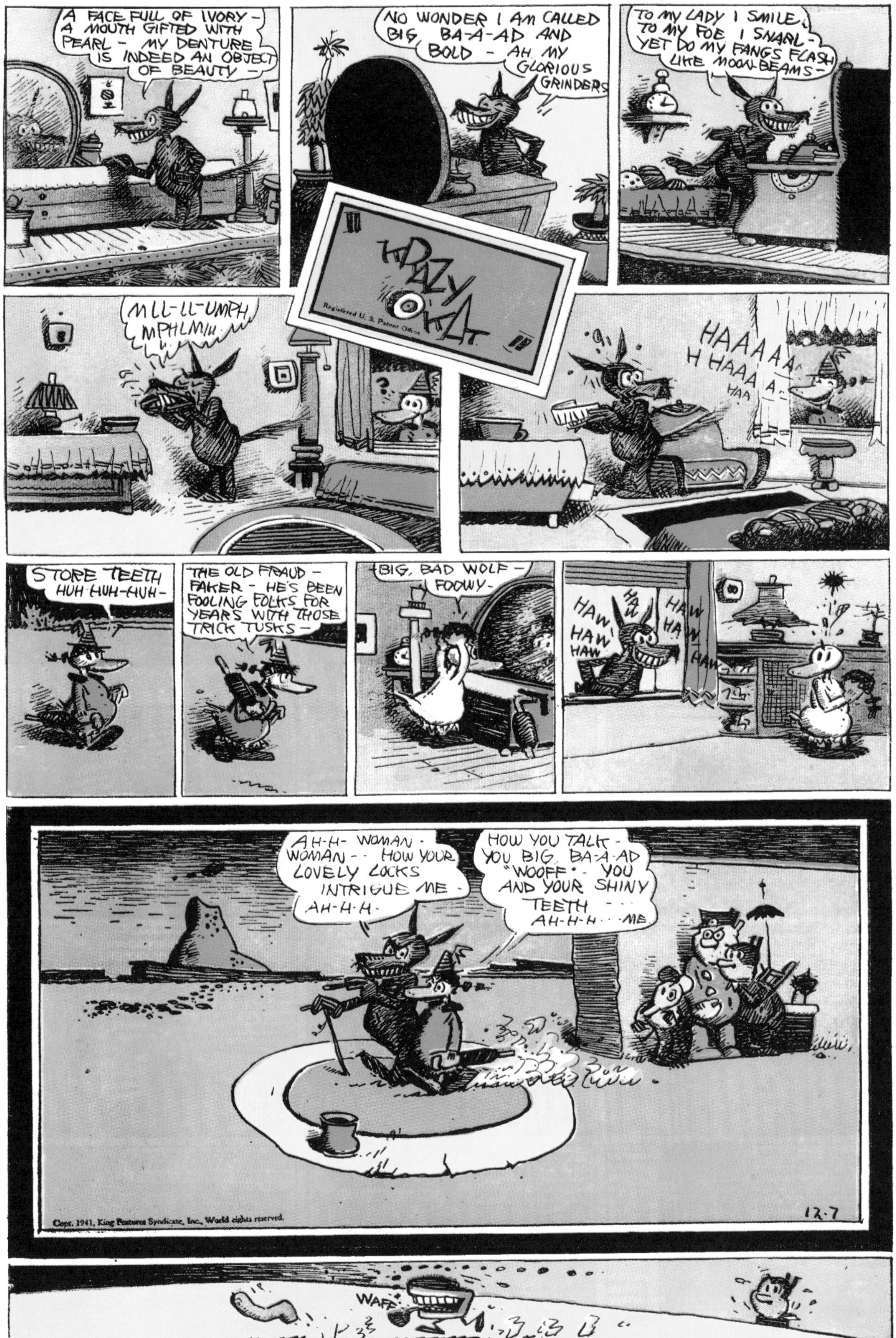
A FACE FULL OF IVORY - A MOUTH GIFTED WITH PEARL - MY DENTURE IS INDEED AN OBJECT OF BEAUTY -
NO WONDER I AM CALLED BIG, BA-A-AD AND BOLD - AH, MY GLORIOUS GRINDERS
TO MY LADY I SMILE, TO MY FOE I SNARL - YET DO MY FANGS FLASH LIKE MOON-BEAMS -
KRAZY KAT
Registered U. S. Patent Office
MLL-LL-UMPH MPHLMM
HAAAAA H HAAA A HAA
STORE TEETH HUH HUH-HUH-
THE OLD FRAUD - FAKER - HE'S BEEN FOOLING FOLKS FOR YEARS WITH THOSE TRICK TUSKS -
BIG, BAD WOLF - FOOWY -
HAW HAW HAW HAW HAW HAW HAW
AH-H- WOMAN - WOMAN -- HOW YOUR LOVELY LOCKS INTRIGUE ME - AH-H-H-
HOW YOU TALK - YOU BIG, BA-A-AD "WOOFF" - YOU AND YOUR SHINY TEETH - - - AH-H-H - - ME
Copr. 1941, King Features Syndicate, Inc., World rights reserved.
12-7
WAP

December 7th, 1941.

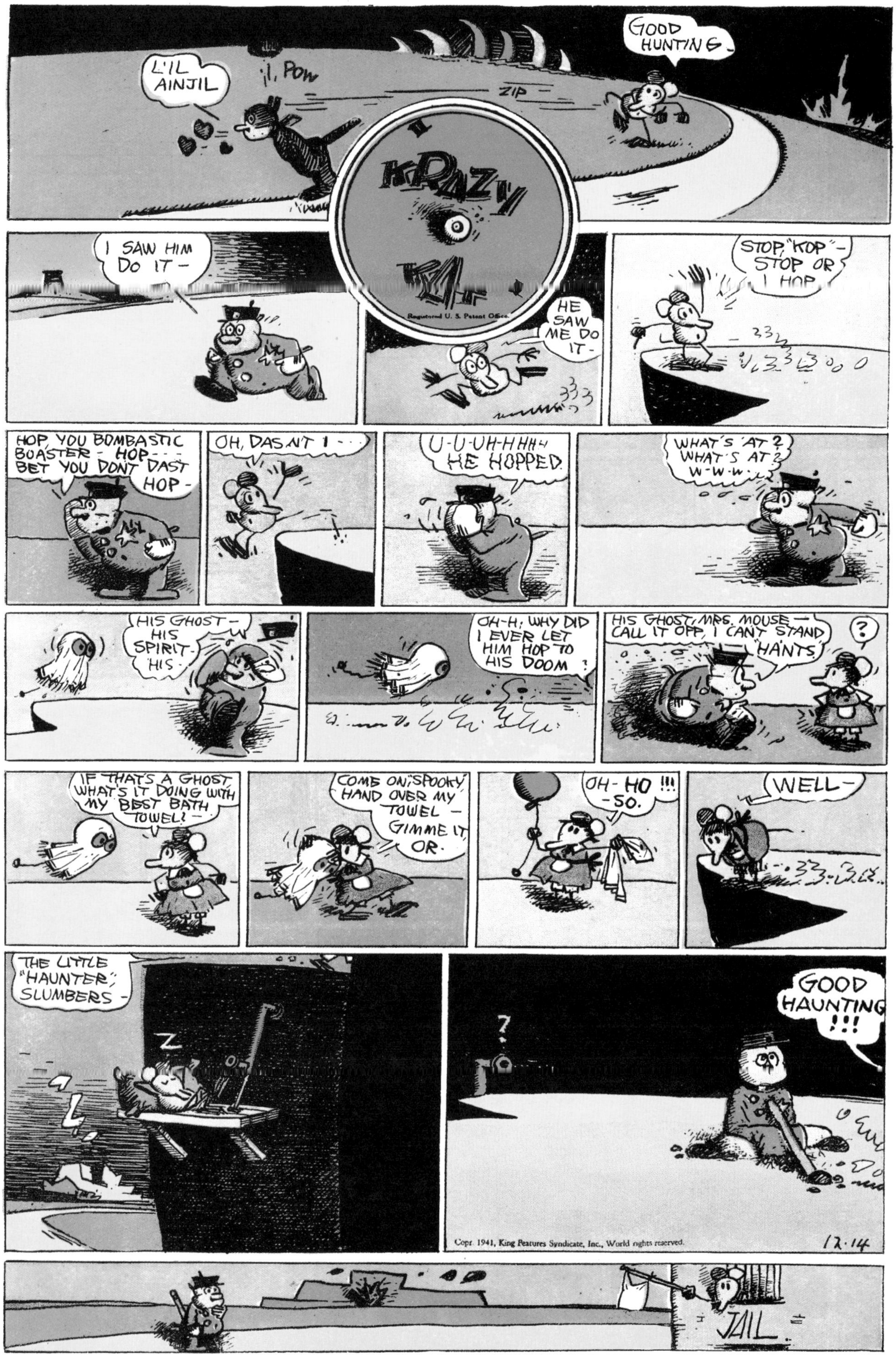
GOOD HUNTING -
L'IL AINJIL
POW
ZIP
KRAZY KAT
Registered U. S. Patent Office
I SAW HIM DO IT -
HE SAW ME DO IT -
STOP, "KOP" - STOP OR I HOP
HOP, YOU BOMBASTIC BOASTER - HOP - - - BET YOU DON'T DAST HOP -
OH, DAS'N'T I - - -
U-U-UH-HHHH HE HOPPED
WHAT'S 'AT? WHAT'S AT? W-W-W-
HIS GHOST - HIS SPIRIT - HIS -
OH-H, WHY DID I EVER LET HIM HOP TO HIS DOOM ?
HIS GHOST, MRS. MOUSE - CALL IT OFF, I CAN'T STAND "HANTS"
?
IF THAT'S A GHOST, WHAT'S IT DOING WITH MY BEST BATH TOWEL? -
COME ON, "SPOOKY" HAND OVER MY TOWEL - GIMME IT OR -
OH - HO !!! - SO.
WELL -
THE LITTLE "HAUNTER" SLUMBERS -
?
GOOD HAUNTING !!!
Copr. 1941, King Features Syndicate, Inc., World rights reserved.
12-14
JAIL

December 14th, 1941.

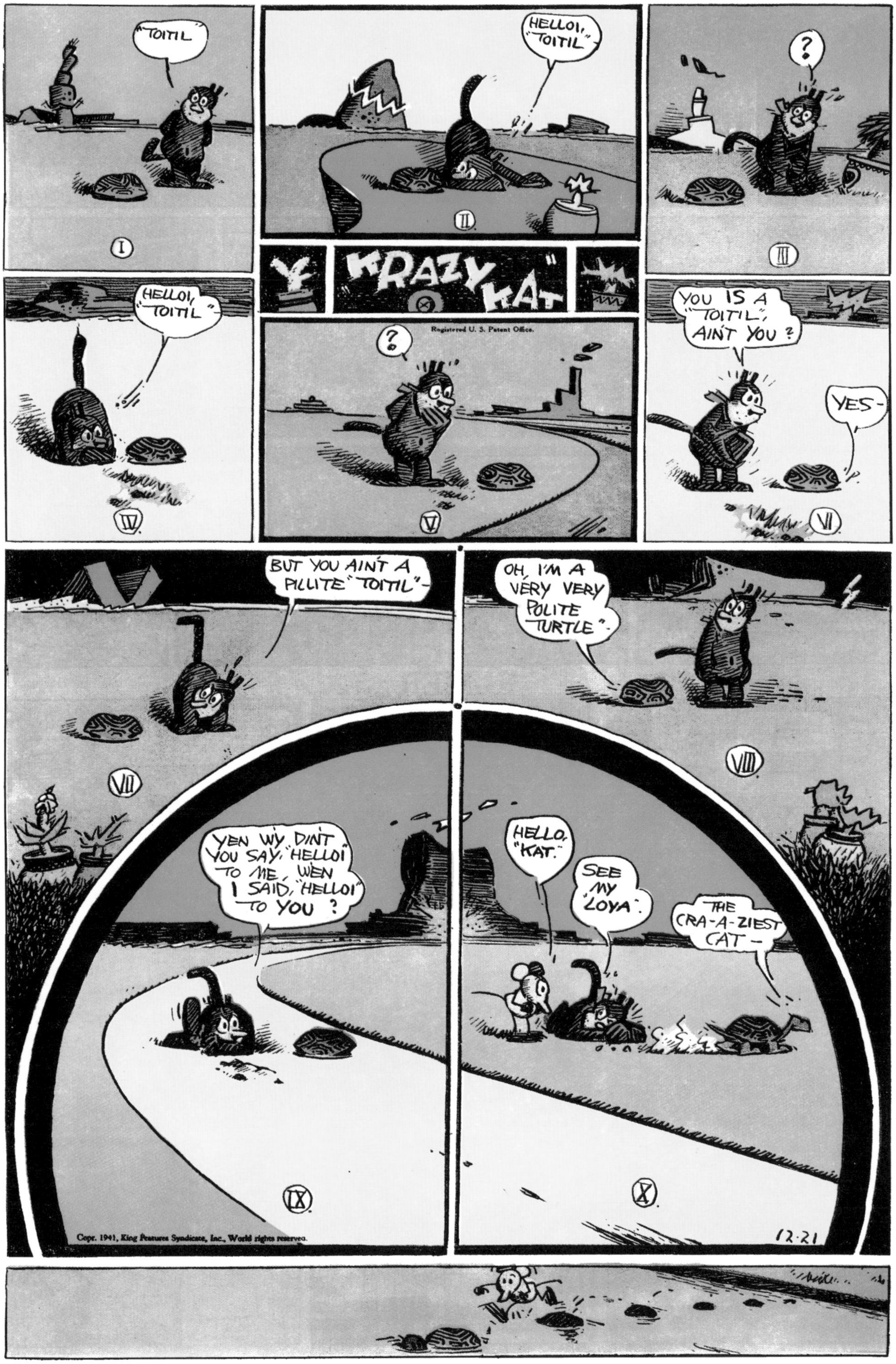
"TOITIL
HELLOI, "TOITIL"
?
"KRAZY KAT"
Registered U. S. Patent Office.
HELLOI, "TOITIL"
?
YOU IS A "TOITIL", AIN'T YOU?
YES-
BUT YOU AIN'T A PILLITE "TOITIL"-
OH, I'M A VERY VERY POLITE TURTLE"-
YEN WY DIN'T YOU SAY, "HELLOI" TO ME, WEN I SAID, "HELLOI" TO YOU ?
HELLO, "KAT."
SEE MY "LOYA".
THE CRA-A-ZIEST CAT -
Copr. 1941, King Features Syndicate, Inc., World rights reserved.
12·21

December 21st, 1941.

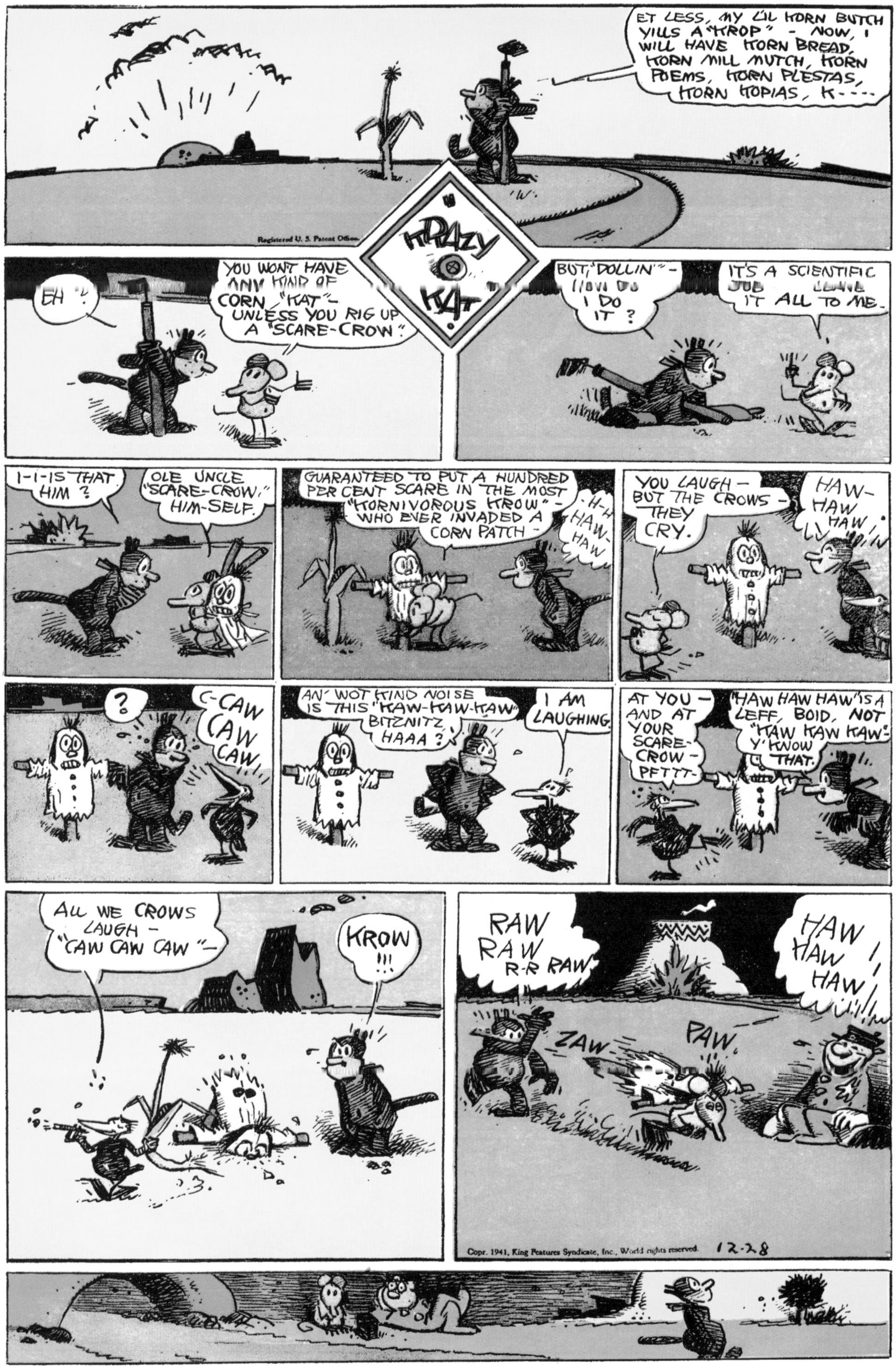
ET LESS, MY L'IL KORN BUTCH YILLS A "KROP" - NOW, I WILL HAVE KORN BREAD, KORN MILL MUTCH, KORN POEMS, KORN PLESTAS, KORN KOPIAS, K----
Registered U. S. Patent Office.
KRAZY KAT
EH ?
YOU WON'T HAVE
CORN "KAT" - UNLESS YOU RIG UP A "SCARE-CROW"
BUT, "DOLLIN" -
I DO IT ?
IT'S A SCIENTIFIC
IT ALL TO ME -
I-I-IS THAT HIM ?
OLE UNCLE "SCARE-CROW," HIM-SELF.
GUARANTEED TO PUT A HUNDRED PER CENT SCARE IN THE MOST "KORNIVOROUS KROW" - WHO EVER INVADED A CORN PATCH -
H-H HAW-HAW
YOU LAUGH - BUT THE CROWS - THEY CRY.
HAW-HAW HAW
?
C-CAW CAW CAW
AN' WOT KIND NOISE IS THIS "KAW-KAW-KAW" BITZNITZ, HAAA ?
I AM LAUGHING.
AT YOU - AND AT YOUR SCARE-CROW - PFTTT-
"HAW HAW HAW" IS A LEFF, BOID, NOT "KAW KAW KAW" - Y'KNOW THAT.
ALL WE CROWS LAUGH - "CAW CAW CAW" -
KROW !!!
RAW RAW R-R RAW
HAW HAW HAW
ZAW
PAW
Copr. 1941, King Features Syndicate, Inc., World rights reserved.
12-28

December 28th, 1941.

1942.

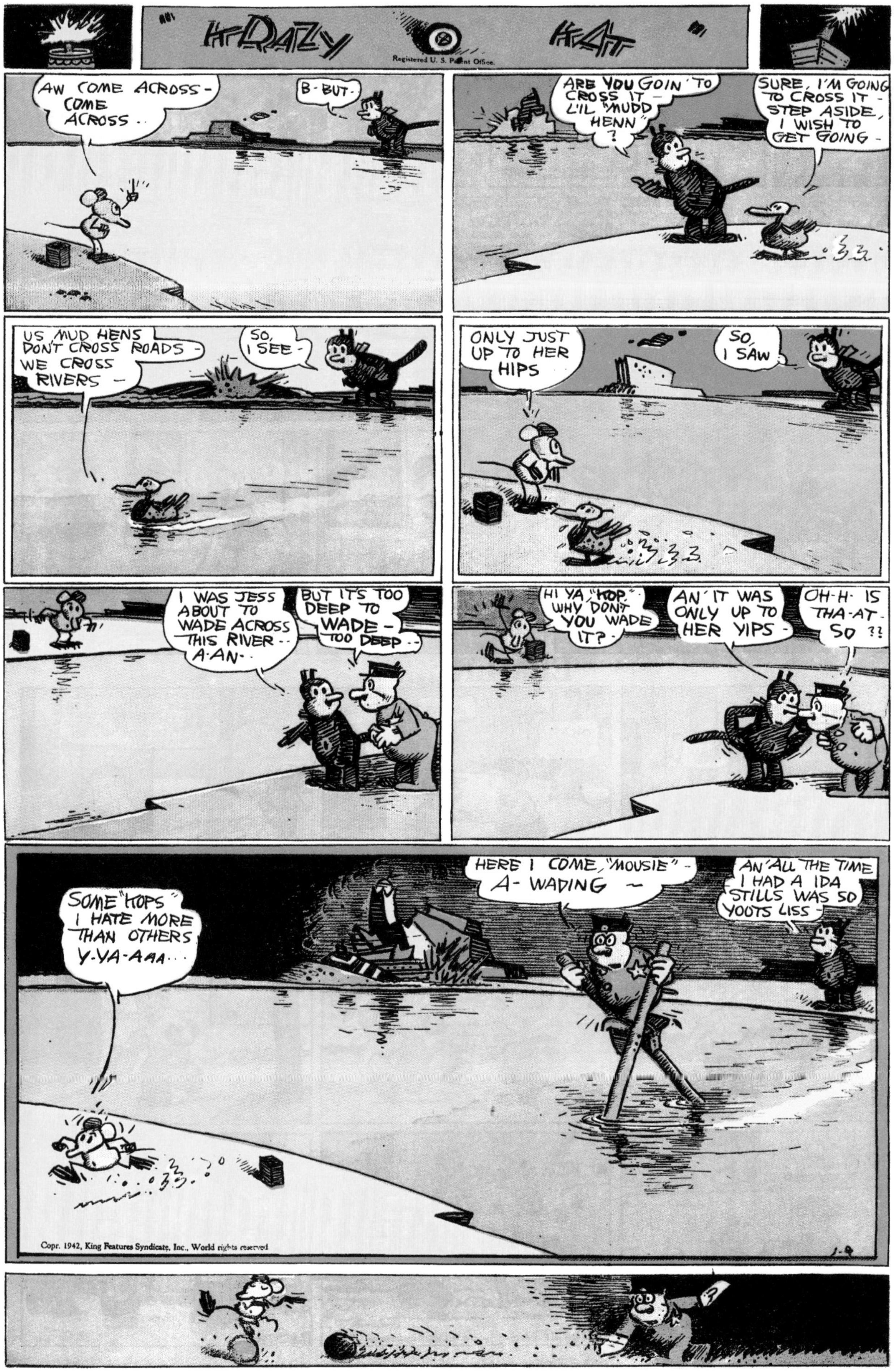
KRAZY KAT
Registered U. S. Patent Office.
AW COME ACROSS - COME ACROSS - -
B-BUT-
ARE YOU GOIN' TO CROSS IT - L'IL "MUDD HENN" ?
SURE, I'M GOING TO CROSS IT - STEP ASIDE, I WISH TO GET GOING -
US MUD HENS DON'T CROSS ROADS - WE CROSS RIVERS -
SO, I SEE -
ONLY JUST UP TO HER HIPS
SO, I SAW
I WAS JESS ABOUT TO WADE ACROSS THIS RIVER - - A-AN- -
BUT IT'S TOO DEEP TO WADE - TOO DEEP - -
HI YA, "KOP" WHY DON'T YOU WADE IT? -
AN' IT WAS ONLY UP TO HER YIPS -
OH-H- IS THA-AT - SO ??
SOME "KOPS" I HATE MORE THAN OTHERS Y-YA-AAA - -
HERE I COME, "MOUSIE" - A-WADING ~
AN' ALL THE TIME I HAD A IDA STILLS WAS SO YOOTS LISS -
Copr. 1942, King Features Syndicate, Inc., World rights reserved.

January 4th, 1942.

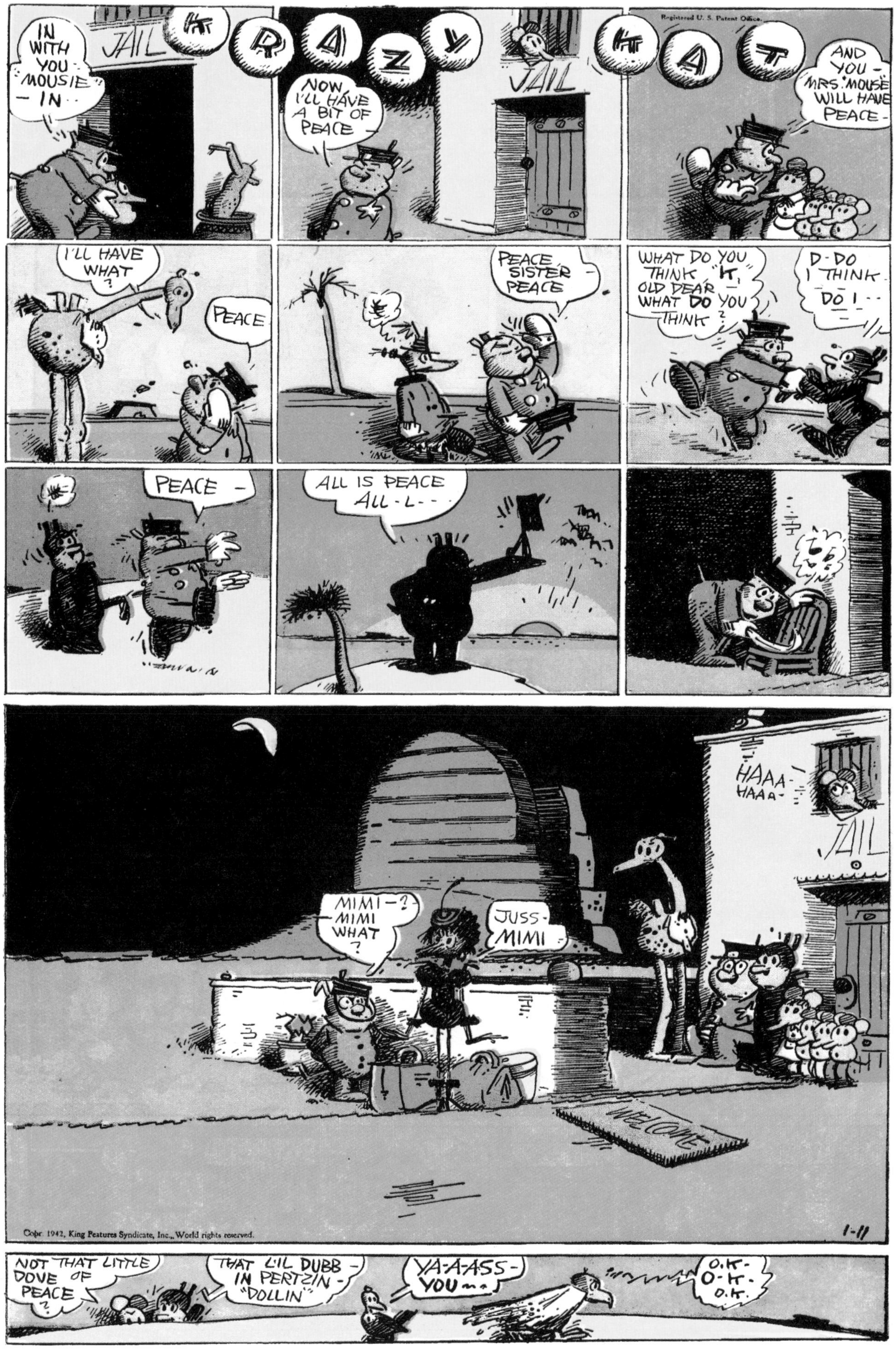
KRAZY KAT
Registered U. S. Patent Office.
IN WITH YOU - MOUSIE - IN -
JAIL
NOW, I'LL HAVE A BIT OF PEACE -
JAIL
AND YOU - MRS. MOUSE WILL HAVE PEACE -
I'LL HAVE WHAT ?
PEACE
PEACE, SISTER PEACE -
WHAT DO YOU THINK "K", OLD DEAR WHAT DO YOU THINK ?
D-DO I THINK - DO I - -
PEACE -
ALL IS PEACE ALL - L - -
HAAA - HAAA -
JAIL
MIMI - ? - MIMI WHAT ?
JUSS - MIMI
WELCOME
Copr. 1942, King Features Syndicate, Inc., World rights reserved.
1-11
NOT THAT LITTLE DOVE OF PEACE ?
THAT LI'L DUBB - IN PERTZIN - "DOLLIN"
YA-A-ASS - YOU - -
O.K. - O-K - O.K.

January 11th, 1942.

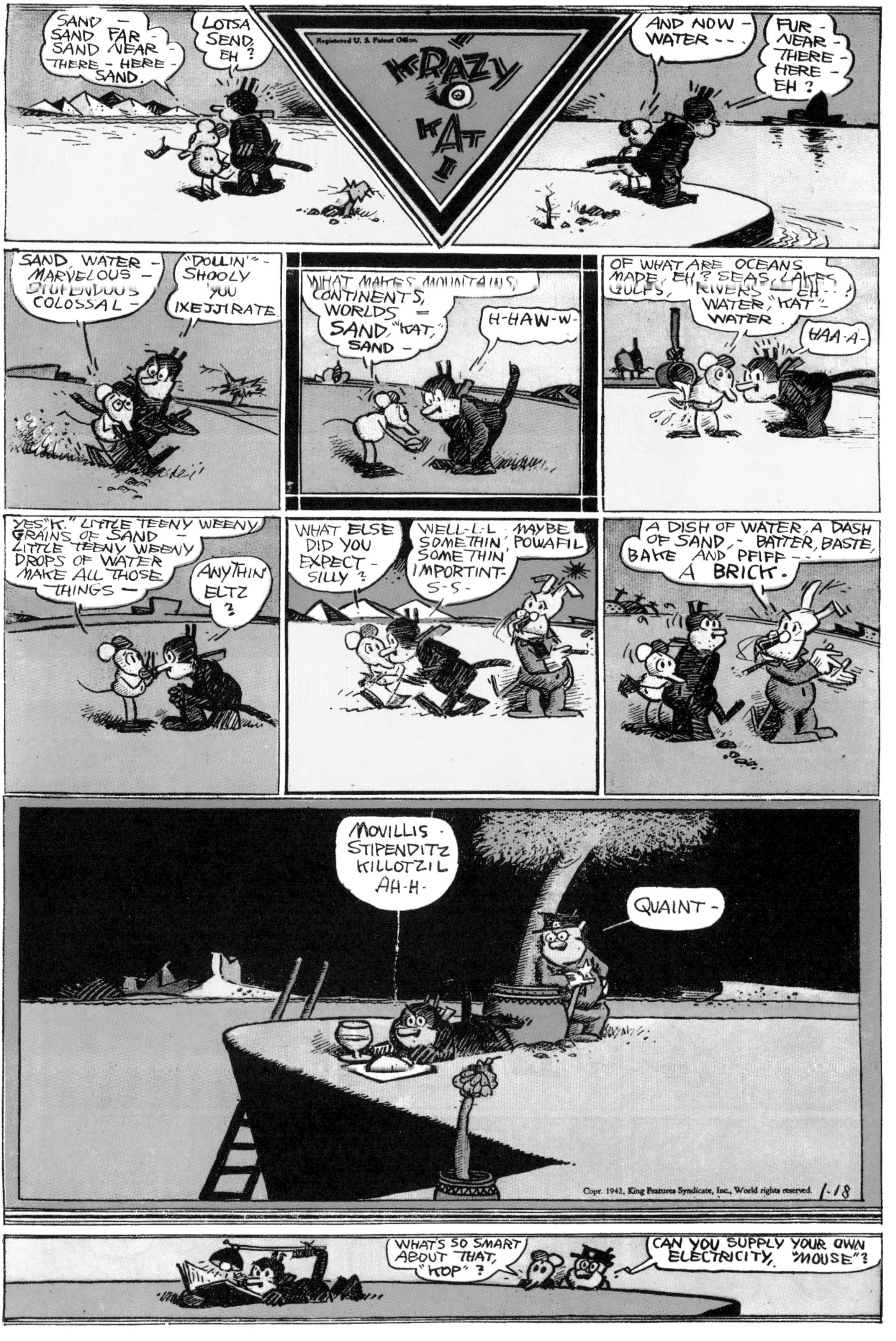

Registered U. S. Patent Office.
KRAZY KAT
SAND – SAND FAR SAND NEAR – THERE – HERE – SAND.
LOTSA SEND, EH?
AND NOW – WATER – – –
FUR – NEAR – THERE – HERE – EH?
SAND, WATER – MARVELOUS – COLOSSAL –
"DOLLIN'" – SHOOLY YOU IXEJJIRATE.
WHAT MAKES MOUNTAINS, CONTINENTS, WORLDS = SAND, "KAT," SAND –
H-HAW-W-
OF WHAT ARE OCEANS MADE, EH? SEAS, LAKES GULFS, RIVERS — EH – – ? WATER, "KAT" – WATER.
HAA-A-
YES, "K." LITTLE TEENY WEENY GRAINS OF SAND – LITTLE TEENY WEENY DROPS OF WATER MAKE ALL THOSE THINGS –
ANYTHIN' ELTZ ?
WHAT ELSE DID YOU EXPECT – SILLY ?
WELL-L-L – MAYBE SOMETHIN', POWAFIL SOMETHIN' IMPORTINT-S-S-
A DISH OF WATER, A DASH OF SAND, – BATTER, BASTE, BAKE AND PFIFF – – – A BRICK.
MOVILLIS – STIPENDITZ KILLOTZIL AH-H-
QUAINT –
Copr. 1942, King Features Syndicate, Inc., World rights reserved.
1-18
WHAT'S SO SMART ABOUT THAT, "KOP"?
CAN YOU SUPPLY YOUR OWN ELECTRICITY, "MOUSE"?

January 18th, 1942.

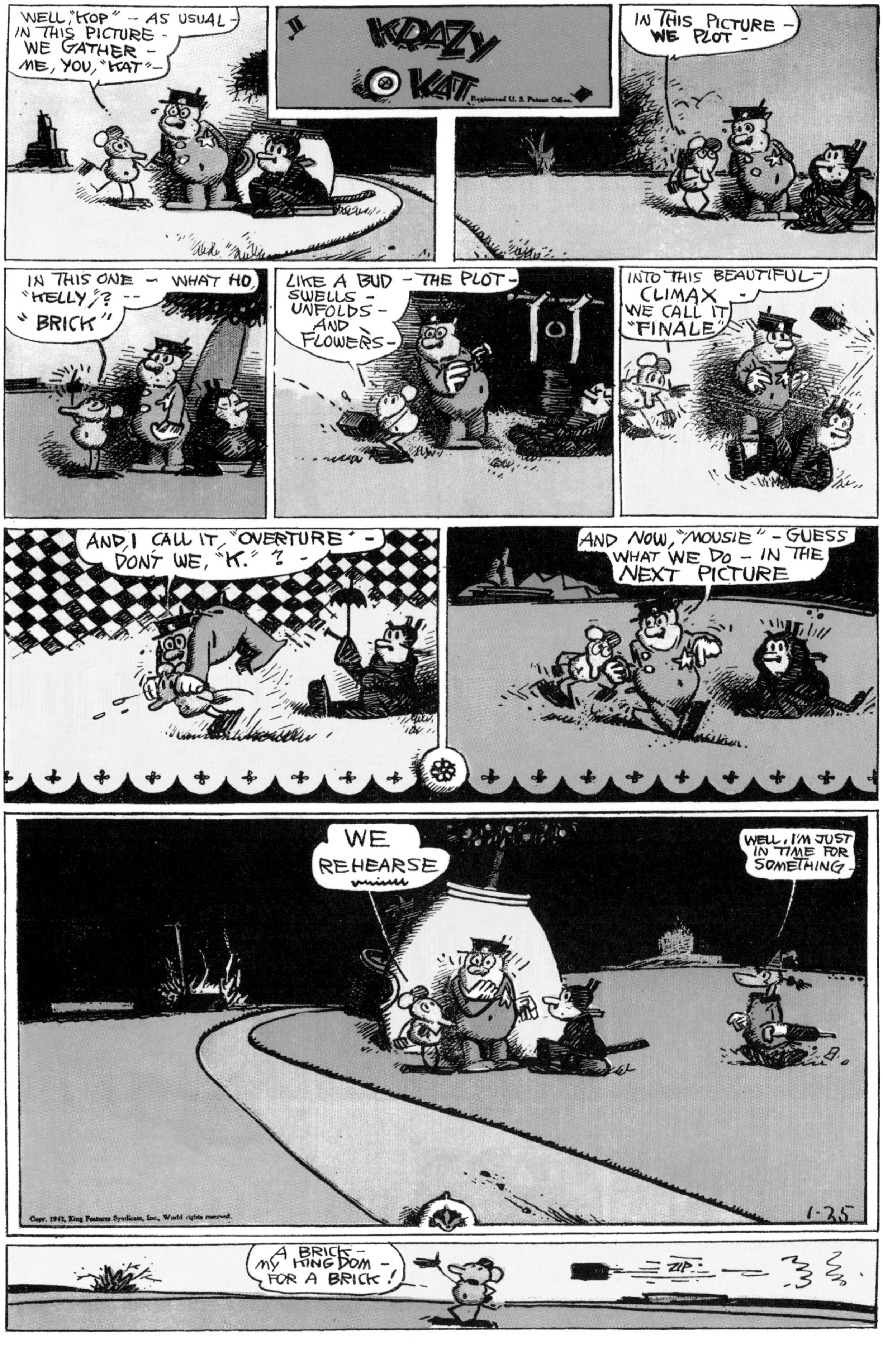
KRAZY KAT
Registered U. S. Patent Office.
WELL, "KOP" - AS USUAL - IN THIS PICTURE - WE GATHER - ME, YOU, "KAT" -
IN THIS PICTURE - WE PLOT -
IN THIS ONE - WHAT HO, "KELLY"? -- "BRICK"
LIKE A BUD - THE PLOT - SWELLS - UNFOLDS - AND FLOWERS -
INTO THIS BEAUTIFUL - CLIMAX - WE CALL IT "FINALE"
AND I CALL IT, "OVERTURE" - DON'T WE, "K."? -
AND NOW, "MOUSIE" - GUESS WHAT WE DO - IN THE NEXT PICTURE
WE REHEARSE
WELL, I'M JUST IN TIME FOR SOMETHING -
Copr. 1942, King Features Syndicate, Inc., World rights reserved.
1-25
A BRICK - MY KINGDOM - FOR A BRICK!
ZIP

January 25th, 1942.

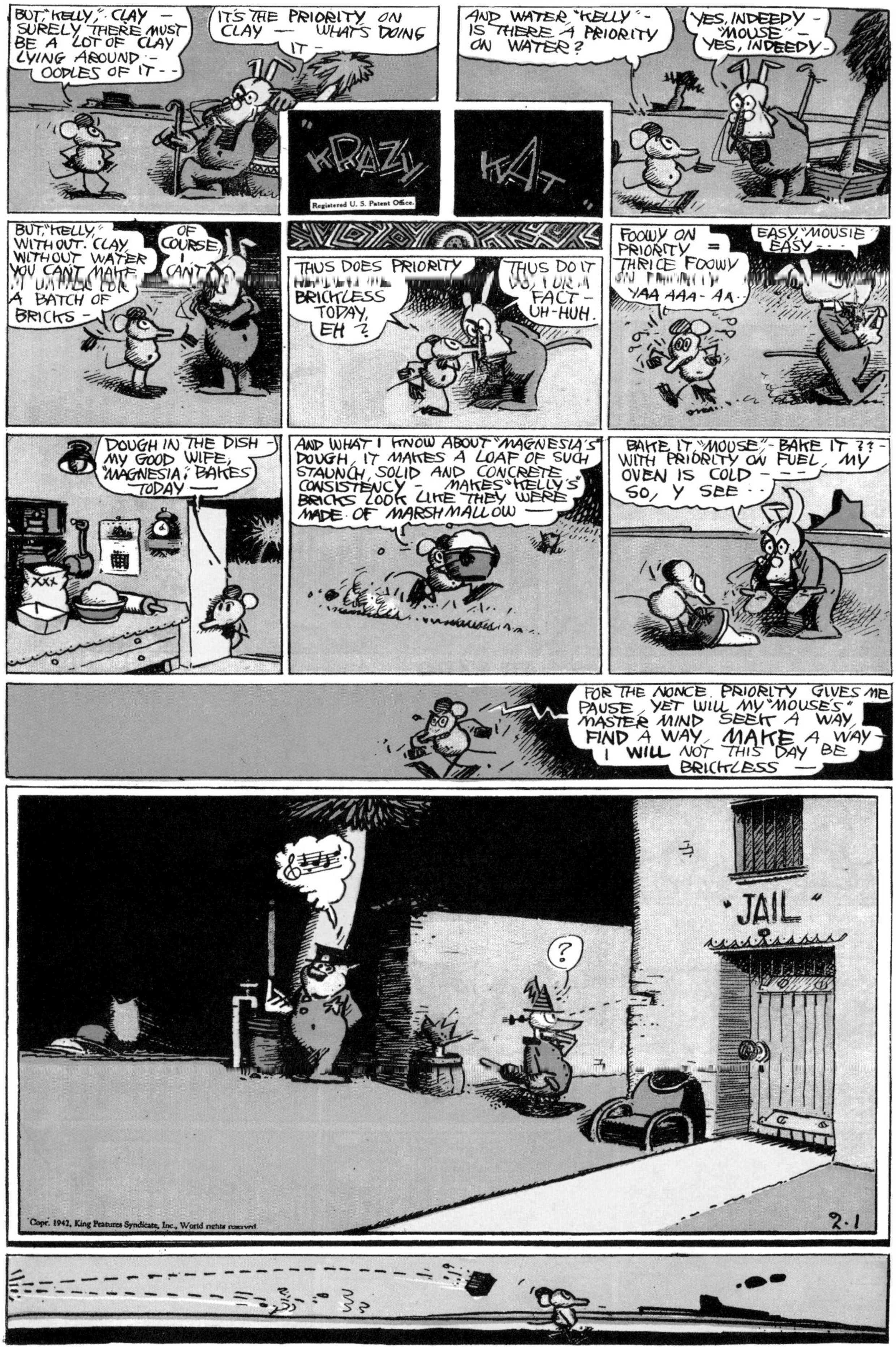
BUT, "KELLY," CLAY — SURELY THERE MUST BE A LOT OF CLAY LYING AROUND — OODLES OF IT — —
IT'S THE PRIORITY ON CLAY — WHAT'S DOING IT —
"KRAZY KAT"
Registered U. S. Patent Office.
AND WATER "KELLY" — IS THERE A PRIORITY ON WATER?
YES, INDEEDY — "MOUSE" — YES, INDEEDY —
BUT, "KELLY," WITHOUT CLAY, WITHOUT WATER YOU CAN'T MAKE A BATCH OF BRICKS —
OF COURSE, I CAN'T
THUS DOES PRIORITY BRICKLESS TODAY, EH?
THUS DO IT FACT — UH-HUH.
FOOWY ON PRIORITY = THRICE FOOWY YAA AAA - AA
EASY, "MOUSIE" EASY — — —
DOUGH IN THE DISH — MY GOOD WIFE, "MAGNESIA," BAKES TODAY —
XXX
AND WHAT I KNOW ABOUT "MAGNESIA'S" DOUGH, IT MAKES A LOAF OF SUCH STAUNCH, SOLID AND CONCRETE CONSISTENCY — MAKES "KELLY'S" BRICKS LOOK LIKE THEY WERE MADE OF MARSHMALLOW —
BAKE IT "MOUSE" — BAKE IT ?? — WITH PRIORITY ON FUEL, MY OVEN IS COLD — — — SO, Y' SEE — —
FOR THE NONCE, PRIORITY GIVES ME PAUSE, YET WILL MY "MOUSE'S" MASTER MIND SEEK A WAY, FIND A WAY, MAKE A WAY — I WILL NOT THIS DAY BE BRICKLESS —
?
"JAIL"
Copr. 1942, King Features Syndicate, Inc., World rights reserved.
2-1

February 1st, 1942.

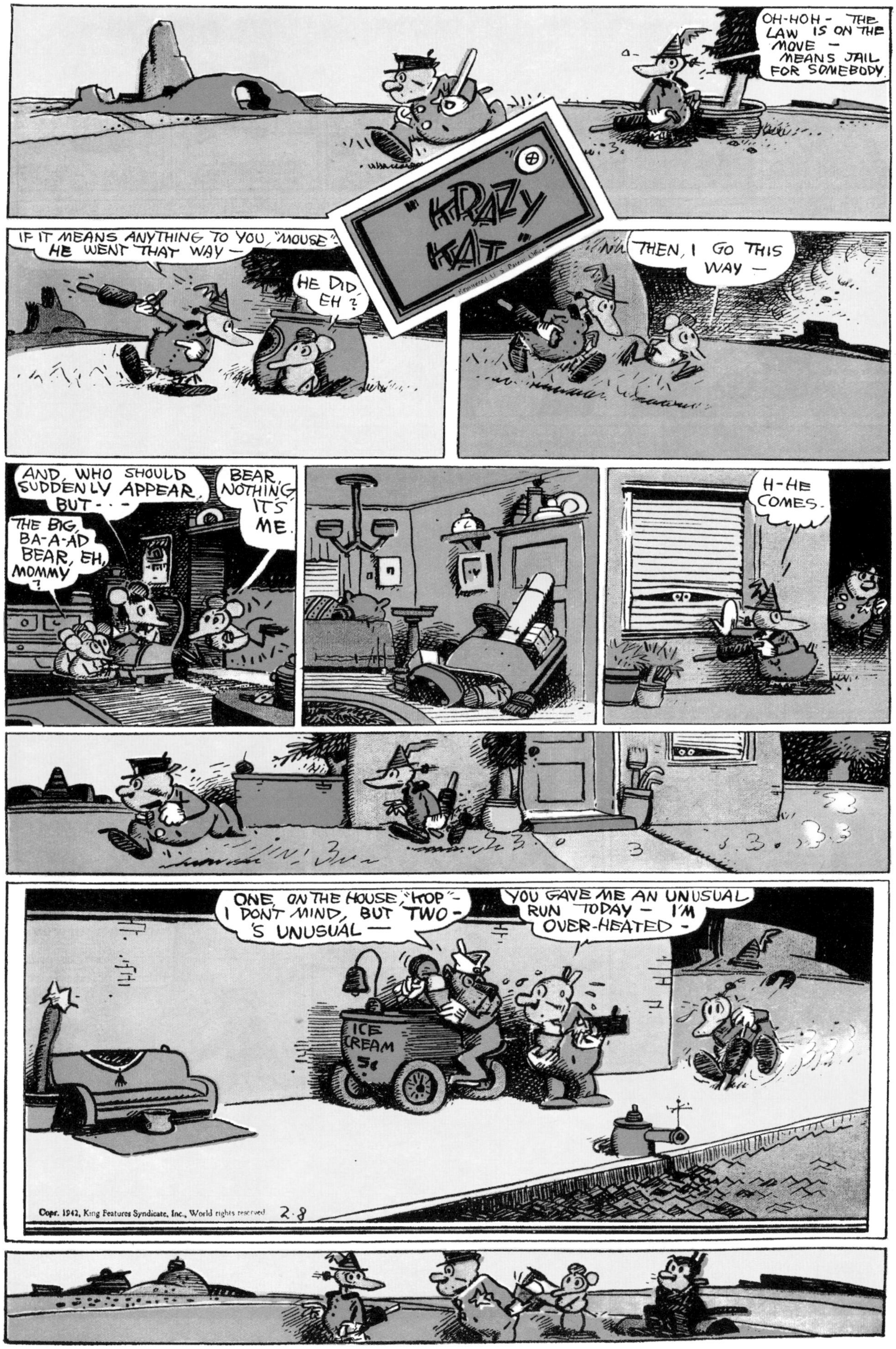
OH-HOH - THE LAW IS ON THE MOVE - MEANS JAIL FOR SOMEBODY.
"KRAZY KAT"
IF IT MEANS ANYTHING TO YOU, "MOUSE" HE WENT THAT WAY -
HE DID, EH?
THEN, I GO THIS WAY -
AND, WHO SHOULD SUDDENLY APPEAR, BUT - - -
THE BIG, BA-A-AD BEAR, EH, MOMMY ?
BEAR, NOTHING, IT'S ME.
H-HE COMES.
ONE, ON THE HOUSE, "KOP" - I DON'T MIND, BUT TWO-'S UNUSUAL -
YOU GAVE ME AN UNUSUAL RUN TODAY - I'M OVER-HEATED -
ICE CREAM 5¢
Copr. 1942, King Features Syndicate, Inc., World rights reserved 2-8

February 8th, 1942.

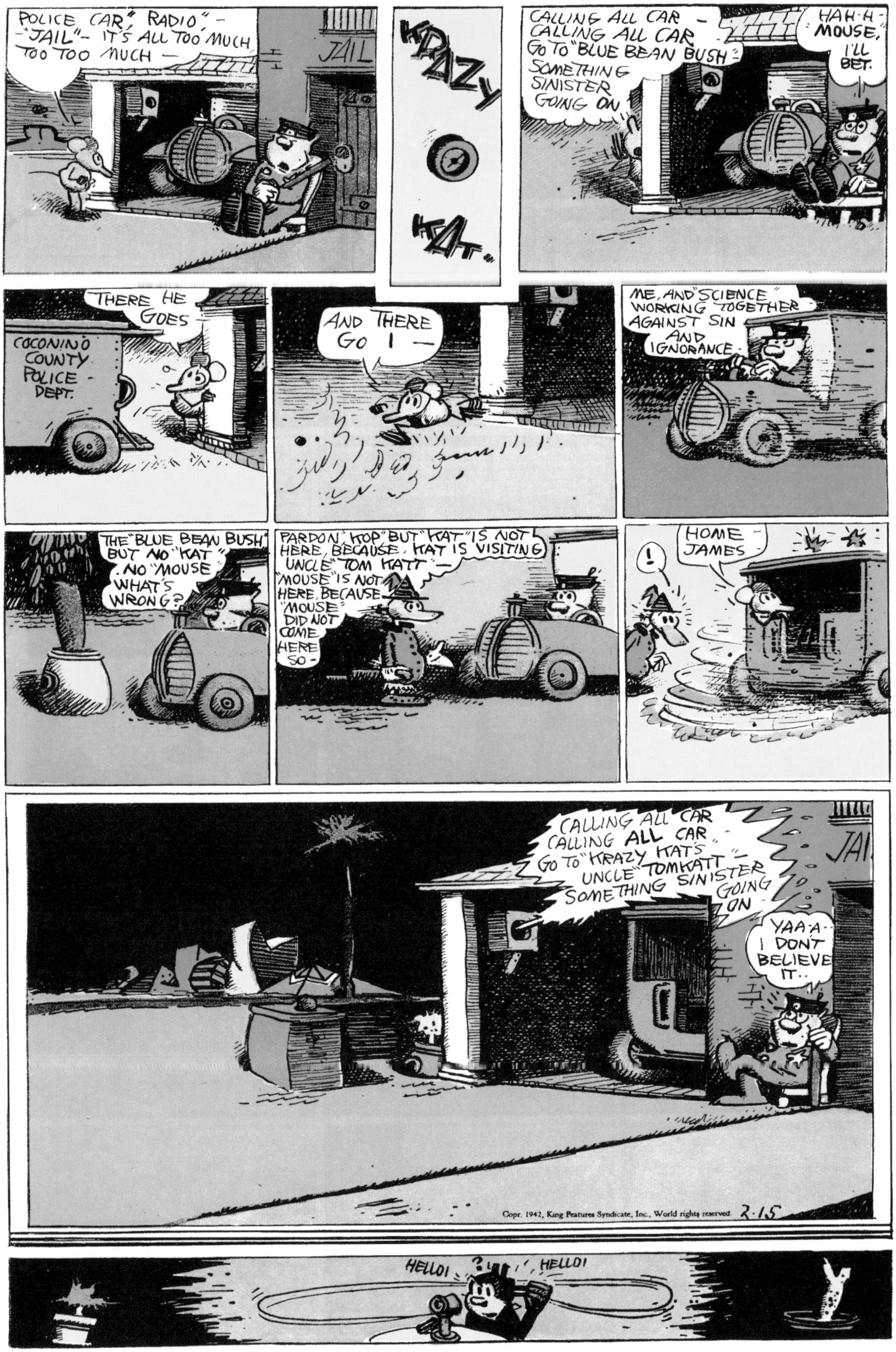

POLICE CAR," RADIO" - "JAIL" - IT'S ALL TOO MUCH TOO TOO MUCH -
JAIL
KRAZY KAT
CALLING ALL CAR - CALLING ALL CAR GO TO "BLUE BEAN BUSH" SOMETHING SINISTER GOING ON
HAH-H MOUSE, I'LL BET.
THERE HE GOES
COCONINO COUNTY POLICE - DEPT.
AND THERE GO I -
ME, AND "SCIENCE" WORKING TOGETHER AGAINST SIN AND IGNORANCE -
THE "BLUE BEAN BUSH" BUT NO "KAT" - NO "MOUSE" WHAT'S WRONG?
PARDON "KOP" BUT "KAT" IS NOT HERE, BECAUSE, KAT IS VISITING UNCLE "TOM KATT" - "MOUSE" IS NOT HERE, BECAUSE "MOUSE" DID NOT COME HERE SO -
HOME JAMES -
!
CALLING ALL CAR CALLING ALL CAR GO TO "KRAZY KAT'S" UNCLE "TOMKATT" SOMETHING SINISTER GOING ON
JAIL
YAA-A - I DON'T BELIEVE IT..
Copr. 1942, King Features Syndicate, Inc., World rights reserved.
2-15
HELLO! ? HELLO!

February 15th, 1942.

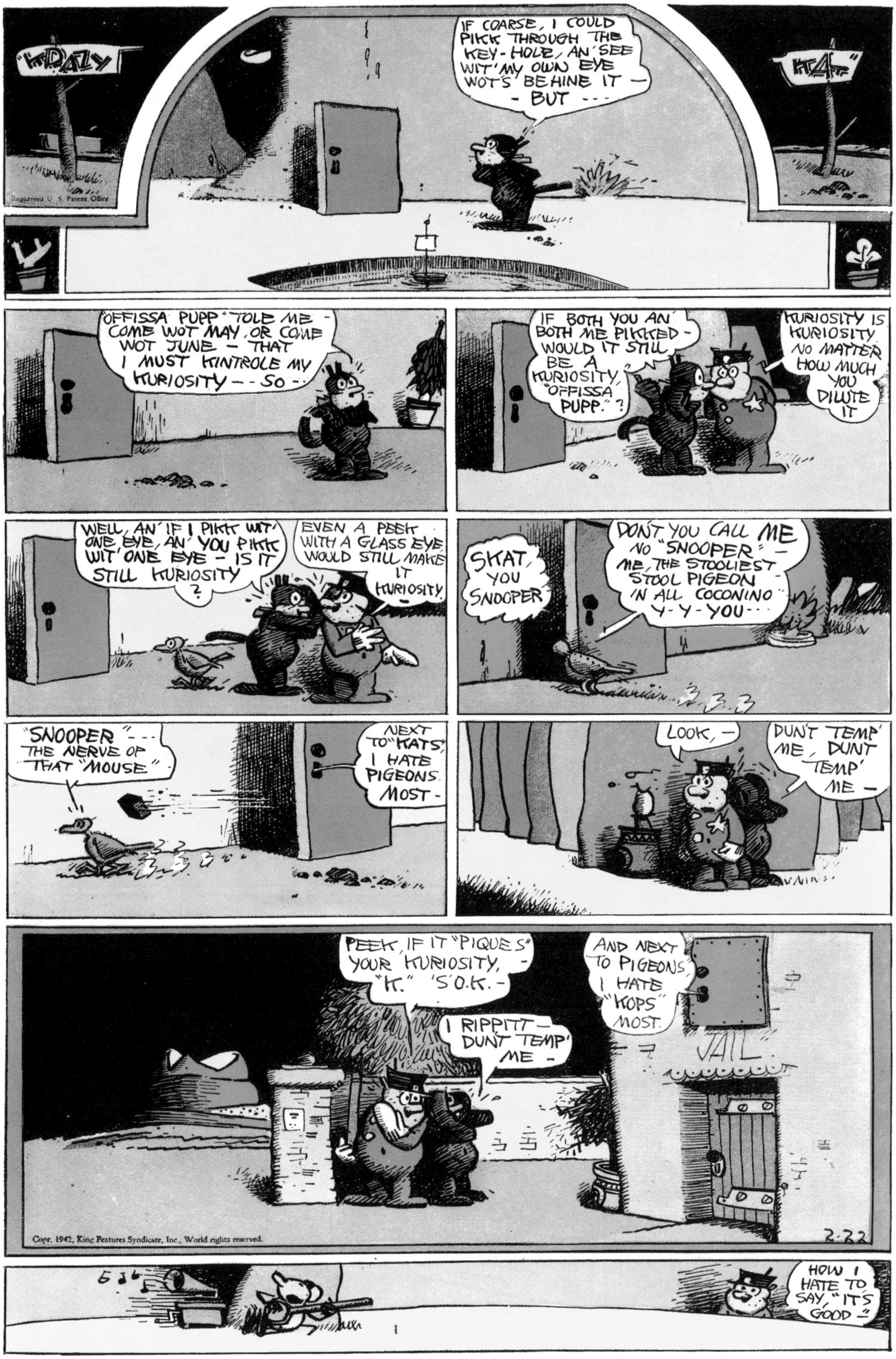
KRAZY
KAT
Registered U. S. Patent Office
IF COARSE, I COULD PIKK THROUGH THE KEY-HOLE, AN' SEE WIT' MY OWN EYE WOT'S BEHINE IT — - BUT ---
"OFFISSA PUPP" TOLE ME - COME WOT MAY, OR COME WOT JUNE — THAT I MUST KINTROLE MY KURIOSITY -- SO -
IF BOTH YOU AN' BOTH ME PIKKED - WOULD IT STILL BE A KURIOSITY, "OFFISSA PUPP." ?
KURIOSITY IS KURIOSITY NO MATTER HOW MUCH YOU DILUTE IT
WELL, AN' IF I PIKK WIT' ONE EYE, AN' YOU PIKK WIT ONE EYE - IS IT STILL KURIOSITY ?
EVEN A PEEK WITH A GLASS EYE WOULD STILL MAKE IT KURIOSITY.
SKAT, YOU SNOOPER
DON'T YOU CALL ME NO "SNOOPER" — ME, THE STOOLIEST STOOL PIGEON IN ALL COCONINO Y-Y-YOU---
"SNOOPER" --- THE NERVE OF THAT "MOUSE" -
NEXT TO "KATS," I HATE PIGEONS MOST -
LOOK, —
DUN'T TEMP' ME, DUNT 'TEMP' ME —
PEEK, IF IT "PIQUES" YOUR KURIOSITY, "K." 'S O.K. -
AND NEXT TO PIGEONS, I HATE "KOPS" MOST.
I RIPPITT — DUN'T TEMP' ME -
JAIL
Copr. 1942, King Features Syndicate, Inc., World rights reserved.
2-22
HOW I HATE TO SAY, "IT'S GOOD -"

February 22nd, 1942.

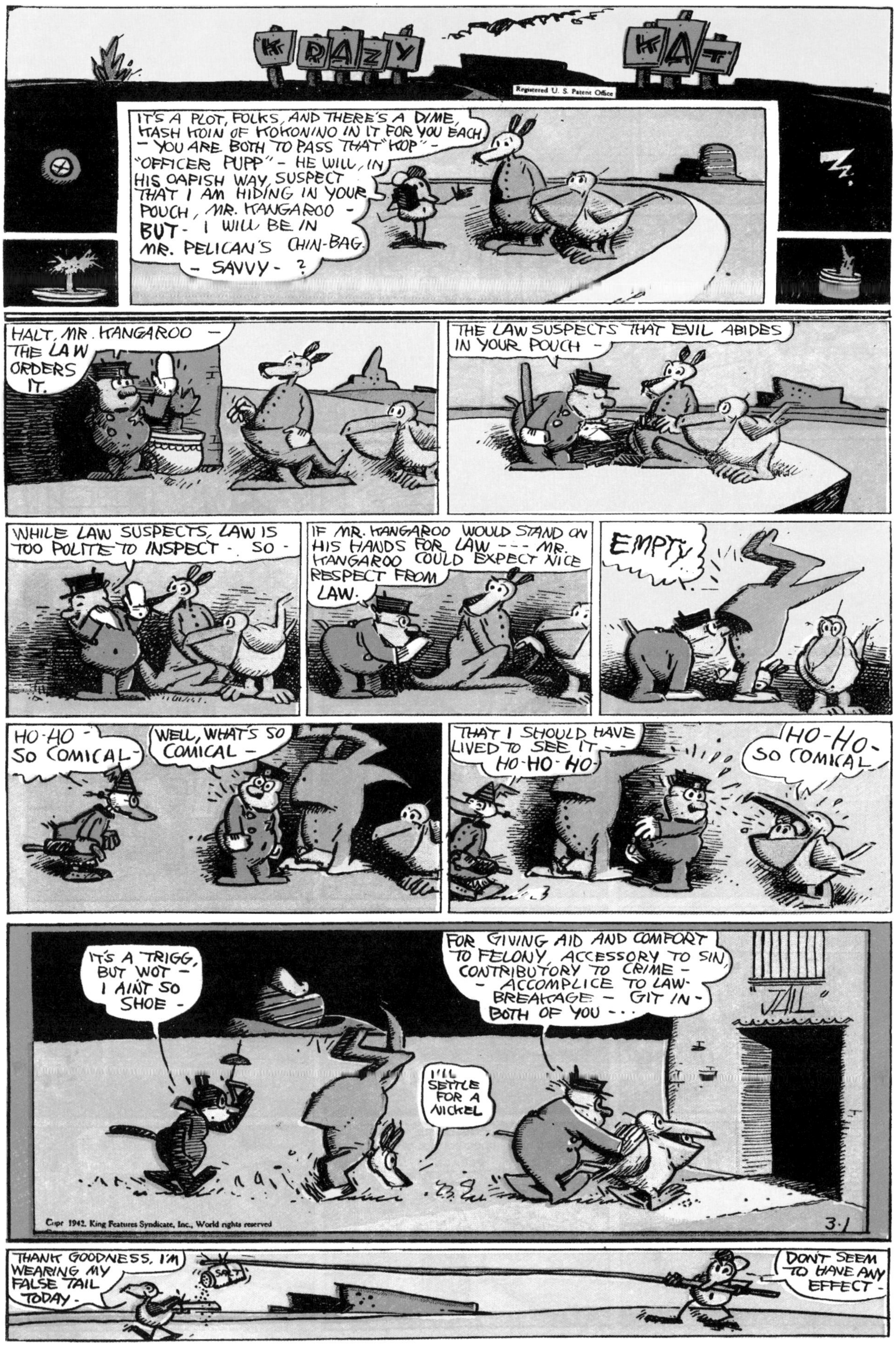
KRAZY KAT
Registered U. S. Patent Office
IT'S A PLOT, FOLKS, AND THERE'S A DIME, KASH KOIN OF KOKONINO IN IT FOR YOU EACH - YOU ARE BOTH TO PASS THAT "KOP" - "OFFICER PUPP" - HE WILL, IN HIS OAFISH WAY, SUSPECT THAT I AM HIDING IN YOUR POUCH, MR. KANGAROO - BUT - I WILL BE IN MR. PELICAN'S CHIN-BAG - SAVVY - ?
HALT, MR. KANGAROO - THE LAW ORDERS IT.
THE LAW SUSPECTS THAT EVIL ABIDES IN YOUR POUCH -
WHILE LAW SUSPECTS, LAW IS TOO POLITE TO INSPECT - SO -
IF MR. KANGAROO WOULD STAND ON HIS HANDS FOR LAW --- MR. KANGAROO COULD EXPECT NICE RESPECT FROM LAW.
EMPTY
HO-HO - SO COMICAL -
WELL, WHAT'S SO COMICAL -
THAT I SHOULD HAVE LIVED TO SEE IT - - HO-HO-HO -
HO-HO - SO COMICAL -
IT'S A TRIGG, BUT WOT - I AIN'T SO SHOE -
FOR GIVING AID AND COMFORT TO FELONY, ACCESSORY TO SIN, CONTRIBUTORY TO CRIME - - ACCOMPLICE TO LAW-BREAKAGE - GIT IN - BOTH OF YOU - - -
"JAIL"
I'LL SETTLE FOR A NICKEL
Copr 1942, King Features Syndicate, Inc., World rights reserved
3-1
THANK GOODNESS, I'M WEARING MY FALSE TAIL TODAY -
SALT
DON'T SEEM TO HAVE ANY EFFECT -

March 1st, 1942.

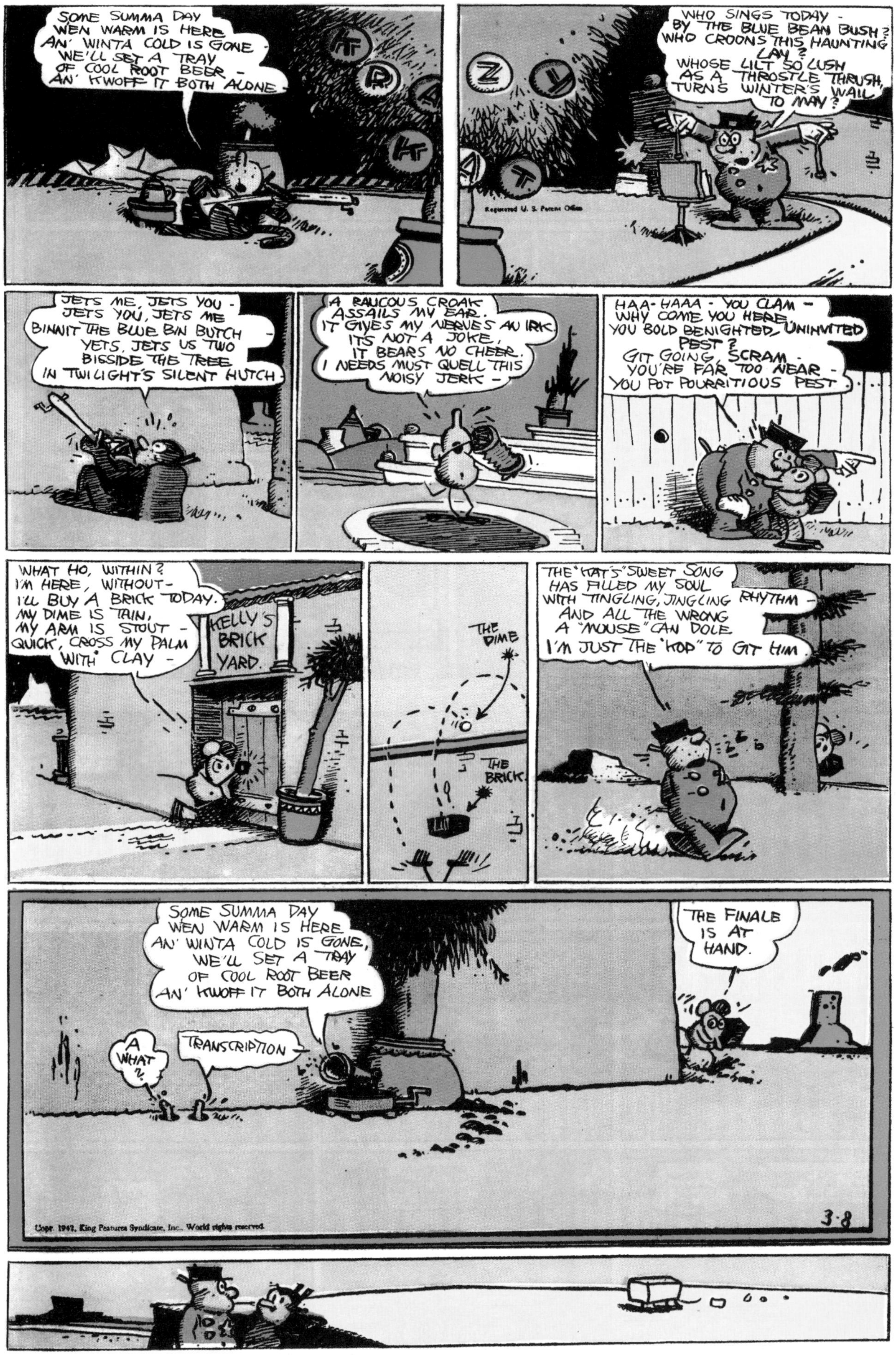
SOME SUMMA DAY WEN WARM IS HERE AN' WINTA COLD IS GONE - WE'LL SET A TRAY OF COOL ROOT BEER - AN' KWOFF IT BOTH ALONE -
KRAZY KAT
Registered U. S. Patent Office
WHO SINGS TODAY - BY THE BLUE BEAN BUSH? WHO CROONS THIS HAUNTING LAY? WHOSE LILT SO LUSH AS A THROSTLE THRUSH, TURNS WINTER'S WAIL TO MAY?
JETS ME, JETS YOU - JETS YOU, JETS ME BINNIT THE BLUE BIN BUTCH - YETS, JETS US TWO BISSIDE THE TREE IN TWILIGHT'S SILENT HUTCH -
A RAUCOUS CROAK ASSAILS MY EAR. IT GIVES MY NERVES AN IRK. ITS NOT A JOKE, IT BEARS NO CHEER. I NEEDS MUST QUELL THIS NOISY JERK -
HAA-HAAA - YOU CLAM - WHY COME YOU HERE, YOU BOLD BENIGHTED, UNINVITED PEST? GIT GOING, SCRAM - YOU'RE FAR TOO NEAR - YOU POT POURRITIOUS PEST
WHAT HO, WITHIN? I'M HERE, WITHOUT - I'LL BUY A BRICK TODAY. MY DIME IS THIN, MY ARM IS STOUT - QUICK, CROSS MY PALM WITH CLAY -
KELLY'S BRICK YARD.
THE DIME
THE BRICK
THE "KAT'S" SWEET SONG HAS FILLED MY SOUL WITH TINGLING, JINGLING RHYTHM - AND ALL THE WRONG A "MOUSE" CAN DOLE I'M JUST THE "KOP" TO GIT HIM
SOME SUMMA DAY WEN WARM IS HERE AN' WINTA COLD IS GONE, WE'LL SET A TRAY OF COOL ROOT BEER AN' KWOFF IT BOTH ALONE
THE FINALE IS AT HAND.
A WHAT?
TRANSCRIPTION -
Copr. 1942, King Features Syndicate, Inc., World rights reserved.
3-8

March 8th, 1942.

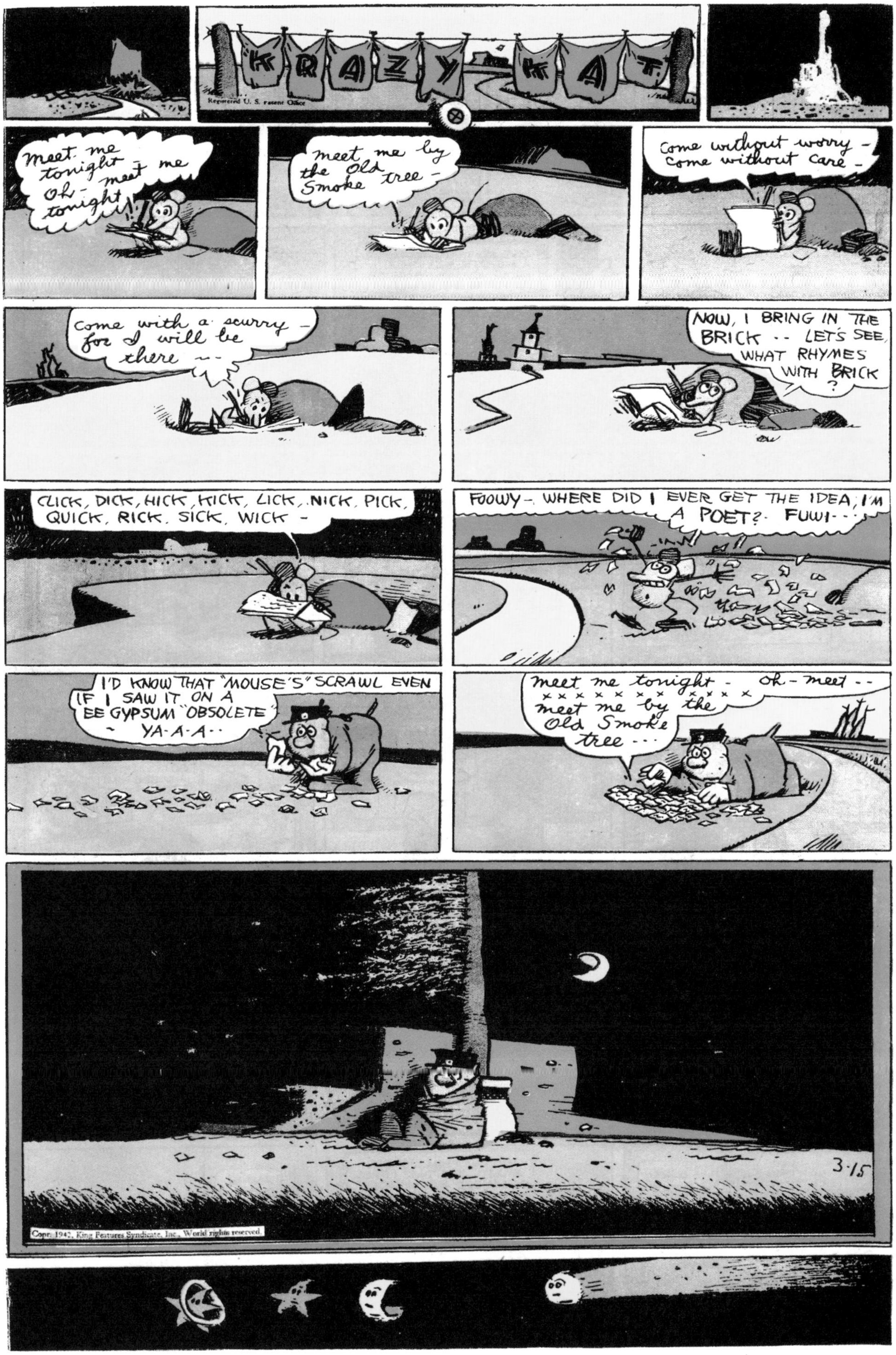
KRAZY KAT
Registered U. S. Patent Office
Meet me tonight Oh - meet me tonight!
meet me by the Old Smoke tree -
Come without worry - Come without care -
Come with a scurry - for I will be there --
NOW, I BRING IN THE BRICK -- LET'S SEE, WHAT RHYMES WITH BRICK ?
CLICK, DICK, HICK, KICK, LICK, NICK, PICK, QUICK, RICK, SICK, WICK -
FOOWY - WHERE DID I EVER GET THE IDEA, I'M A POET? - FUWI---
I'D KNOW THAT "MOUSE'S" SCRAWL EVEN IF I SAW IT ON A EE GYPSUM "OBSOLETE" - YA-A-A--
meet me tonight - oh - meet -- meet me by the Old Smoke tree ---
3·15
Copr. 1942, King Features Syndicate, Inc., World rights reserved.

March 15th, 1942.

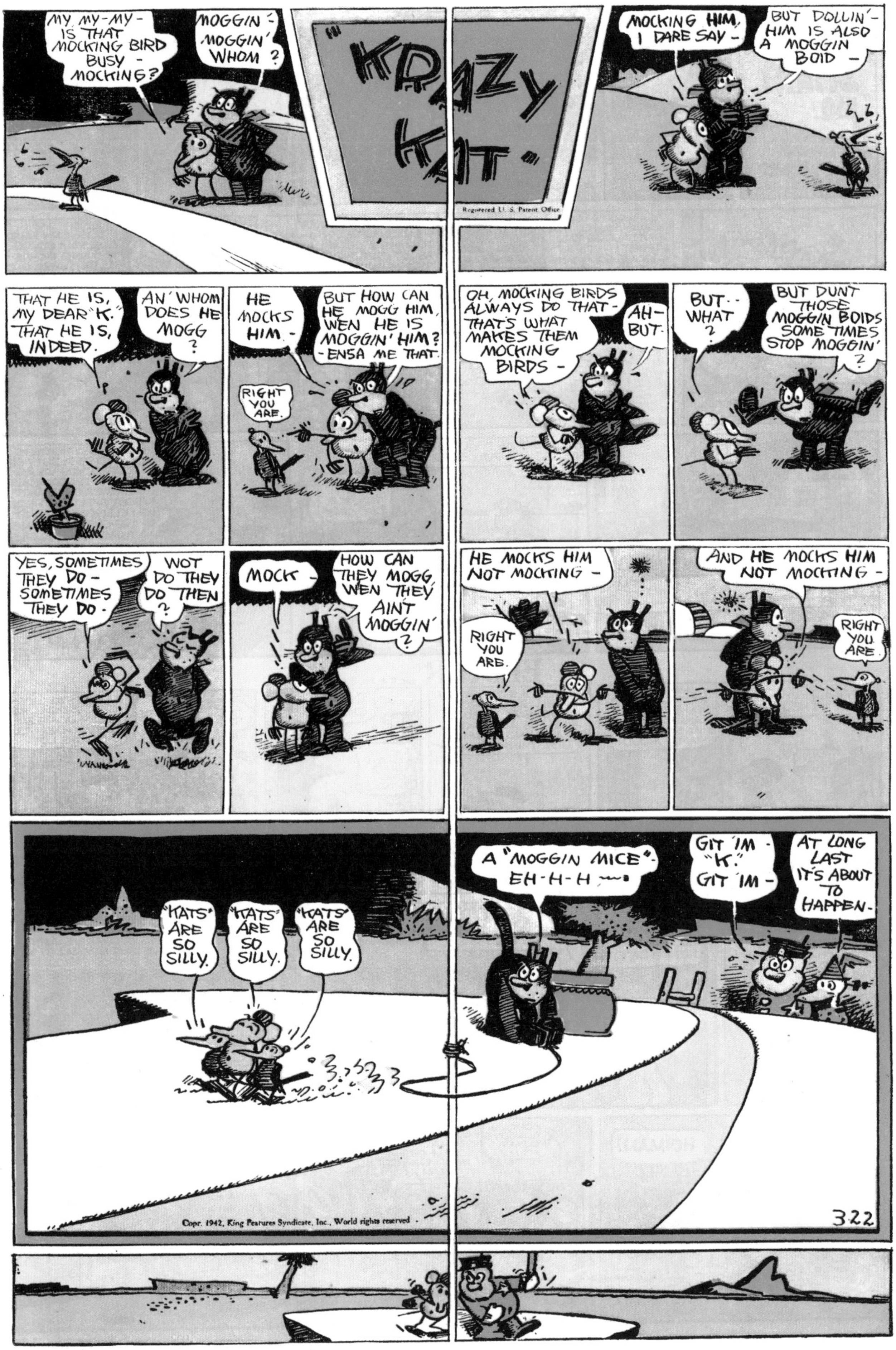
MY MY-MY - IS THAT MOCKING BIRD BUSY - MOCKING?
MOGGIN - MOGGIN' WHOM ?
KRAZY KAT.
Registered U. S. Patent Office
MOCKING HIM, I DARE SAY -
BUT DOLLIN' - HIM IS ALSO A MOGGIN BOID -
THAT HE IS, MY DEAR "K." THAT HE IS, INDEED.
AN' WHOM DOES HE MOGG ?
HE MOCKS HIM -
BUT HOW CAN HE MOGG HIM, WEN HE IS MOGGIN' HIM? - ENSA ME THAT.
RIGHT YOU ARE.
OH, MOCKING BIRDS ALWAYS DO THAT - THAT'S WHAT MAKES THEM MOCKING BIRDS -
AH-BUT-
BUT - WHAT ?
BUT DUNT THOSE MOGGIN BOIDS SOME TIMES STOP MOGGIN' ?
YES, SOMETIMES THEY DO - SOMETIMES THEY DO -
WOT DO THEY DO THEN ?
MOCK -
HOW CAN THEY MOGG, WEN THEY AINT MOGGIN' ?
HE MOCKS HIM NOT MOCKING -
RIGHT YOU ARE.
AND HE MOCKS HIM NOT MOCKING -
RIGHT YOU ARE.
"KATS" ARE SO SILLY.
"KATS" ARE SO SILLY.
"KATS" ARE SO SILLY.
A "MOGGIN MICE" - EH-H-H
GIT 'IM - "K." GIT 'IM -
AT LONG LAST IT'S ABOUT TO HAPPEN -
Copr. 1942, King Features Syndicate, Inc., World rights reserved
3.22

March 22nd, 1942.

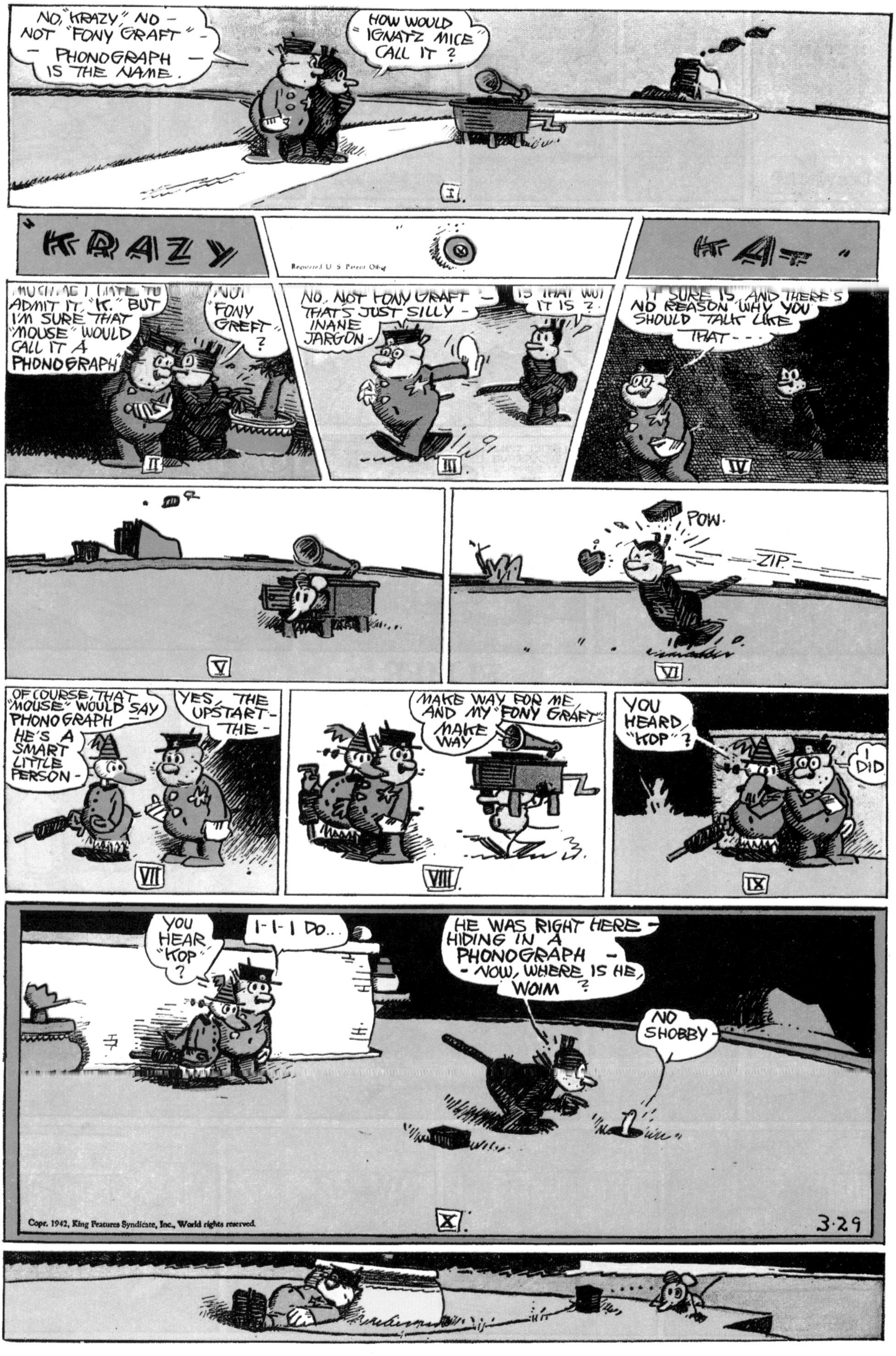
NO, "KRAZY," NO — NOT "FONY GRAFT" — — PHONOGRAPH — IS THE NAME.
HOW WOULD IGNATZ MICE CALL IT ?
"KRAZY KAT"
Registered U. S. Patent Office
ADMIT IT, "K." BUT I'M SURE THAT "MOUSE" WOULD CALL IT A PHONOGRAPH"
FONY GREFT ?
NO, NOT FONY GRAFT — THAT'S JUST SILLY — INANE JARGON —
IT IS ?
IT SURE IS, AND THERE'S NO REASON WHY YOU SHOULD TALK LIKE THAT - - -
POW
ZIP
OF COURSE, THAT "MOUSE" WOULD SAY PHONOGRAPH — HE'S A SMART LITTLE PERSON —
YES, THE UPSTART — THE —
MAKE WAY FOR ME, AND MY "FONY GRAFT" — MAKE WAY
YOU HEARD, "KOP" ?
I DID
YOU HEAR "KOP" ?
I-I-I DO..
HE WAS RIGHT HERE — HIDING IN A PHONOGRAPH — — NOW, WHERE IS HE, WOIM ?
NO SHOBBY —
Copr. 1942, King Features Syndicate, Inc., World rights reserved.
3·29

March 29th, 1942.

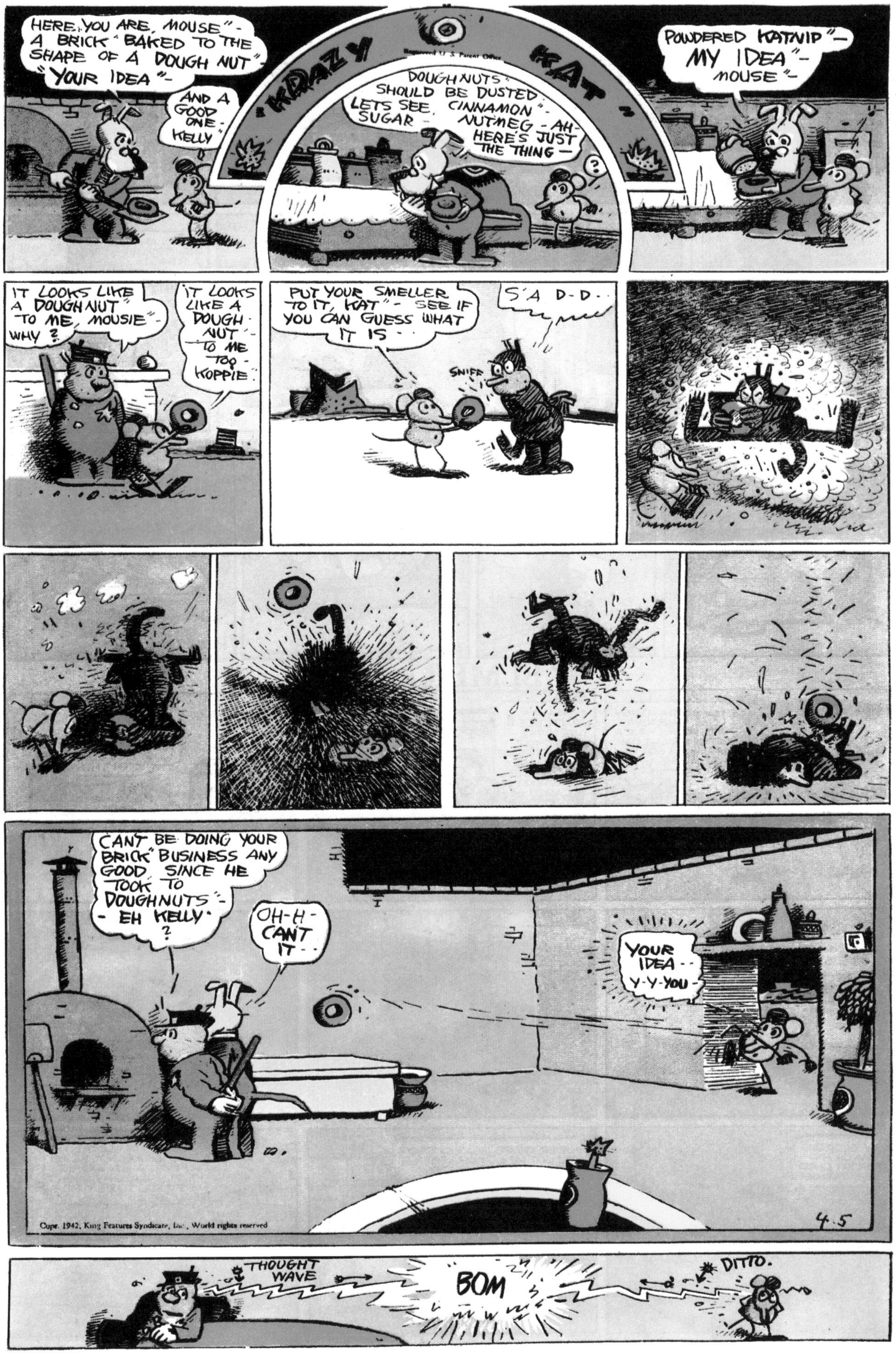

HERE YOU ARE, MOUSE" - A BRICK" BAKED TO THE SHAPE OF A DOUGH NUT" "YOUR IDEA" -
AND A GOOD ONE - KELLY
KRAZY KAT
Registered U. S. Patent Office
DOUGHNUTS SHOULD BE DUSTED - LETS SEE, CINNAMON - SUGAR - NUTMEG - AH - HERE'S JUST THE THING -
?
POWDERED KATNIP" - MY IDEA" - MOUSE" -
IT LOOKS LIKE A DOUGHNUT" TO ME, MOUSIE" - WHY ?
IT LOOKS LIKE A DOUGHNUT TO ME TOO - KOPPIE.
PUT YOUR SMELLER TO IT, KAT" - SEE IF YOU CAN GUESS WHAT IT IS -
SNIFF
S'A D-D-
CAN'T BE DOING YOUR BRICK" BUSINESS ANY GOOD, SINCE HE TOOK TO DOUGHNUTS - EH KELLY ?
OH-H - CAN'T IT -
YOUR IDEA - Y-Y-YOU -
Copr. 1942, King Features Syndicate, Inc., World rights reserved
4.5
THOUGHT WAVE
BOM
DITTO.

April 5th, 1942.

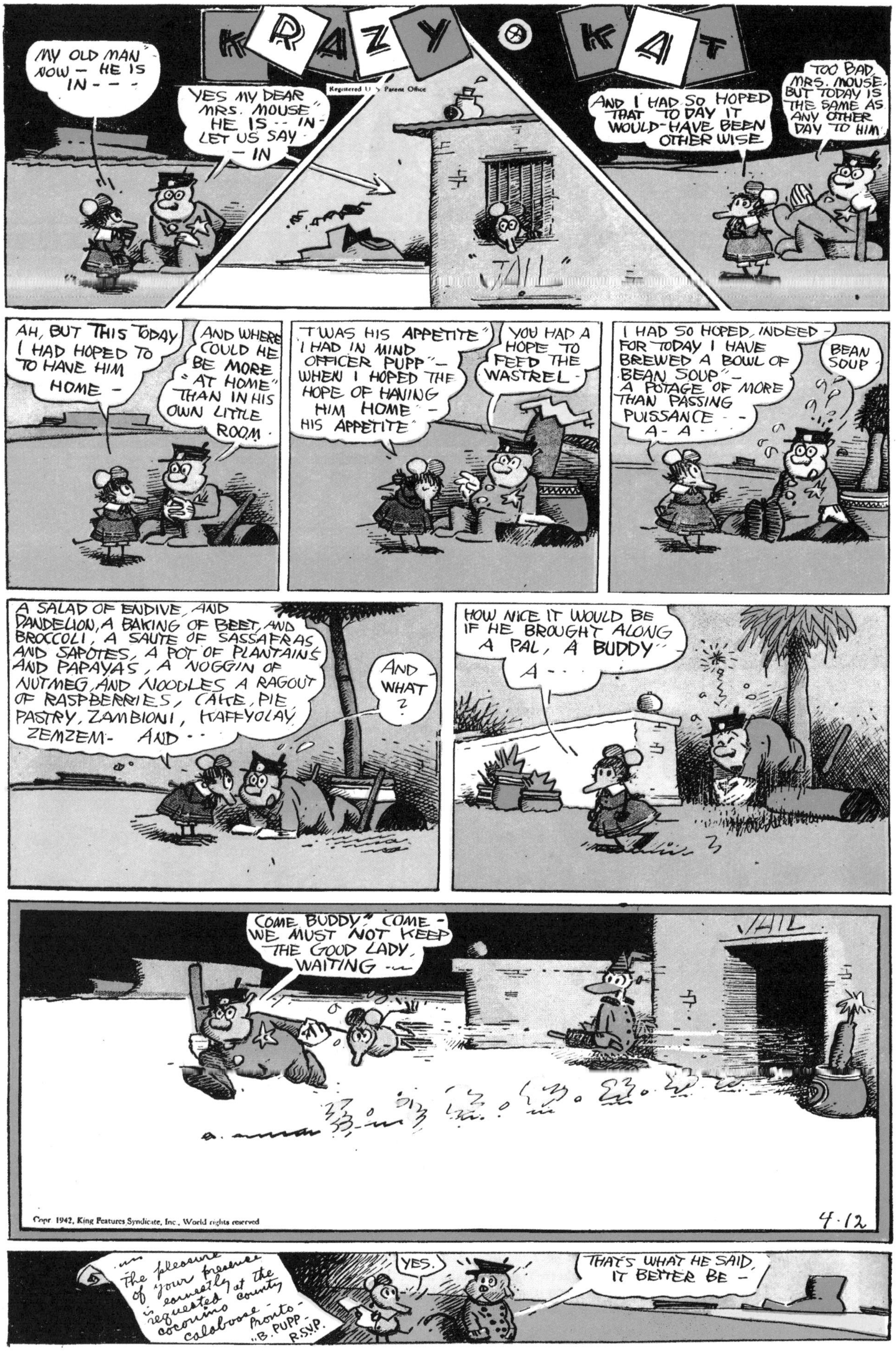
KRAZY KAT
Registered U.S. Patent Office
MY OLD MAN NOW — HE IS IN - - -
YES MY DEAR MRS. MOUSE HE IS - - IN LET US SAY — IN
JAIL
AND I HAD SO HOPED THAT TO DAY IT WOULD-HAVE BEEN OTHER WISE
TOO BAD, MRS. MOUSE, BUT TODAY IS THE SAME AS ANY OTHER DAY TO HIM
AH, BUT THIS TODAY I HAD HOPED TO TO HAVE HIM HOME -
AND WHERE COULD HE BE MORE "AT HOME" THAN IN HIS OWN LITTLE ROOM.
T'WAS HIS APPETITE I HAD IN MIND OFFICER PUPP — WHEN I HOPED THE HOPE OF HAVING HIM HOME — HIS APPETITE
YOU HAD A HOPE TO FEED THE WASTREL -
I HAD SO HOPED, INDEED — FOR TODAY I HAVE BREWED A BOWL OF BEAN SOUP — A POTAGE OF MORE THAN PASSING PUISSANCE - - A - A -
BEAN SOUP
A SALAD OF ENDIVE, AND DANDELION, A BAKING OF BEET, AND BROCCOLI, A SAUTE OF SASSAFRAS AND SAPOTES, A POT OF PLANTAINS AND PAPAYAS, A NOGGIN OF NUTMEG, AND NOODLES A RAGOUT OF RASPBERRIES, CAKE, PIE PASTRY, ZAMBIONI, KAFFYOLAY ZEMZEM - AND - -
AND WHAT ?
HOW NICE IT WOULD BE IF HE BROUGHT ALONG A PAL, A BUDDY - A - -
COME BUDDY, COME - WE MUST NOT KEEP THE GOOD LADY WAITING -
JAIL
4·12
... pleasure of your presence is earnestly requested at the coconino county calaboose Pronto - B. PUPP R.S.V.P.
YES.
THAT'S WHAT HE SAID, IT BETTER BE -

April 12th, 1942.

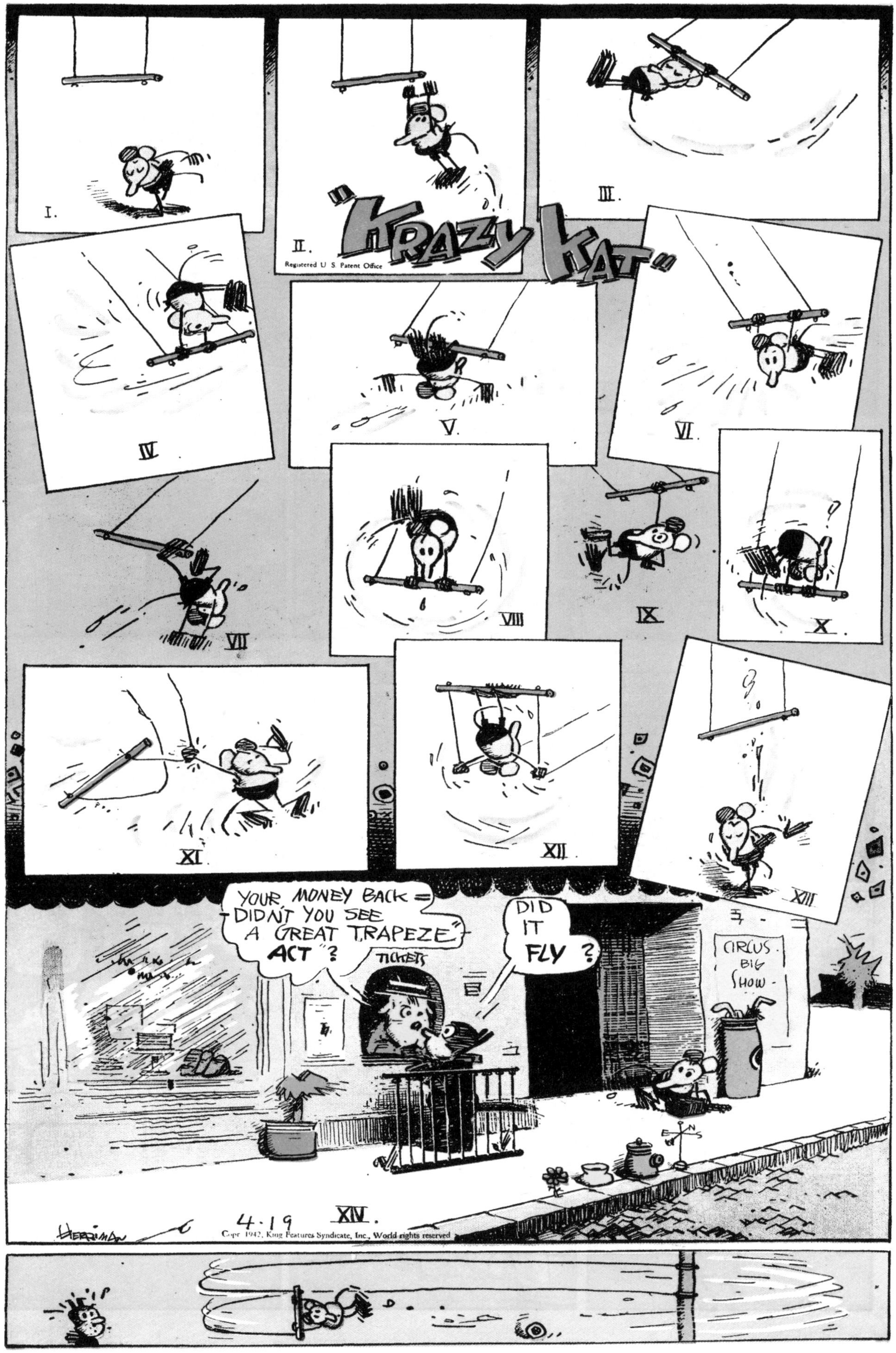
"KRAZY KAT"
Registered U. S. Patent Office
I.
II.
III.
IV
V.
VI.
VII
VIII
IX
X.
XI.
XII.
XIII
YOUR MONEY BACK = DIDN'T YOU SEE A GREAT TRAPEZE ACT ?
TICKETS
DID IT FLY ?
CIRCUS BIG SHOW
HERRIMAN
4-19
XIV.
Copr. 1942, King Features Syndicate, Inc., World rights reserved

April 19th, 1942.

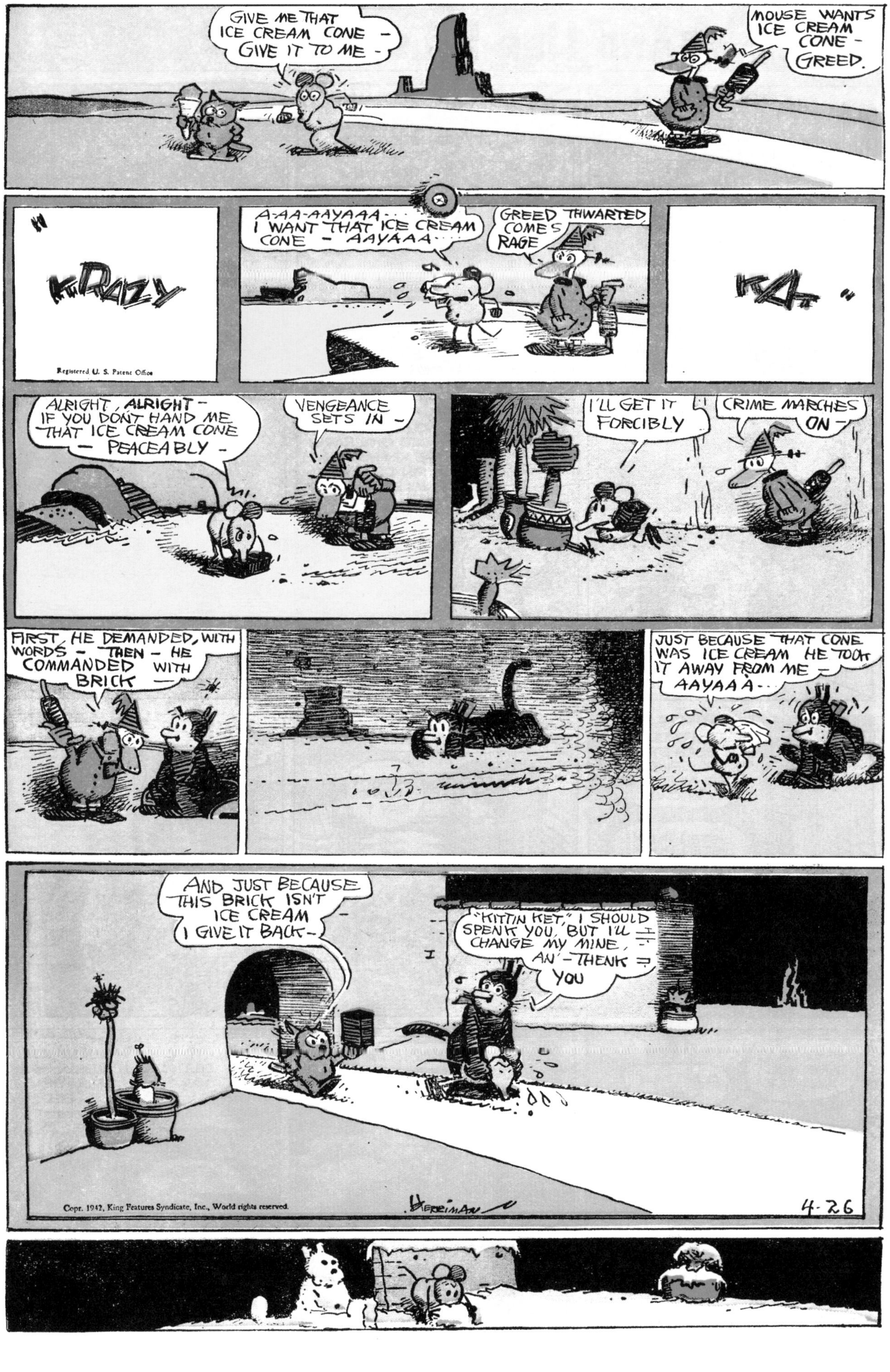
GIVE ME THAT ICE CREAM CONE - GIVE IT TO ME -
MOUSE WANTS ICE CREAM CONE - GREED.
KRAZY
Registered U. S. Patent Office
A-AA-AAYAAA - I WANT THAT ICE CREAM CONE - AAYAAA -
GREED THWARTED COMES RAGE
KAT
ALRIGHT, ALRIGHT - IF YOU DON'T HAND ME THAT ICE CREAM CONE - PEACEABLY -
VENGEANCE SETS IN -
I'LL GET IT FORCIBLY
CRIME MARCHES ON -
FIRST, HE DEMANDED, WITH WORDS - THEN - HE COMMANDED WITH BRICK -
JUST BECAUSE THAT CONE WAS ICE CREAM HE TOOK IT AWAY FROM ME - AAYAAA -
AND JUST BECAUSE THIS BRICK ISN'T ICE CREAM I GIVE IT BACK -
"KITTIN KET," I SHOULD SPENK YOU, BUT I'LL CHANGE MY MINE, AN' - THENK YOU
Copr. 1942, King Features Syndicate, Inc., World rights reserved.
HERRIMAN
4-26

April 26th, 1942.

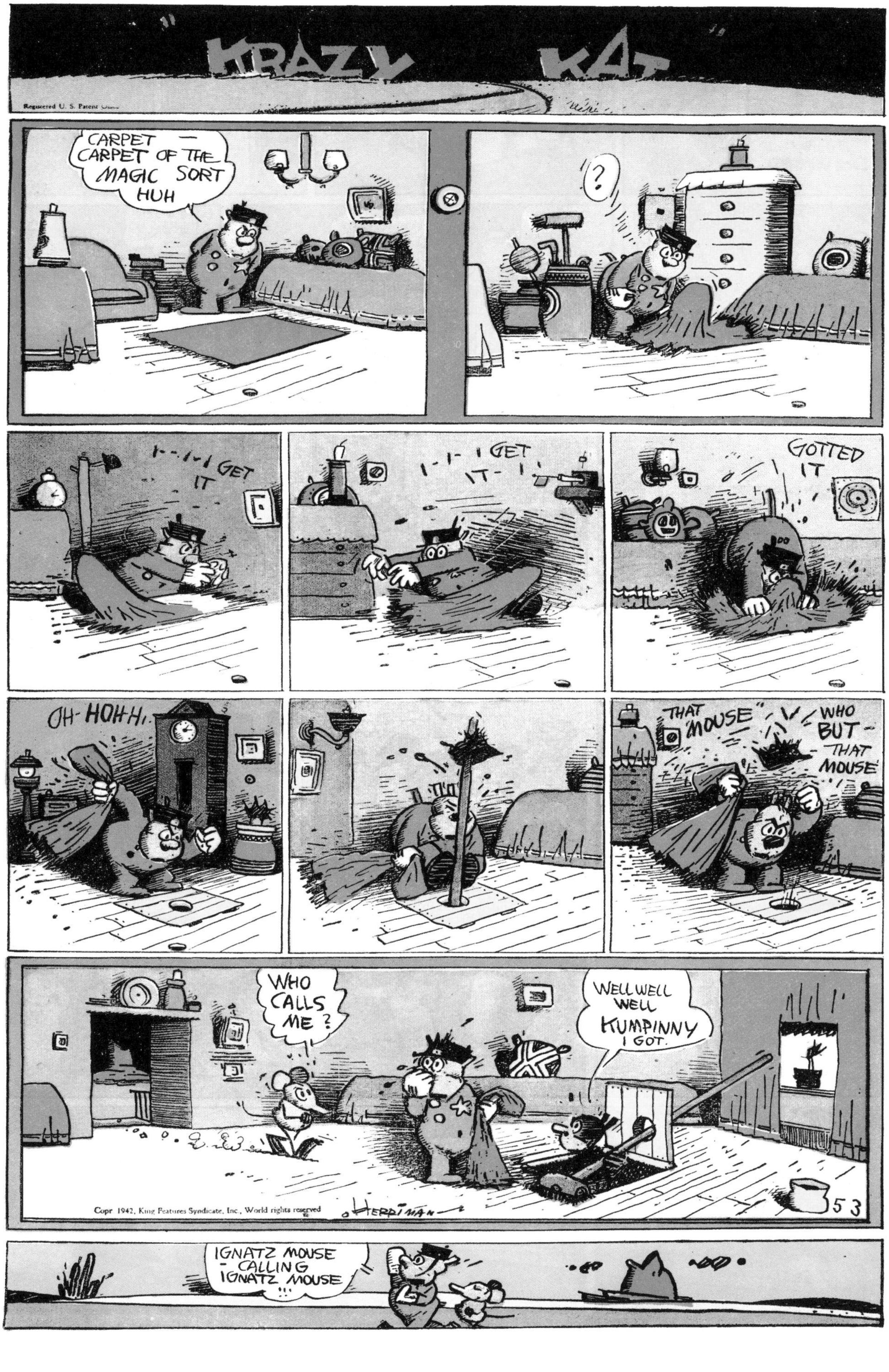
"KRAZY KAT"
Registered U. S. Patent Office
CARPET — CARPET OF THE MAGIC SORT HUH
?
I-I-I GET IT
I-I-I GET IT-I
GOTTED IT
OH-HOHH
"THAT "MOUSE" — WHO BUT — THAT MOUSE
WHO CALLS ME?
WELL WELL WELL KUMPINNY I GOT.
Copr 1942, King Features Syndicate, Inc., World rights reserved
HERRIMAN
5 3
IGNATZ MOUSE — CALLING IGNATZ MOUSE !!!

May 3rd, 1942.

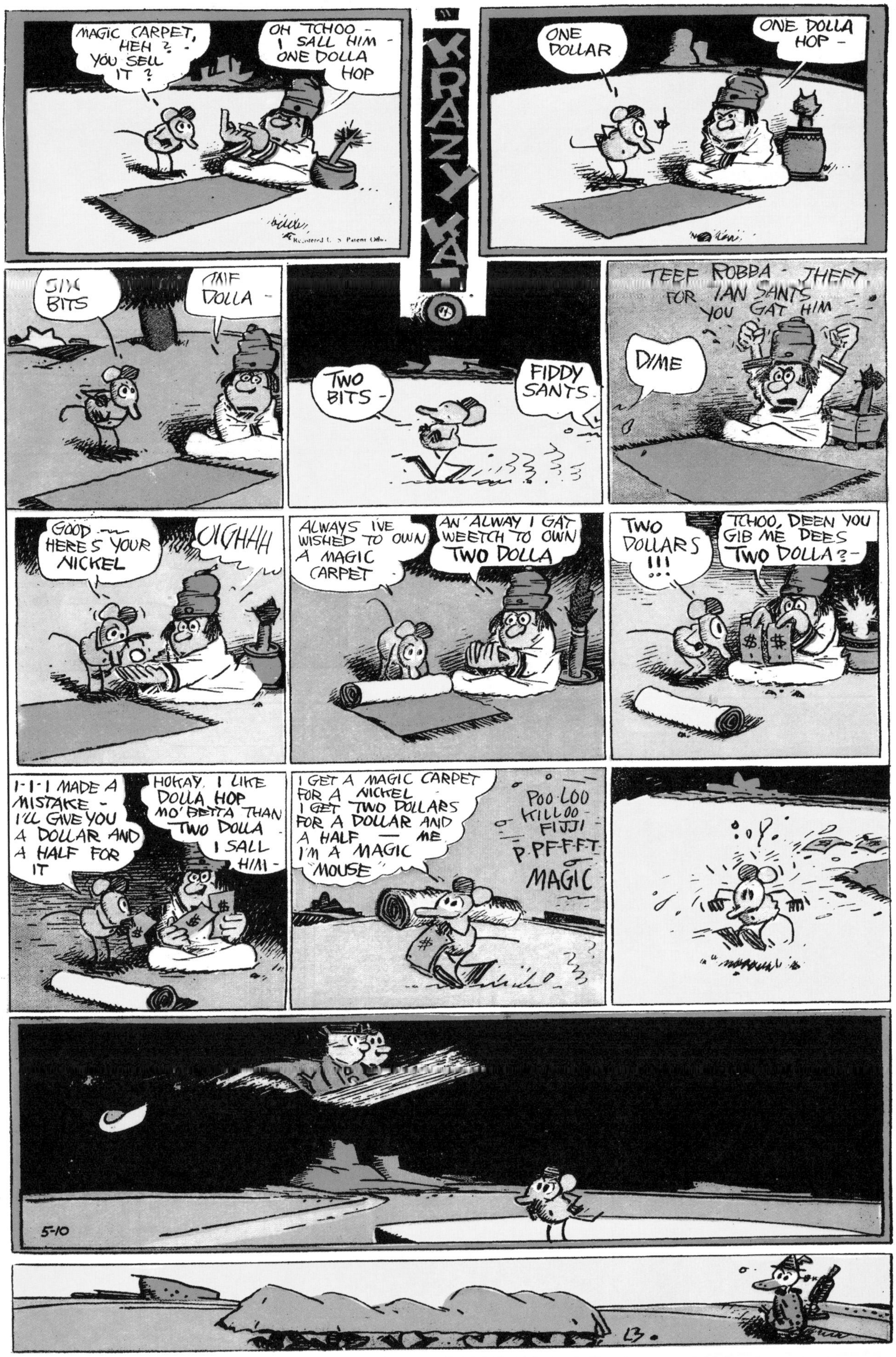
KRAZY KAT
MAGIC CARPET, HEH ? YOU SELL IT ?
OH TCHOO - I SALL HIM ONE DOLLA HOP
Registered U. S. Patent Office
ONE DOLLAR
ONE DOLLA HOP -
SIX BITS
HAIF DOLLA -
TWO BITS -
FIDDY SANTS
TEEF ROBBA - THEFT FOR IAN SANTS YOU GAT HIM
DIME
GOOD - HERE'S YOUR NICKEL
UGHHH
ALWAYS I'VE WISHED TO OWN A MAGIC CARPET
AN' ALWAY I GAT WEETCH TO OWN TWO DOLLA
TWO DOLLARS !!!
TCHOO, DEEN YOU GIB ME DEES TWO DOLLA ? -
I-I-I MADE A MISTAKE - I'LL GIVE YOU A DOLLAR AND A HALF FOR IT
HOKAY, I LIKE DOLLA HOP MO' BETTA THAN TWO DOLLA - I SALL HIM -
I GET A MAGIC CARPET FOR A NICKEL I GET TWO DOLLARS FOR A DOLLAR AND A HALF — ME, I'M A MAGIC MOUSE
POO LOO KILLOO FIJJI P-PF-F-F-T MAGIC
5-10

May 10th, 1942.

"KRAZY KAT"
Registered U.S. Patent Office
MY TREASURE –
PATT PATT PATT
BEING SPRINGTIME HE MAY HAVE PLANTED A SEED OR SOMETHING – BUT THAT, I DO, INDEED, DOUBT –
–WELL–WELL– WOULD YOU LOOK?.. I SUSPECTED JUST THIS –
THUS DO I UPROOT THEE –
ZOOM
SEED OF SIN –
ZOOM
ZOOM
BOOM
HIS BRICK CROP WILL BE A SWEET FAILURE THIS SEASON –
ZOOM
ZOOM
BOOM
ZOOM
HUH, IT MUST HAVE BEEN A "GOLD BRICK" THE WAY YOU CARRY-ON –
"RUBBER," WOMAN – SOLID "RUBBER"
ZOOM
© 1942, King Features Syndicate, Inc., World rights reserved.
HERRIMAN
5-17
A "B." MADE OF "C." – NOW WHAT SORT OF JIBBERJIBBER IS THIS?
A B-R-I-C-K MADE OF C-L-A-Y – A CODE, Y'SEE "K."?
ALL BUT THE "C.," "K."

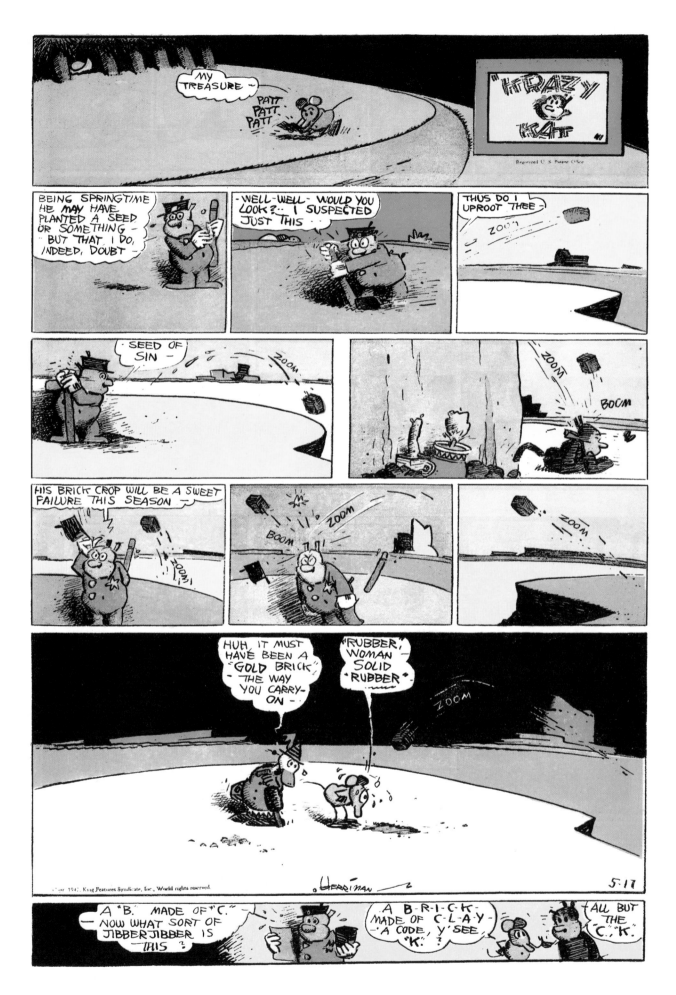

May 17th, 1942.

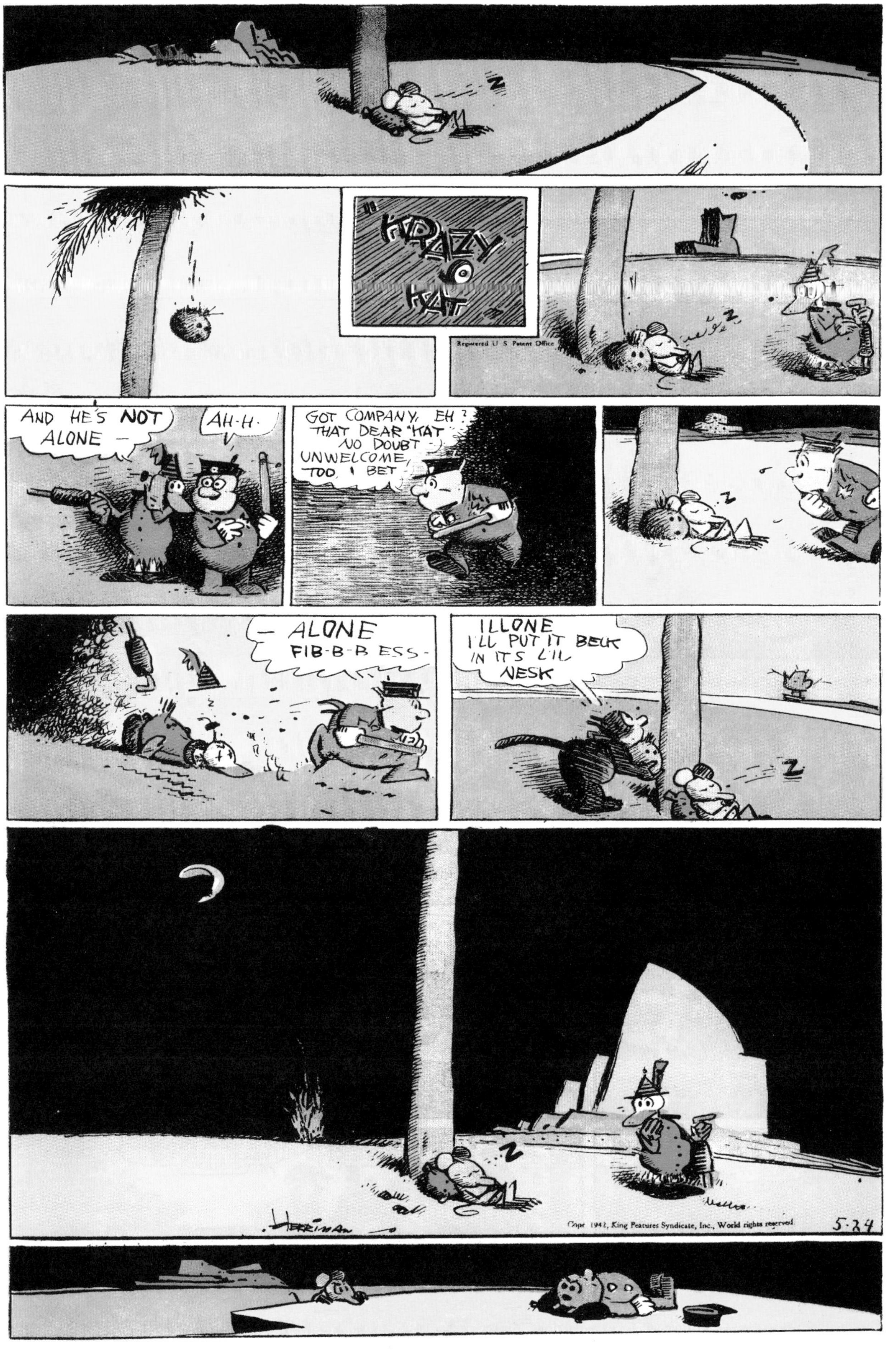
KRAZY KAT
Registered U S Patent Office
AND HE'S NOT ALONE —
AH-H.
GOT COMPANY, EH? THAT DEAR "KAT" NO DOUBT UNWELCOME, TOO, I BET
— ALONE FIB-B-B ESS-
ILLONE I'LL PUT IT BECK IN ITS L'IL NESK
HERRIMAN
Copr 1942, King Features Syndicate, Inc., World rights reserved.
5-24

May 24th, 1942.

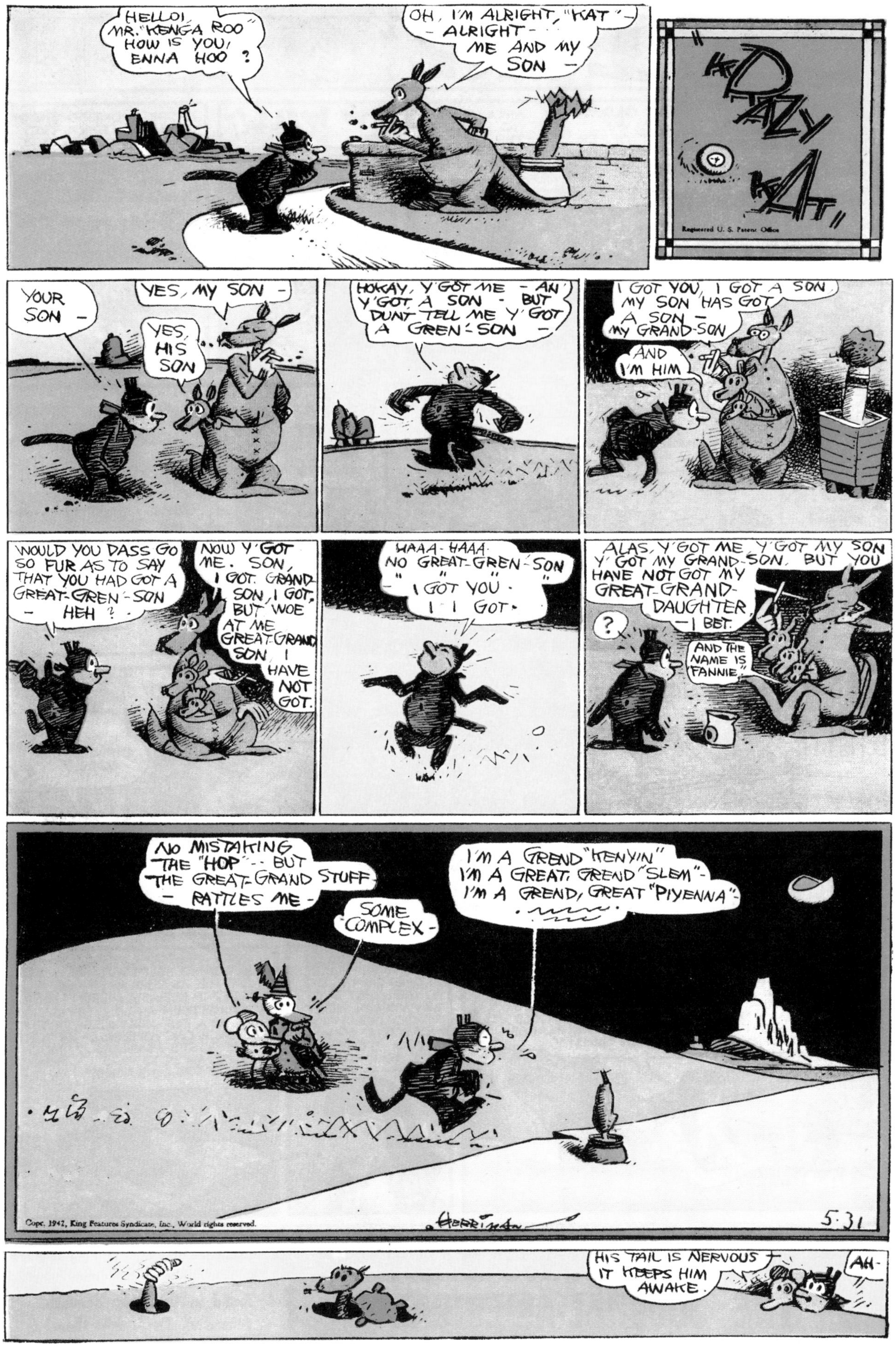

HELLO!, MR. KENGA ROO HOW IS YOU, ENNA HOO ?
OH, I'M ALRIGHT, "KAT" - - ALRIGHT - ME AND MY SON -
KRAZY KAT
Registered U. S. Patent Office
YOUR SON -
YES, MY SON -
YES, HIS SON
HOKAY, Y'GOT ME - AN' Y'GOT A SON - BUT DUNT TELL ME Y'GOT A GREN-SON -
I GOT YOU, I GOT A SON. MY SON HAS GOT A SON - MY GRAND-SON
AND I'M HIM
WOULD YOU DASS GO SO FUR AS TO SAY THAT YOU HAD GOT A GREAT-GREN-SON - HEH ?
NOW Y'GOT ME. SON, I GOT. GRAND-SON, I GOT, BUT WOE AT ME GREAT-GRAND SON I HAVE NOT GOT.
HAAA-HAAA NO GREAT-GREN-SON - " I GOT YOU " I - I GOT -
ALAS, Y'GOT ME, Y'GOT MY SON Y'GOT MY GRAND-SON, BUT YOU HAVE NOT GOT MY GREAT-GRAND-DAUGHTER, - I BET.
?
AND THE NAME IS "FANNIE."
NO MISTAKING THE "HOP" - BUT THE GREAT-GRAND STUFF - RATTLES ME -
SOME COMPLEX -
I'M A GREND "KENYIN" I'M A GREAT, GREND "SLEM" - I'M A GREND, GREAT "PIYENNA" -
Copr. 1942, King Features Syndicate, Inc., World rights reserved.
HERRIMAN
5.31
HIS TAIL IS NERVOUS - IT KEEPS HIM AWAKE.
AH-

May 31st, 1942.

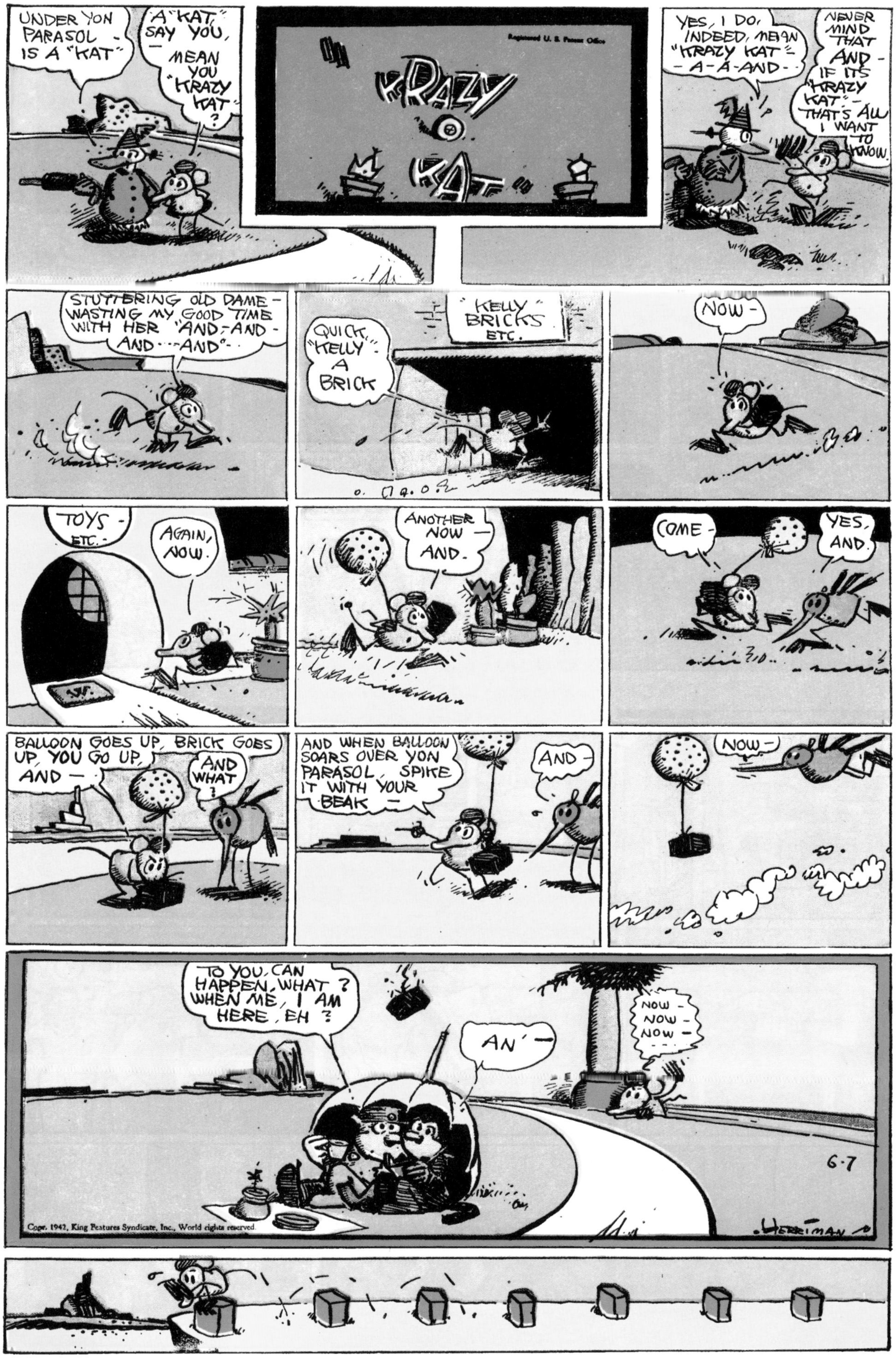
UNDER YON PARASOL - IS A "KAT"
"A KAT," SAY YOU, — MEAN YOU "KRAZY KAT" ?
Registered U. S. Patent Office
KRAZY KAT
YES, I DO, INDEED, MEAN "KRAZY KAT" - A-A-AND -
NEVER MIND THAT AND - IF ITS "KRAZY KAT" - THAT'S ALL I WANT TO KNOW.
STUTTERING OLD DAME - WASTING MY GOOD TIME WITH HER "AND-AND AND --- AND" -
KELLY BRICKS ETC.
QUICK, "KELLY" - A BRICK
NOW -
TOYS - ETC. -
AGAIN, NOW.
ANOTHER NOW — AND.
COME -
YES, AND.
BALLOON GOES UP, BRICK GOES UP, YOU GO UP, AND —
AND WHAT ?
AND WHEN BALLOON SOARS OVER YON PARASOL, SPIKE IT WITH YOUR BEAK —
AND -
NOW -
TO YOU, CAN HAPPEN, WHAT ? WHEN ME, I AM HERE, EH ?
AN' —
NOW - NOW - NOW - - -
6-7
Copr. 1942, King Features Syndicate, Inc., World rights reserved.
HERRIMAN

June 7th, 1942.

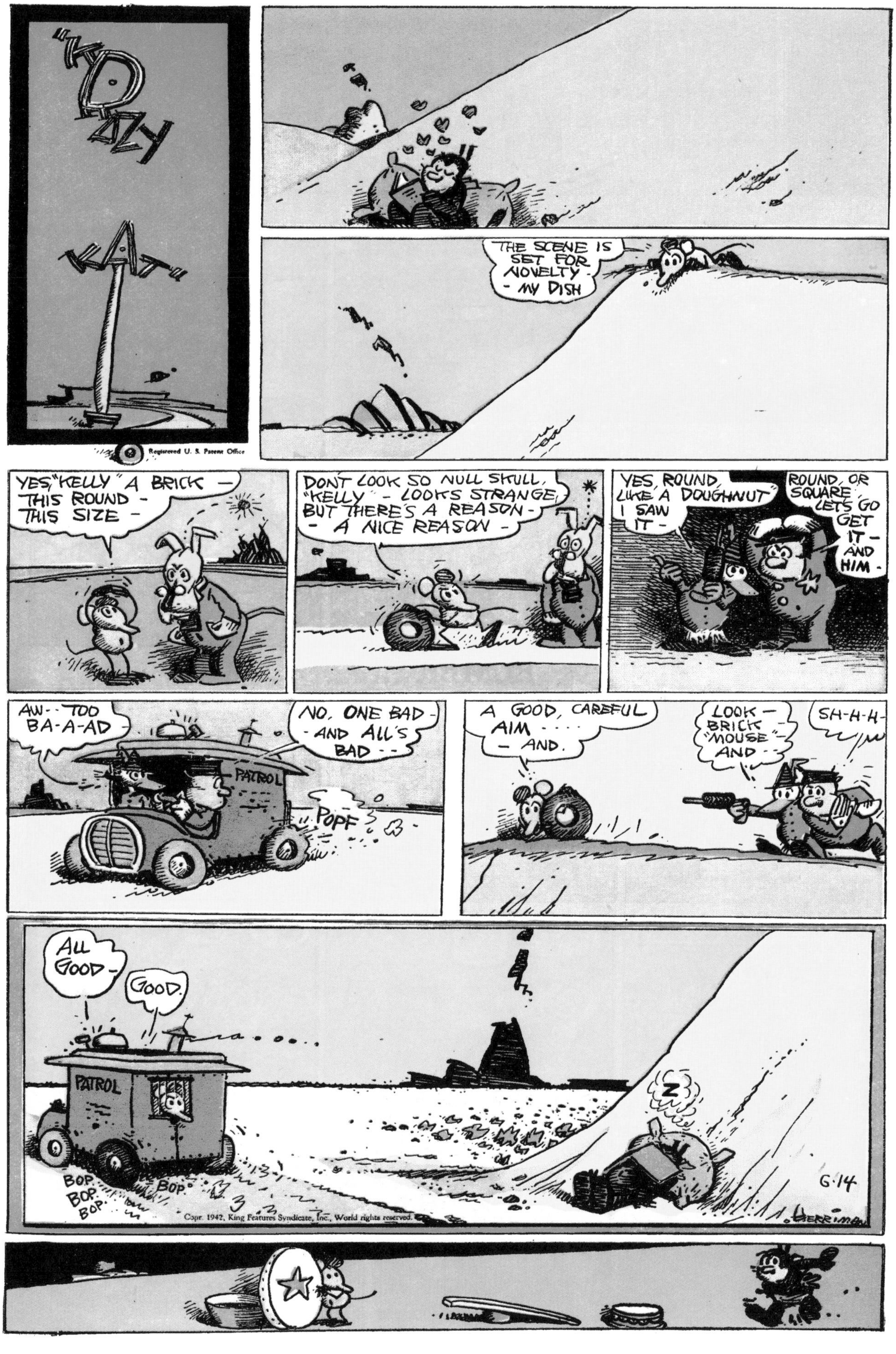
"KRAZY KAT"
Registered U. S. Patent Office
THE SCENE IS SET FOR NOVELTY - MY DISH
YES, "KELLY" A BRICK - THIS ROUND - THIS SIZE -
DON'T LOOK SO NULL SKULL, "KELLY" - LOOKS STRANGE, BUT THERE'S A REASON - - A NICE REASON -
YES, ROUND, LIKE A DOUGHNUT I SAW IT -
ROUND, OR SQUARE LET'S GO GET IT - AND HIM -
AW-- TOO BA-A-AD
NO, ONE BAD - AND ALL'S BAD --
PATROL
POPF
A GOOD, CAREFUL AIM - AND.
LOOK - BRICK "MOUSE" AND -
SH-H-H-
ALL GOOD -
GOOD.
PATROL
Z
BOP. BOP. BOP. BOP.
G·14
Copr. 1942, King Features Syndicate, Inc., World rights reserved.
HERRIMAN

June 14th, 1942.

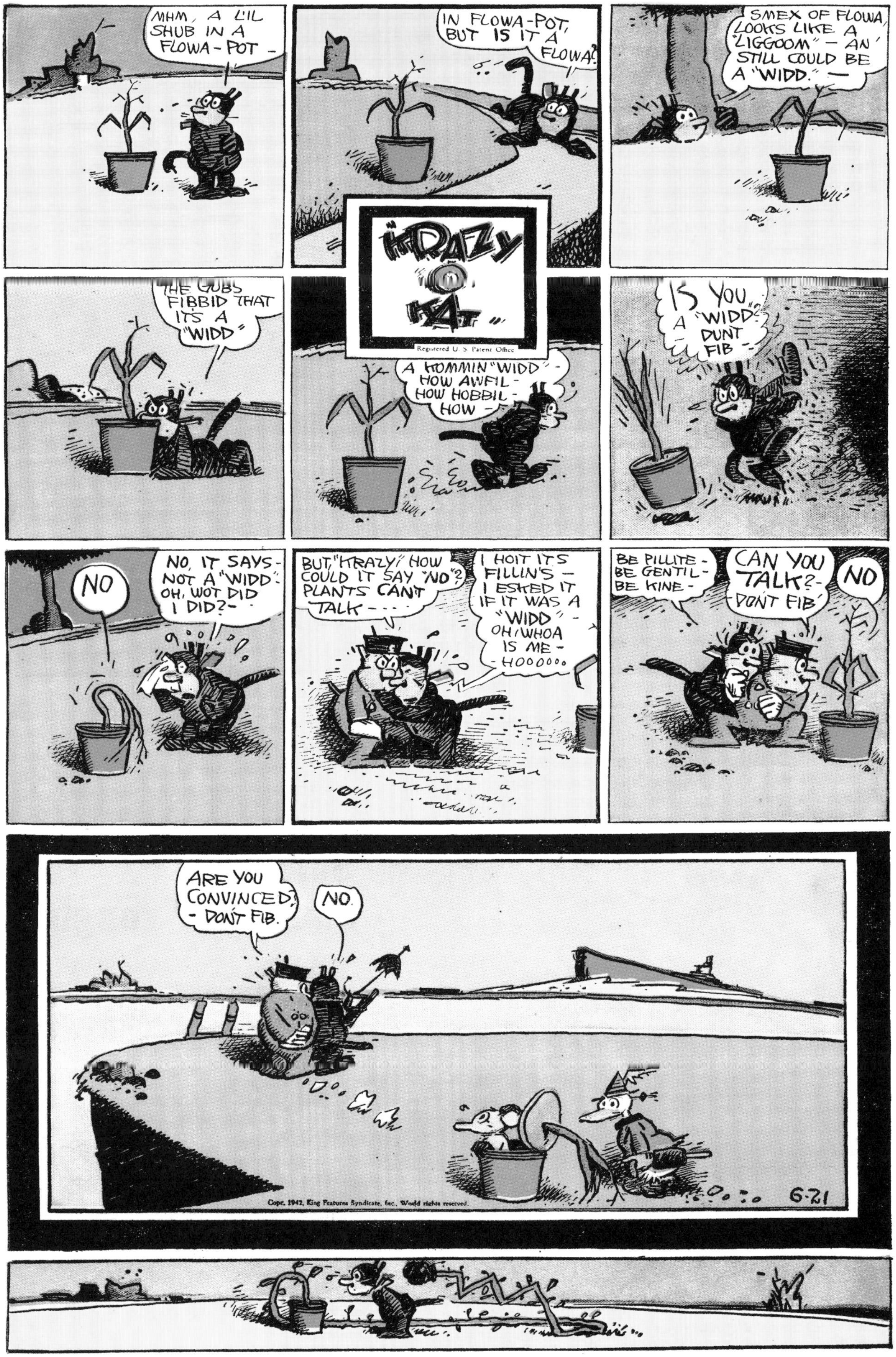
MHM, A L'IL SHUB IN A FLOWA-POT -
IN FLOWA-POT, BUT IS IT A FLOWA?
SMEX OF FLOWA, LOOKS LIKE A "LIGGOOM" - AN' STILL COULD BE A "WIDD." -
"KRAZY" "N" "KAT"
Registered U. S. Patent Office
THE GUBS FIBBID THAT ITS A "WIDD"
A "KOMMIN" "WIDD" - HOW AWFIL - HOW HOBBIL - HOW -
IS YOU A "WIDD"? - DUNT FIB -
NO
NO, IT SAYS - NOT A "WIDD" - OH, WOT DID I DID? -
BUT, "KRAZY," HOW COULD IT SAY "NO"? PLANTS CAN'T TALK - - -
I HOIT ITS FILLIN'S - I ESKED IT IF IT WAS A "WIDD" - OH, WHOA IS ME - HOOOOOO
BE PILLITE - BE GENTIL - BE KINE -
CAN YOU TALK? - DON'T FIB
NO
ARE YOU CONVINCED? - DON'T FIB.
NO.
Copr. 1942, King Features Syndicate, Inc., World rights reserved.
6-21

June 21st, 1942.

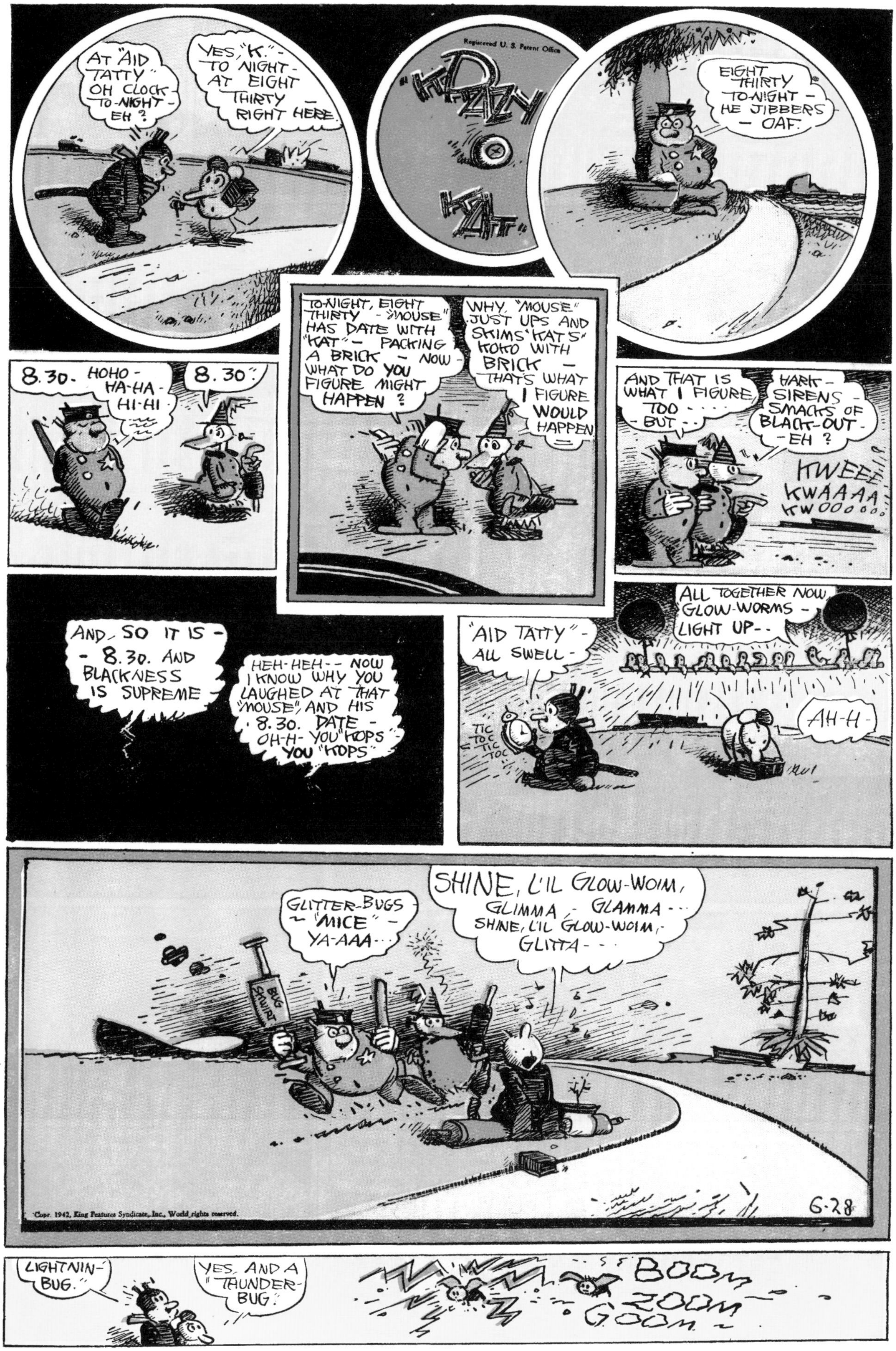
AT "AID TATTY" OH CLOCK TO-NIGHT - EH ?
YES, "K." - TO NIGHT - AT EIGHT THIRTY - RIGHT HERE.
"KRAZY KAT"
EIGHT THIRTY TO-NIGHT - HE JIBBERS - OAF.
8.30 -
HOHO - HA-HA HI-HI
8.30
TO-NIGHT, EIGHT THIRTY - "MOUSE" HAS DATE WITH "KAT" - PACKING A BRICK - NOW - WHAT DO YOU FIGURE MIGHT HAPPEN ?
WHY, "MOUSE" JUST UPS AND SKIMS "KAT'S" KOKO WITH BRICK - THAT'S WHAT I FIGURE WOULD HAPPEN
AND THAT IS WHAT I FIGURE, TOO - BUT - -
HARK - SIRENS - SMACKS OF BLACK-OUT - EH ?
KWEEE KWAAAA KWOOOOO
AND SO IT IS - 8.30. AND BLACKNESS IS SUPREME
HEH-HEH - - NOW I KNOW WHY YOU LAUGHED AT THAT "MOUSE", AND HIS 8.30. DATE - OH-H- YOU "KOPS" YOU "KOPS"
ALL TOGETHER NOW, GLOW-WORMS - LIGHT UP - -
"AID TATTY" - ALL SWELL -
TIC TOC TIC TOC
AH-H -
GLITTER-BUGS - "MICE" - YA-AAA - -
SHINE, L'IL GLOW-WOIM, GLIMMA, GLAMMA - - SHINE, L'IL GLOW-WOIM, GLITTA - -
BUG SQUIRT
6-28
Copr. 1942, King Features Syndicate, Inc., World rights reserved.
LIGHTNIN-BUG.
YES, AND A "THUNDER-BUG."
BOOM - ZOOM - GOOM -

June 28th, 1942.

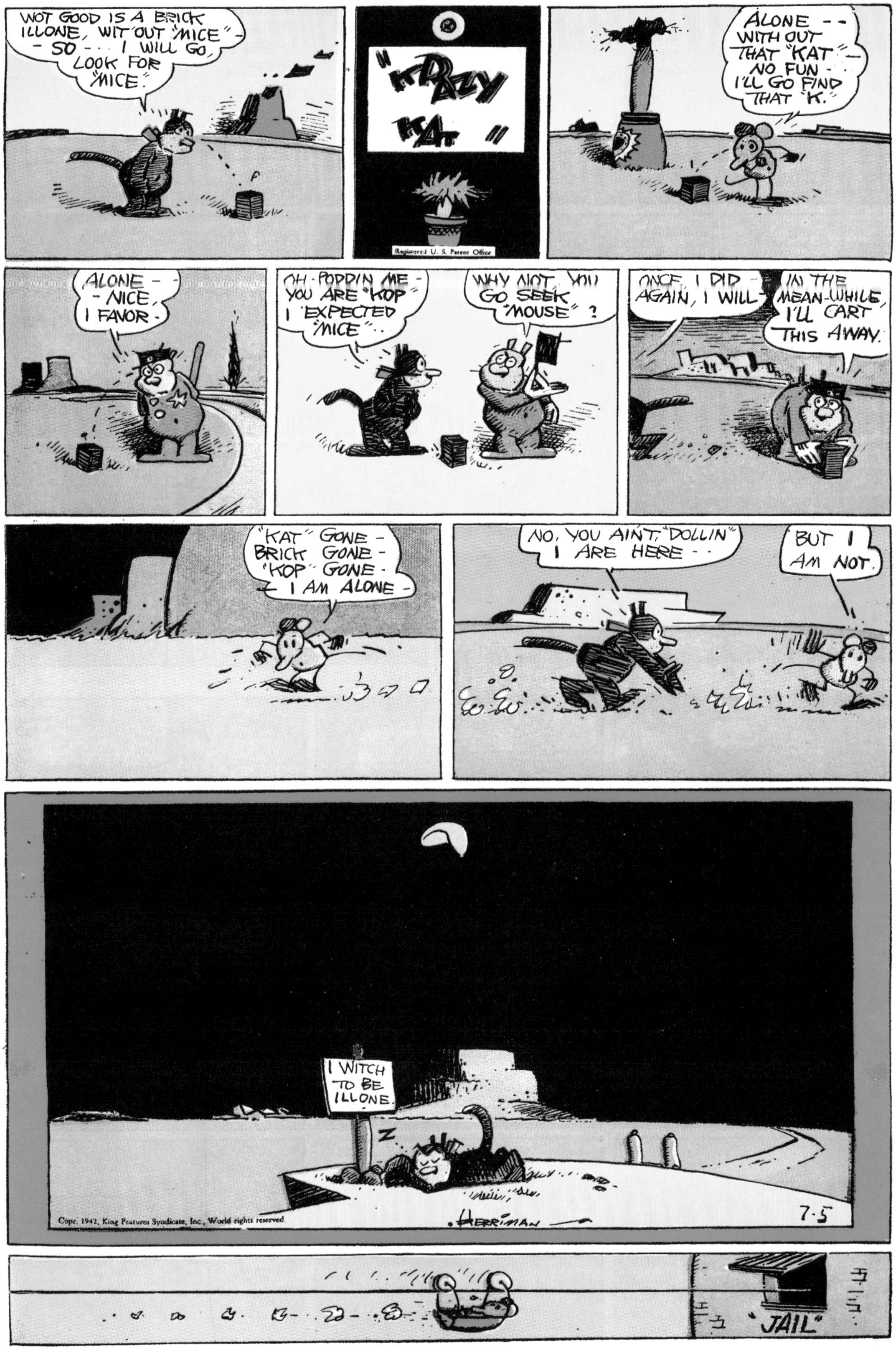
WOT GOOD IS A BRICK ILLONE, WIT OUT "MICE" - - SO - - I WILL GO, LOOK FOR "MICE."
"KRAZY KAT"
Registered U. S. Patent Office
ALONE - - WITH OUT THAT "KAT" - NO FUN - I'LL GO FIND THAT "K."
ALONE - - - NICE, I FAVOR -
OH - PODDIN ME - YOU ARE "KOP" I EXPECTED "MICE" -
WHY NOT, YOU GO SEEK "MOUSE" ?
ONCE, I DID - AGAIN, I WILL -
IN THE MEAN-WHILE, I'LL CART THIS AWAY.
"KAT" GONE - BRICK GONE - "KOP" GONE - I AM ALONE -
NO, YOU AINT, "DOLLIN" I ARE HERE - -
BUT I AM NOT.
I WITCH TO BE ILLONE.
Z
Copr. 1942, King Features Syndicate, Inc., World rights reserved.
HERRIMAN
7-5
"JAIL"

July 5th, 1942.

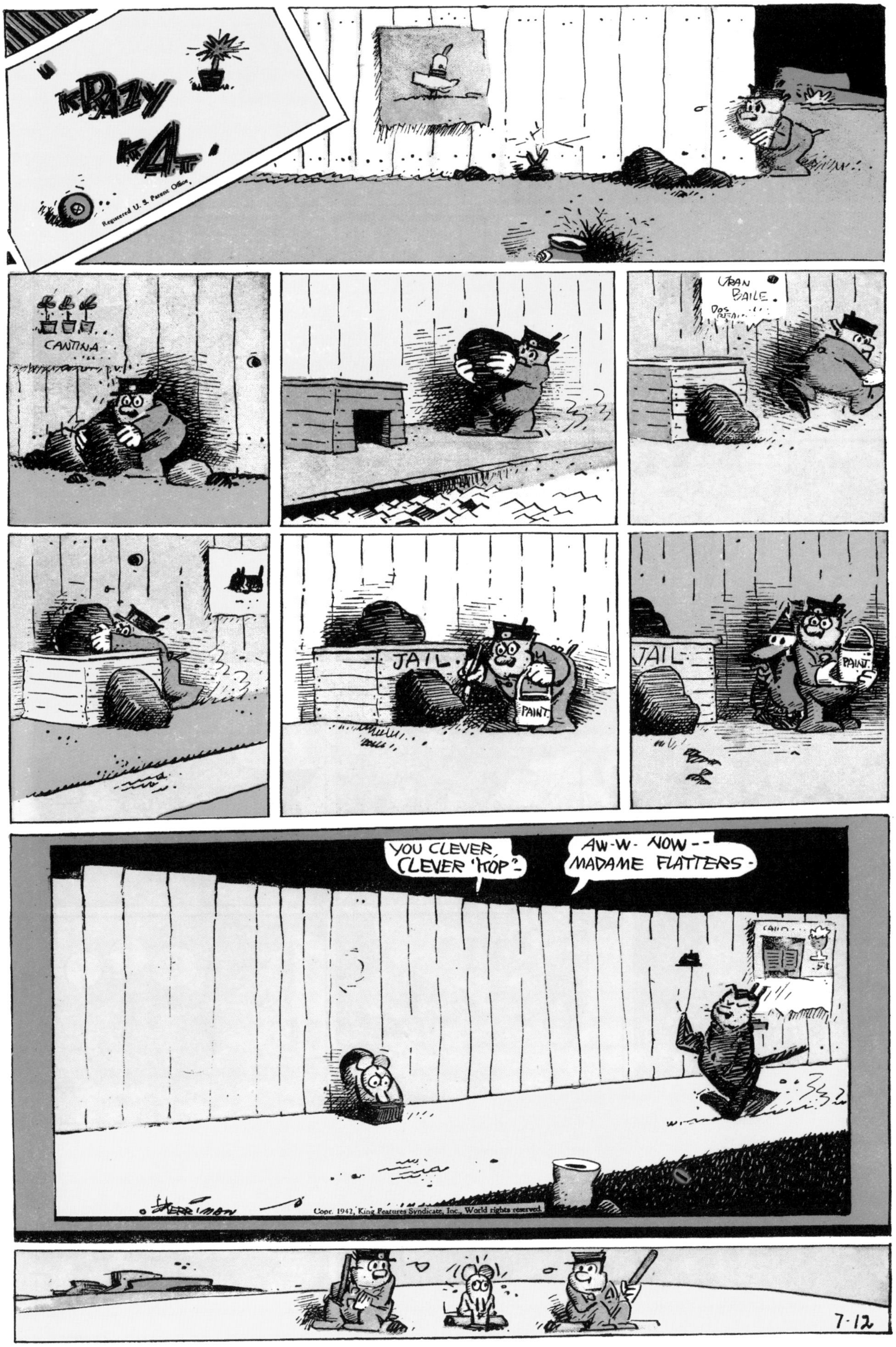
KRAZY KAT
Registered U. S. Patent Office
CANTINA
GRAN BAILE
JAIL
PAINT
JAIL
PAINT
YOU CLEVER, CLEVER 'KOP'-
AW-W- NOW-- MADAME FLATTERS-
HERRIMAN
Copr. 1942, King Features Syndicate, Inc., World rights reserved.
7-12

July 12th, 1942.

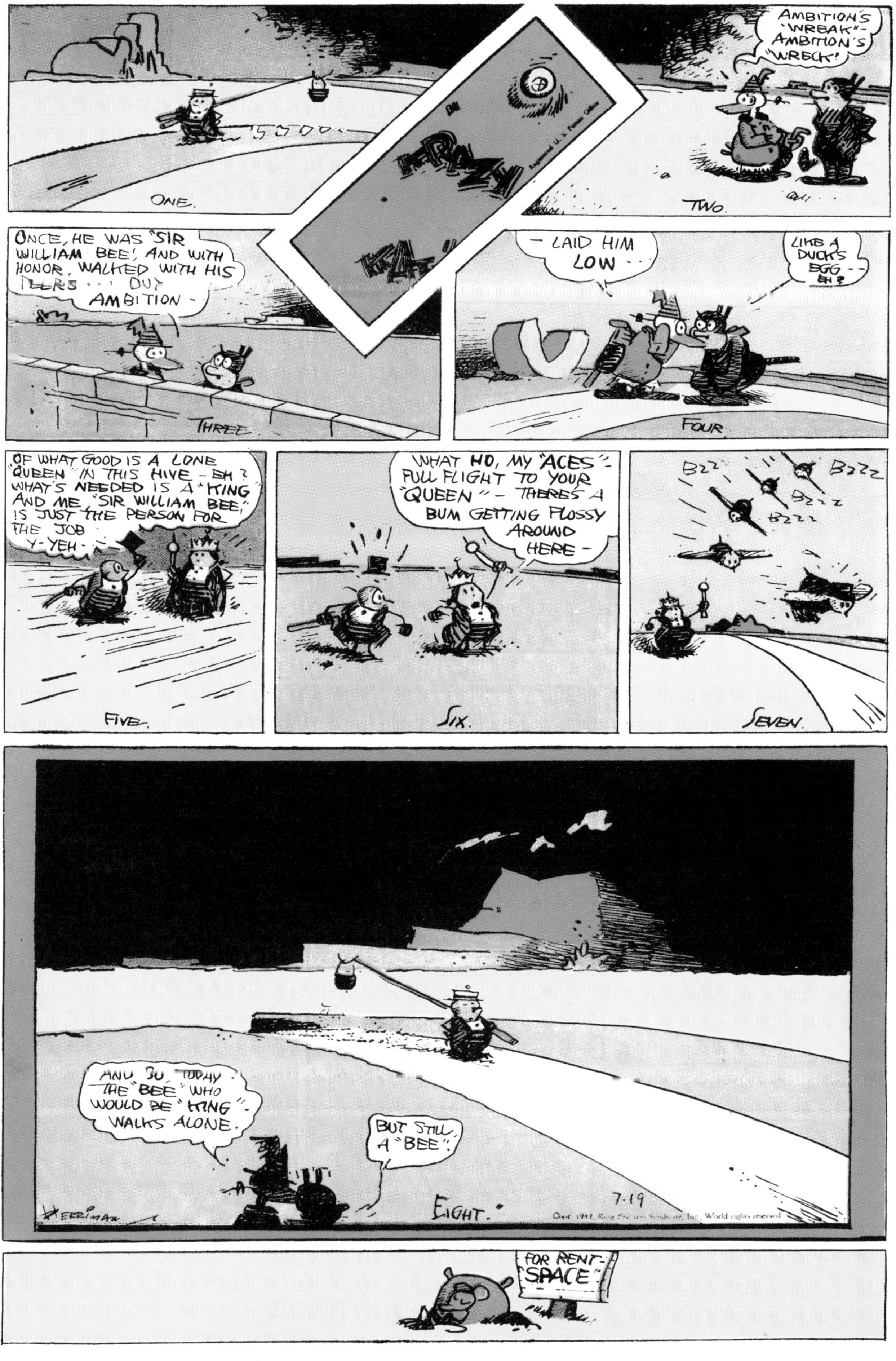
KRAZY KAT
Registered U. S. Patent Office
ONE.
AMBITION'S "WREAK" - AMBITION'S "WRECK"!
TWO.
ONCE, HE WAS "SIR WILLIAM BEE," AND WITH HONOR, WALKED WITH HIS
AMBITION -
THREE.
- LAID HIM LOW - -
LIKE A DUCK'S EGG - - EH?
FOUR.
OF WHAT GOOD IS A LONE "QUEEN" IN THIS HIVE - EH? WHAT'S NEEDED IS A "KING" AND ME, "SIR WILLIAM BEE," IS JUST THE PERSON FOR THE JOB - Y-YEH -
FIVE.
WHAT HO, MY "ACES" - FULL FLIGHT TO YOUR "QUEEN" - THERE'S A BUM GETTING FLOSSY AROUND HERE -
SIX.
BZZ
BZZZ
BZZZ
BZZZ
SEVEN.
AND SO, TODAY THE "BEE" WHO WOULD BE "KING" WALKS ALONE.
BUT STILL A "BEE".
EIGHT.
7.19
HERRIMAN
FOR RENT - "SPACE"

July 19th, 1942.

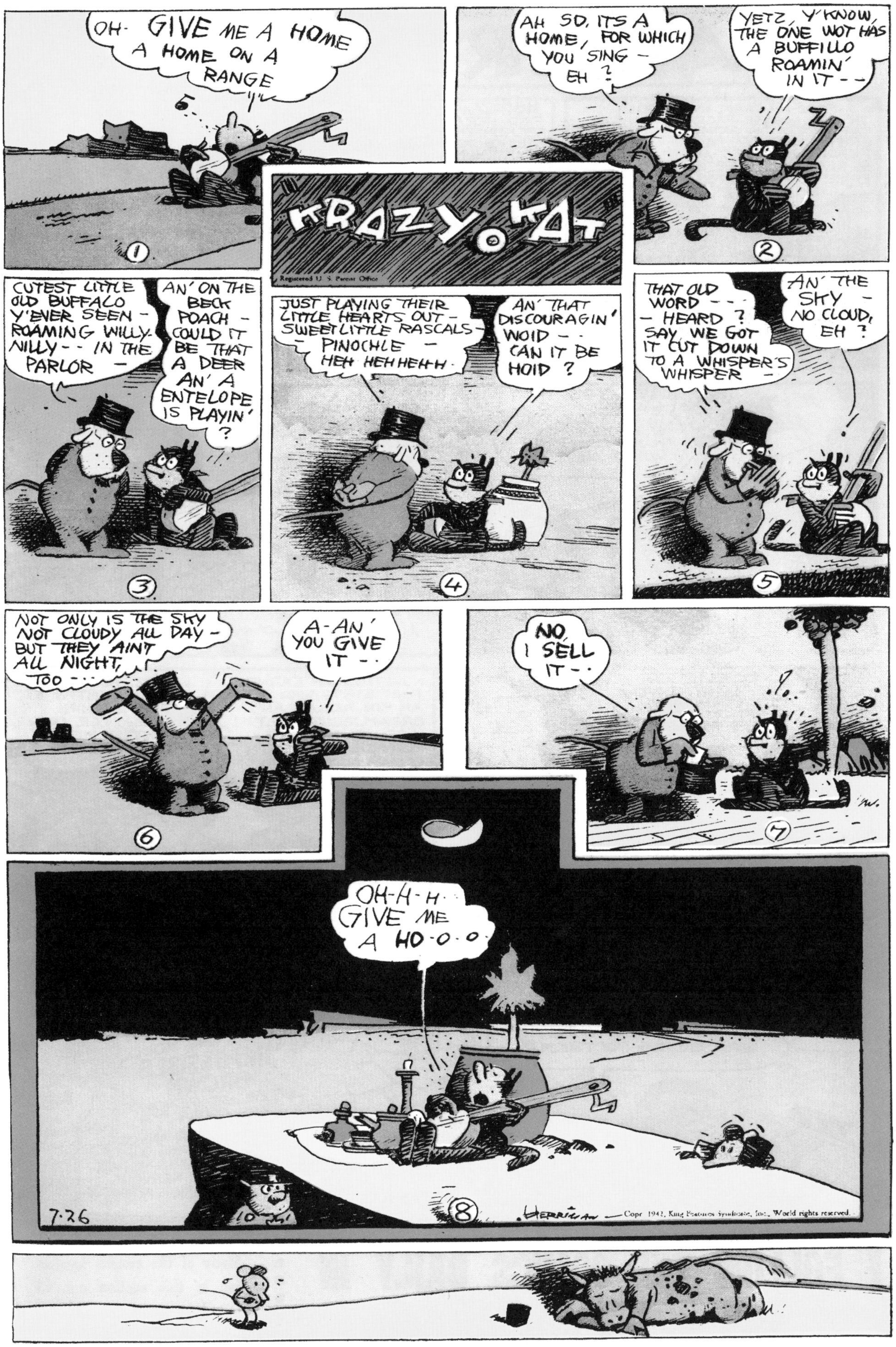

OH- GIVE ME A HOME A HOME ON A RANGE
AH SO, ITS A HOME, FOR WHICH YOU SING - EH ?
YETZ, Y'KNOW, THE ONE WOT HAS A BUFFILLO ROAMIN' IN IT - -
KRAZY KAT
Registered U. S. Patent Office
CUTEST LITTLE OLD BUFFALO Y'EVER SEEN - ROAMING WILLY-NILLY - - IN THE PARLOR -
AN' ON THE BECK POACH - COULD IT BE THAT A DEER AN' A ENTELOPE IS PLAYIN' ?
JUST PLAYING THEIR LITTLE HEARTS OUT - SWEET LITTLE RASCALS - PINOCHLE - HEH HEH HEH HEH -
AN' THAT DISCOURAGIN' WOID - - CAN IT BE HOID ?
THAT OLD WORD - - - HEARD ? SAY WE GOT IT CUT DOWN TO A WHISPER'S WHISPER -
AN' THE SKY - NO CLOUD, EH ?
NOT ONLY IS THE SKY NOT CLOUDY ALL DAY - BUT THEY AINT ALL NIGHT, TOO - - -
A-AN' YOU GIVE IT - -
NO, I SELL IT - -
OH-H-H GIVE ME A HO-O-O
7.26
HERRIMAN
Copr. 1942, King Features Syndicate, Inc., World rights reserved.

July 26th, 1942.

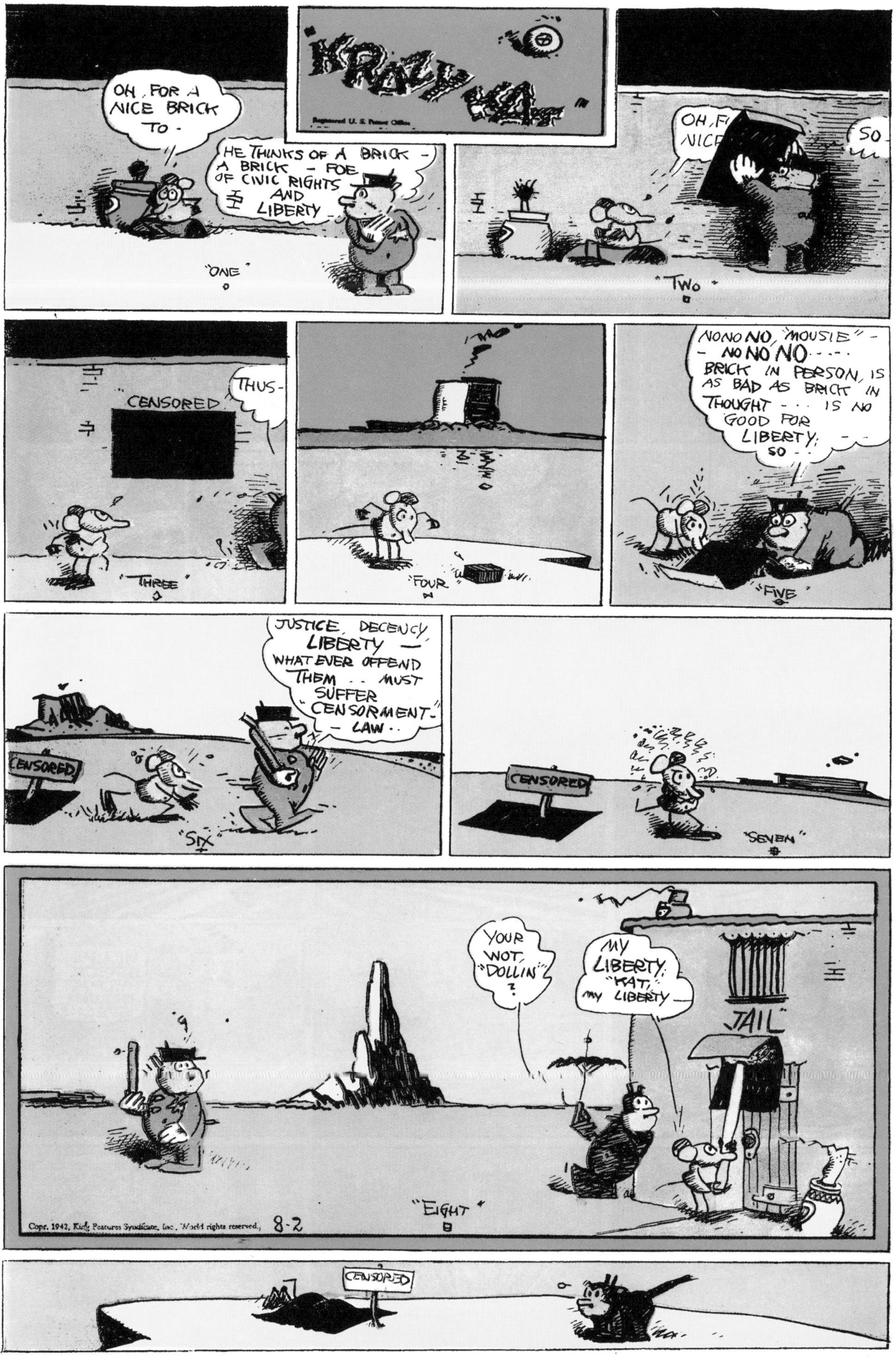
"KRAZY KAT"
Registered U. S. Patent Office
OH, FOR A NICE BRICK TO -
HE THINKS OF A BRICK - A BRICK - FOE OF CIVIC RIGHTS AND LIBERTY
"ONE"
OH, F
NICE
SO
"TWO"
"CENSORED"
THUS-
"THREE"
"FOUR"
NONONO, "MOUSIE" - - NO NO NO - - - - BRICK IN PERSON, IS AS BAD AS BRICK IN THOUGHT - - - IS NO GOOD FOR LIBERTY, - - SO - -
"FIVE"
JUSTICE, DECENCY, LIBERTY - WHAT EVER OFFEND THEM - - MUST SUFFER "CENSORMENT" - LAW - -
CENSORED
"SIX"
CENSORED
"SEVEN"
YOUR WOT, "DOLLIN" ?
MY LIBERTY, "KAT," MY LIBERTY -
"JAIL"
"EIGHT"
Copr. 1942, King Features Syndicate, Inc. World rights reserved. 8-2
CENSORED

August 2nd, 1942.

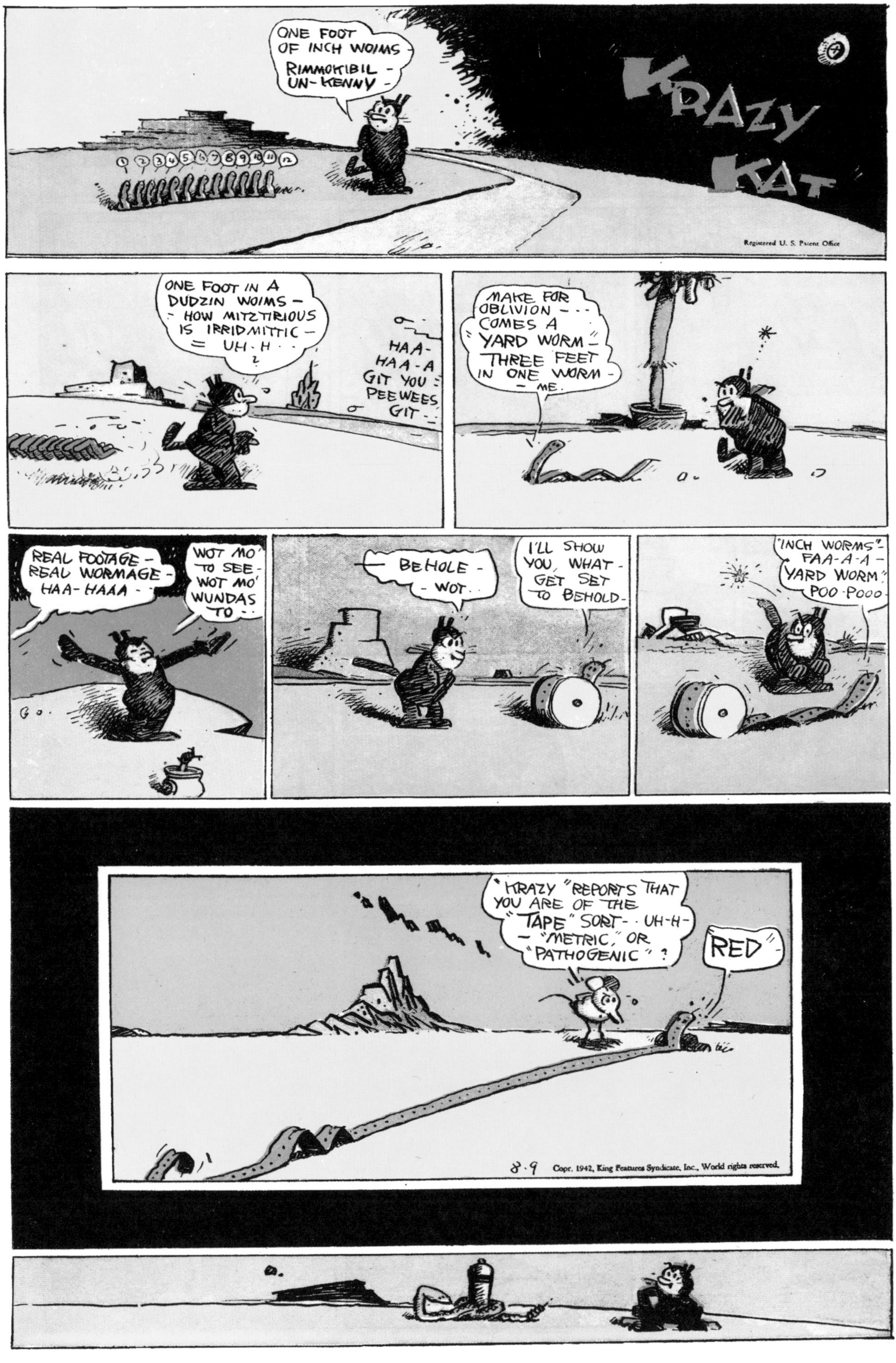
ONE FOOT OF INCH WOIMS - RIMMOKIBIL - UN-KENNY -
KRAZY KAT
Registered U. S. Patent Office
ONE FOOT IN A DUDZIN WOIMS - - HOW MITZTIRIOUS IS IRRIDMITTIC - = UH - H - - ?
HAA-HAA-A GIT YOU PEEWEES GIT - -
MAKE FOR OBLIVION - - - COMES A YARD WORM - THREE FEET IN ONE WORM - - ME.
REAL FOOTAGE - REAL WORMAGE - HAA - HAAA - -
WOT MO' TO SEE - WOT MO' WUNDAS TO - -
- BE HOLE - - WOT - -
I'LL SHOW YOU, WHAT - GET SET TO BEHOLD -
"INCH WORMS" - FAA-A-A - YARD WORM" POO-POOO -
"KRAZY" REPORTS THAT YOU ARE OF THE "TAPE" SORT - - UH-H - - "METRIC," OR "PATHOGENIC" ?
RED
8-9 Copr. 1942, King Features Syndicate, Inc., World rights reserved.

August 9th, 1942.

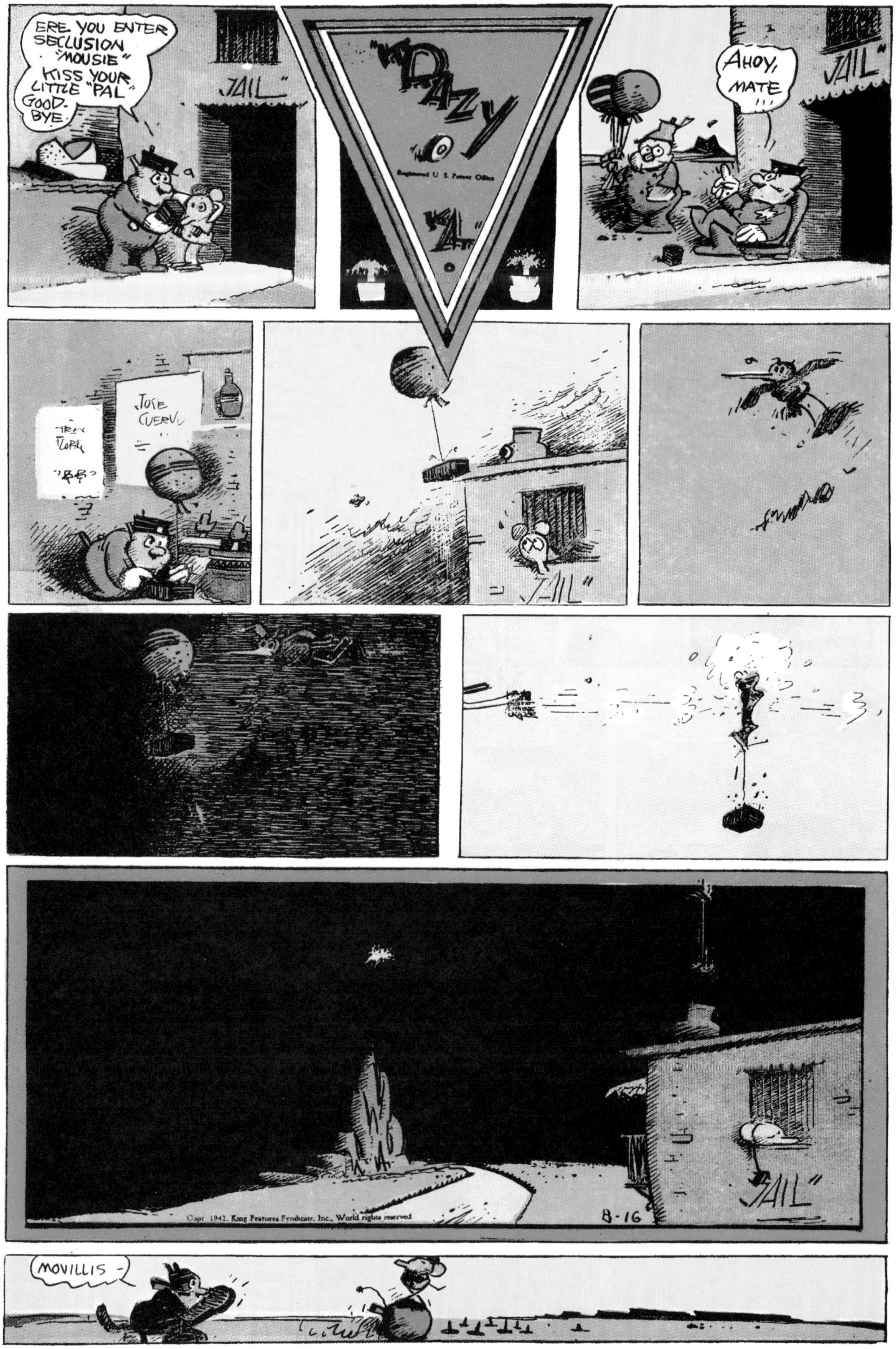
ERE YOU ENTER SECLUSION "MOUSIE" KISS YOUR LITTLE "PAL" GOOD-BYE.
"JAIL"
"KRAZY KAT"
Registered U. S. Patent Office
AHOY, MATE !!!
"JAIL"
JOSE CUERV
"JAIL"
Copr 1942, King Features Syndicate, Inc., World rights reserved
8-16
"JAIL"
MOVILLIS -

August 16th, 1942.

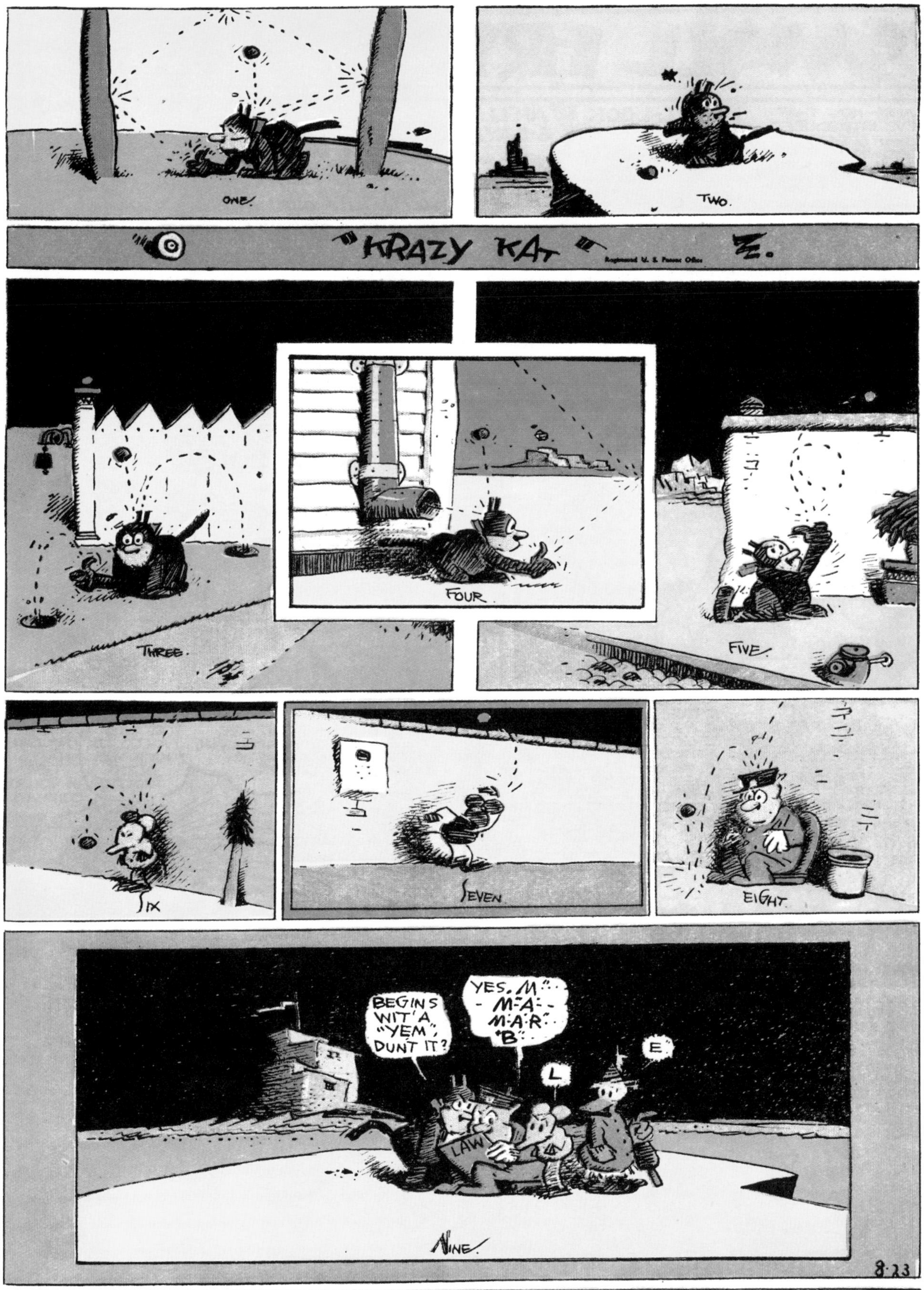
ONE.
TWO.
"KRAZY KAT"
THREE.
FOUR.
FIVE.
SIX
SEVEN
EIGHT.
BEGINS WIT A "YEM", DUNT IT?
YES. M - M-A M-A-R "B"
L
E
LAW
NINE.
8-23
LOOK, DOLLIN - ME, TOO, I CAN DO IT - -
A-AAH - BET YOU CHEATED.

August 23rd, 1942.

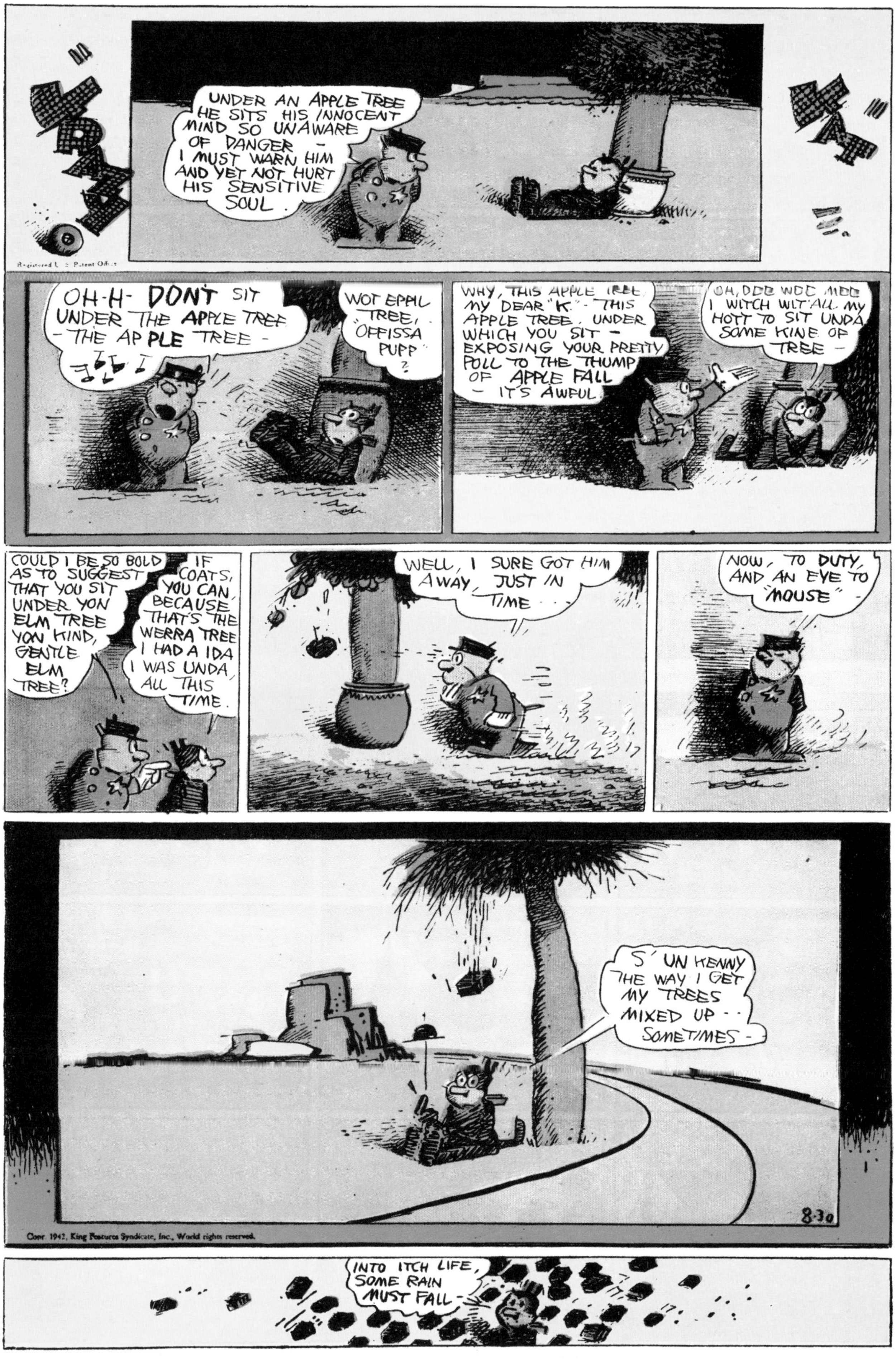
KRAZY KAT
UNDER AN APPLE TREE HE SITS HIS INNOCENT MIND SO UNAWARE OF DANGER - I MUST WARN HIM AND YET NOT HURT HIS SENSITIVE SOUL.
Registered U.S. Patent Office
OH-H- DON'T SIT UNDER THE APPLE TREE - THE APPLE TREE -
WOT EPPIL TREE, OFFISSA PUPP?
WHY, THIS APPLE TREE. MY DEAR "K." - THIS APPLE TREE, UNDER WHICH YOU SIT - EXPOSING YOUR PRETTY POLL TO THE THUMP OF APPLE FALL - IT'S AWFUL.
OH, DEE WEE MEE I WITCH WIT ALL MY HOTT TO SIT UNDA SOME KINE OF TREE -
COULD I BE SO BOLD AS TO SUGGEST THAT YOU SIT UNDER YON ELM TREE YON KIND, GENTLE ELM TREE?
IF COATS, YOU CAN, BECAUSE THAT'S THE WERRA TREE I HAD A IDA I WAS UNDA, ALL THIS TIME.
WELL, I SURE GOT HIM AWAY, JUST IN TIME...
NOW, TO DUTY, AND AN EYE TO "MOUSE" -
S'UN KENNY THE WAY I GET MY TREES MIXED UP - - SOMETIMES -
8-30
Copr. 1942, King Features Syndicate, Inc., World rights reserved.
INTO ITCH LIFE, SOME RAIN MUST FALL -

August 30th, 1942.

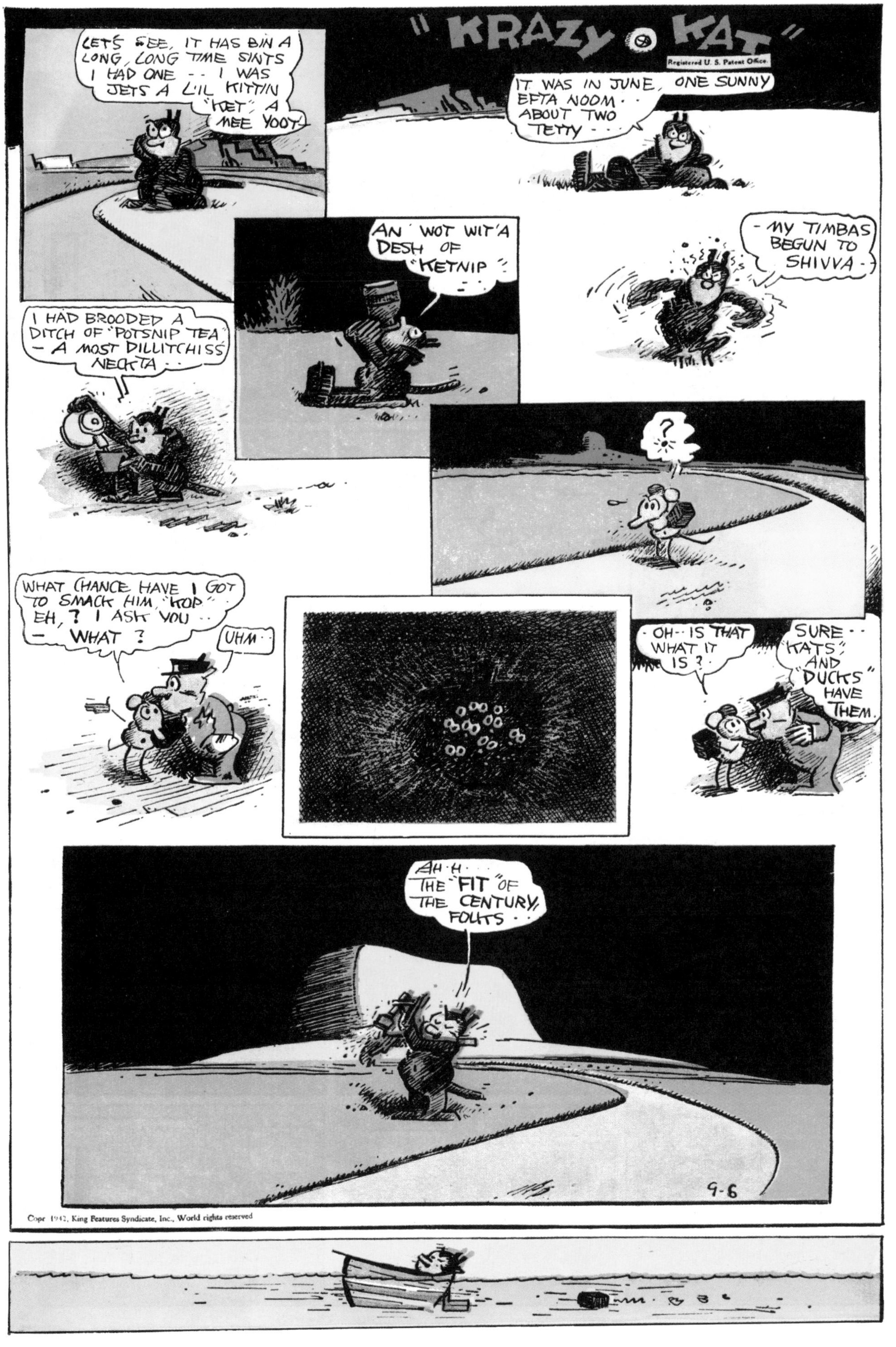
"KRAZY KAT"
Registered U. S. Patent Office.
LET'S SEE, IT HAS BIN A LONG, LONG TIME SINTS I HAD ONE -- I WAS JETS A LIL KITTIN "KET," A MEE YOOT.
IT WAS IN JUNE, ONE SUNNY EFTA NOOM · · ABOUT TWO TETTY - · ·
AN' WOT WIT 'A DESH OF "KETNIP"
- MY TIMBAS BEGUN TO SHIVVA -
I HAD BROODED A DITCH OF "POTSNIP TEA" - A MOST DILLITCHISS NECKTA · ·
?
WHAT CHANCE HAVE I GOT TO SMACK HIM, "KOP" EH, ? I ASK YOU - WHAT ?
UHM · ·
· OH · · IS THAT WHAT IT IS ? ·
SURE · · "KATS" AND "DUCKS" HAVE THEM.
AH · H · · THE "FIT" OF THE CENTURY, FOLKS · ·
9-6
Copr 1942, King Features Syndicate, Inc., World rights reserved

September 6th, 1942.

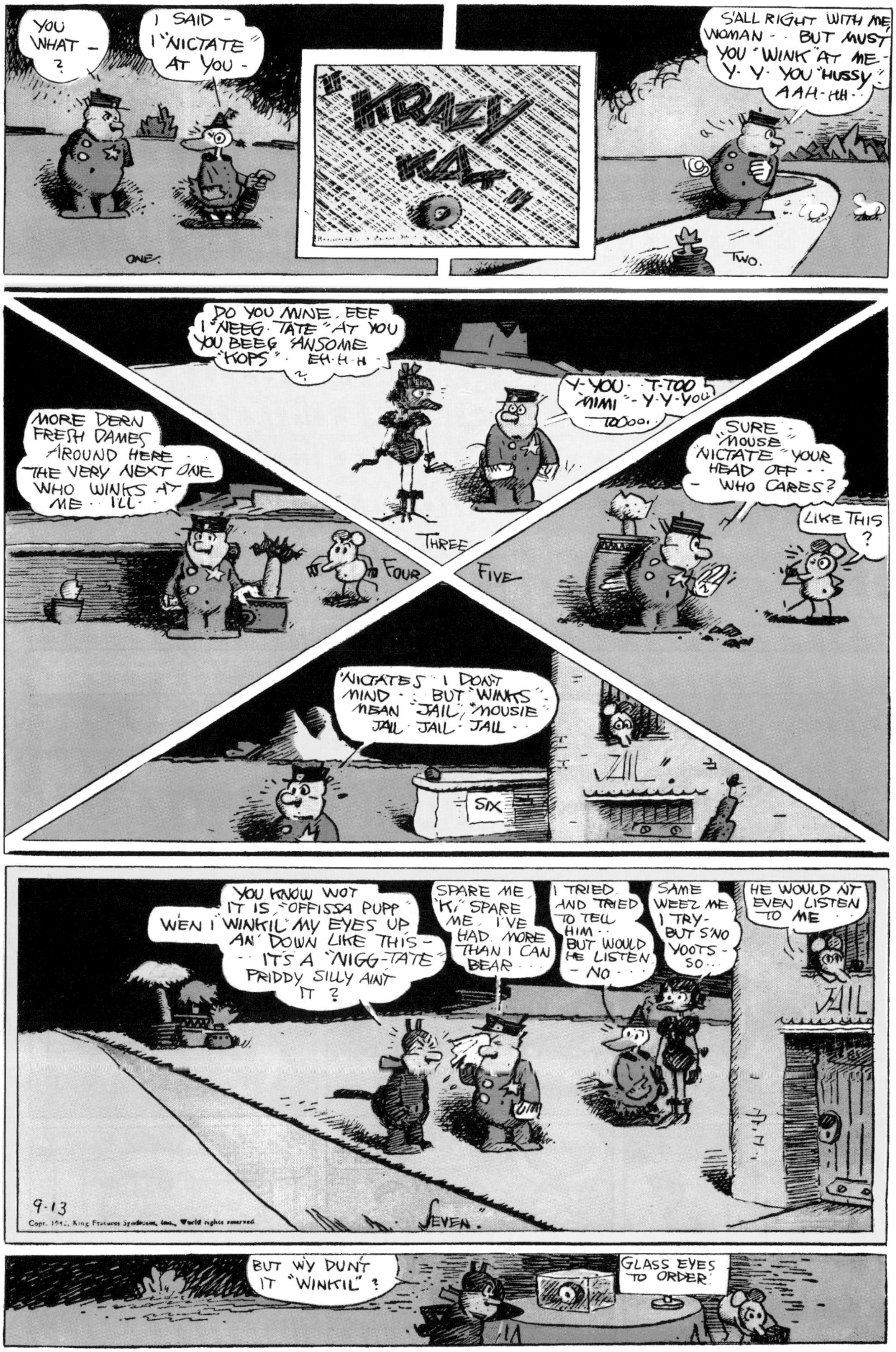
YOU WHAT - ?
I SAID - I "NICTATE AT YOU -
"KRAZY KAT"
S'ALL RIGHT WITH ME WOMAN - - BUT MUST YOU "WINK" AT ME - Y- Y- YOU "HUSSY" AAH-HH
ONE.
TWO.
DO YOU MINE EEF I "NEEG TATE" AT YOU YOU BEEG 'ANSOME "KOPS" EH-H-H ?
Y-YOU - T-TOO MIMI - Y-Y-YOU TOOOO.
MORE DERN FRESH DAMES AROUND HERE THE VERY NEXT ONE WHO WINKS AT ME - I'LL -
THREE
FOUR
FIVE
SURE MOUSE "NICTATE" YOUR HEAD OFF - - WHO CARES?
LIKE THIS ?
"NICTATES" I DON'T MIND - - BUT "WINKS" MEAN "JAIL" "MOUSIE" JAIL - JAIL - JAIL - -
"JAIL"
SIX
YOU KNOW WOT IT IS, "OFFISSA PUPP" WEN I "WINKIL" MY EYES UP AN' DOWN LIKE THIS - - IT'S A "NIGG-TATE" PRIDDY SILLY AINT IT ?
SPARE ME "K," SPARE ME. I'VE HAD MORE THAN I CAN BEAR
I TRIED AND TRIED TO TELL HIM - BUT WOULD HE LISTEN - NO -
SAME WEEZ ME I TRY - BUT S'NO YOOTS - SO - -
HE WOULD N'T EVEN LISTEN TO ME
JAIL
9-13
Copr. 1942, King Features Syndicate, Inc., World rights reserved
SEVEN.
BUT WY DUN'T IT "WINKIL" ?
GLASS EYES TO ORDER

September 13th, 1942.

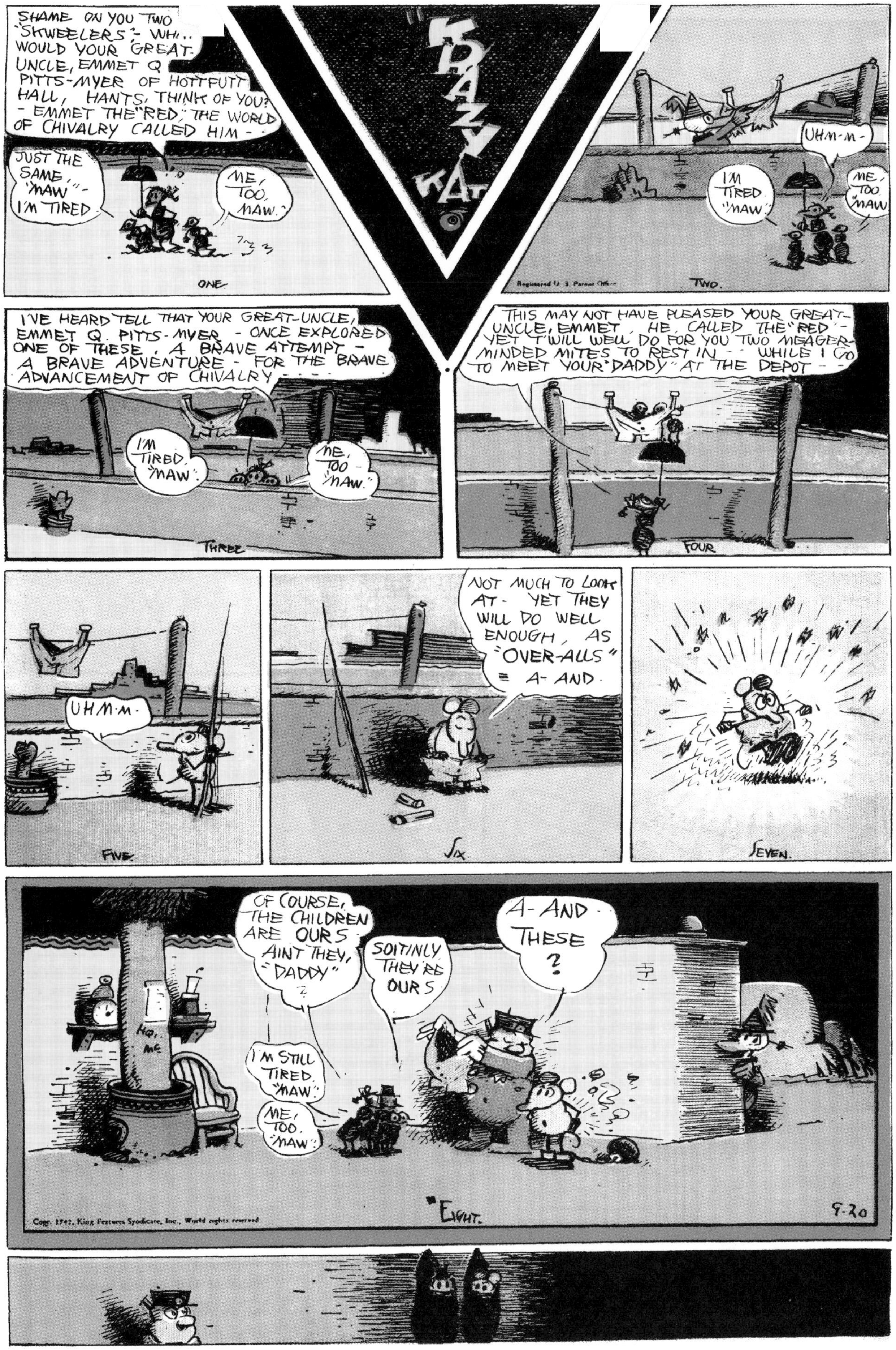

KRAZY KAT
SHAME ON YOU TWO "SKWEELERS" - WH.. WOULD YOUR GREAT-UNCLE, EMMET Q PITTS-MYER OF HOTTFUTT HALL, HANTS, THINK OF YOU? - EMMET THE "RED," THE WORLD OF CHIVALRY CALLED HIM -
JUST THE SAME, "MAW" - I'M TIRED
ME, TOO, MAW.
ONE.
Registered U. S. Patent Office
UHM-M-
I'M TIRED "MAW"
ME, TOO "MAW"
TWO.
I'VE HEARD TELL THAT YOUR GREAT-UNCLE, EMMET Q. PITTS-MYER - ONCE EXPLORED ONE OF THESE, A BRAVE ATTEMPT - A BRAVE ADVENTURE - FOR THE BRAVE ADVANCEMENT OF CHIVALRY - - -
I'M TIRED. "MAW"
ME, TOO - "MAW."
THREE
THIS MAY NOT HAVE PLEASED YOUR GREAT-UNCLE, EMMET, HE, CALLED THE "RED" - YET T'WILL WELL DO FOR YOU TWO MEAGER-MINDED MITES TO REST IN - - WHILE I GO TO MEET YOUR "DADDY" AT THE DEPOT - -
FOUR
UHM-M.
FIVE.
NOT MUCH TO LOOK AT - YET THEY WILL DO WELL ENOUGH, AS "OVER-ALLS" = A- AND -
SIX.
SEVEN.
OF COURSE, THE CHILDREN ARE OURS AINT THEY, "DADDY"
SOITINLY THEY'RE OURS
A- AND - THESE ?
I'M STILL TIRED. "MAW"
ME, TOO. "MAW"
Copr. 1942, King Features Syndicate, Inc., World rights reserved.
EIGHT.
9-20

September 20th, 1942.

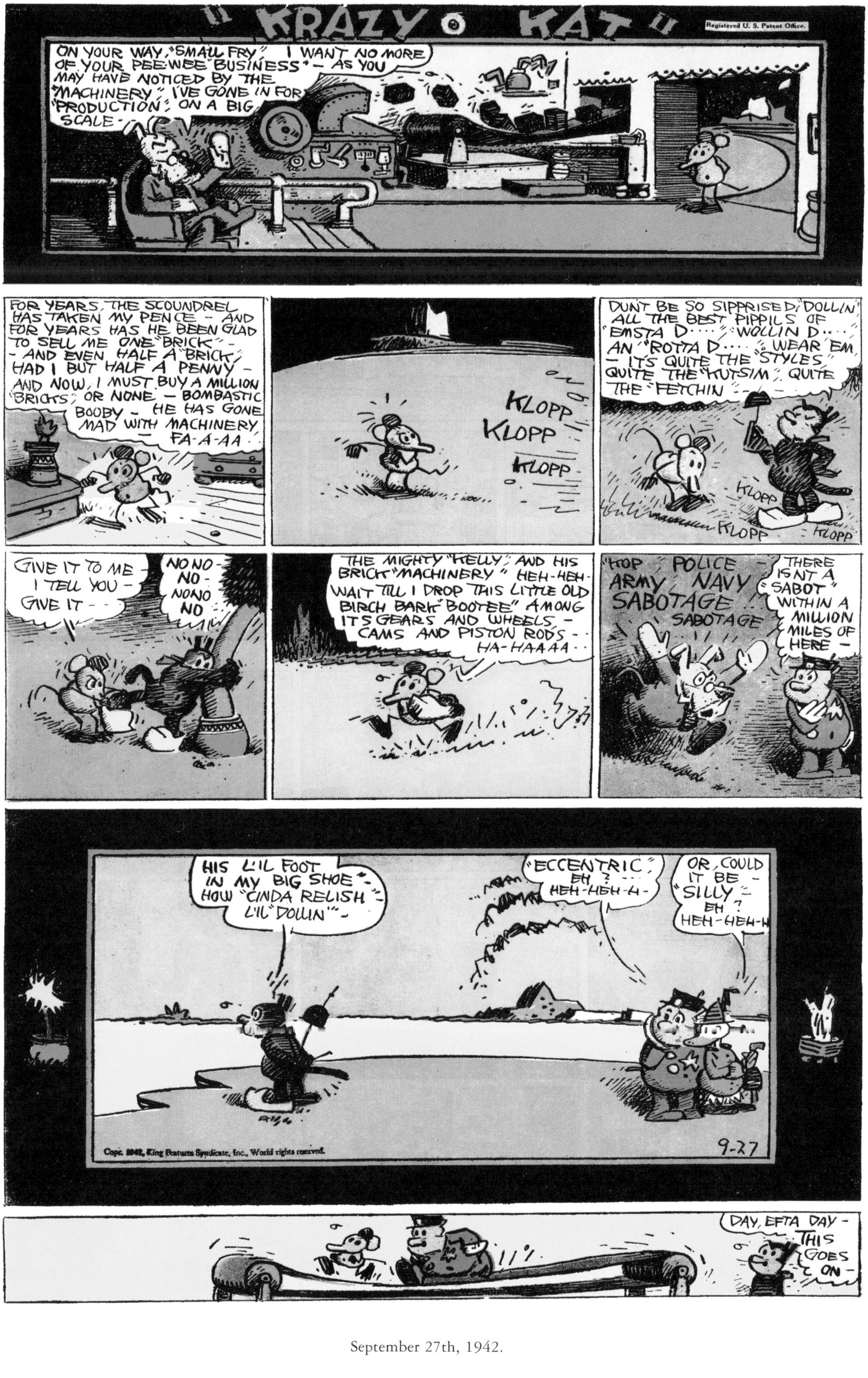
KRAZY KAT
Registered U. S. Patent Office.
ON YOUR WAY, "SMALL FRY" I WANT NO MORE OF YOUR "PEE-WEE" BUSINESS" - AS YOU MAY HAVE NOTICED BY THE "MACHINERY" I'VE GONE IN FOR "PRODUCTION" ON A BIG SCALE -
FOR YEARS, THE SCOUNDREL HAS TAKEN MY PENCE - AND FOR YEARS HAS HE BEEN GLAD TO SELL ME ONE "BRICK" - - AND EVEN HALF A "BRICK" HAD I BUT HALF A PENNY - AND NOW, I MUST BUY A MILLION "BRICKS", OR NONE - BOMBASTIC BOOBY - HE HAS GONE MAD WITH MACHINERY - FA-A-AA
KLOPP
KLOPP
KLOPP
DUNT BE SO SIPPRISED, DOLLIN' ALL THE BEST PIPPILS OF "EMSTA D...." "WOLLIN D...." AN "ROTTA D...." WEAR EM - ITS QUITE THE "STYLES" QUITE THE "HUTSIM" QUITE THE "FETCHIN"
KLOPP
KLOPP
KLOPP
GIVE IT TO ME I TELL YOU - GIVE IT - -
NO NO - NO - NO NO NO
THE MIGHTY "KELLY" AND HIS BRICK "MACHINERY" HEH-HEH WAIT TILL I DROP THIS LITTLE OLD BIRCH BARK "BOOTEE" AMONG ITS GEARS AND WHEELS - CAMS AND PISTON RODS - - HA-HAAAA -
"HOP" POLICE ARMY NAVY SABOTAGE SABOTAGE
THERE IS N'T A "SABOT" WITHIN A MILLION MILES OF HERE -
HIS L'IL FOOT IN MY BIG SHOE - HOW "CINDA RELISH L'IL DOLLIN" -
"ECCENTRIC", EH ? HEH-HEH-H -
OR, COULD IT BE - "SILLY" EH ? HEH-HEH-H
Copr. 1942, King Features Syndicate, Inc., World rights reserved.
9-27
DAY, EFTA DAY - THIS GOES ON -

September 27th, 1942.

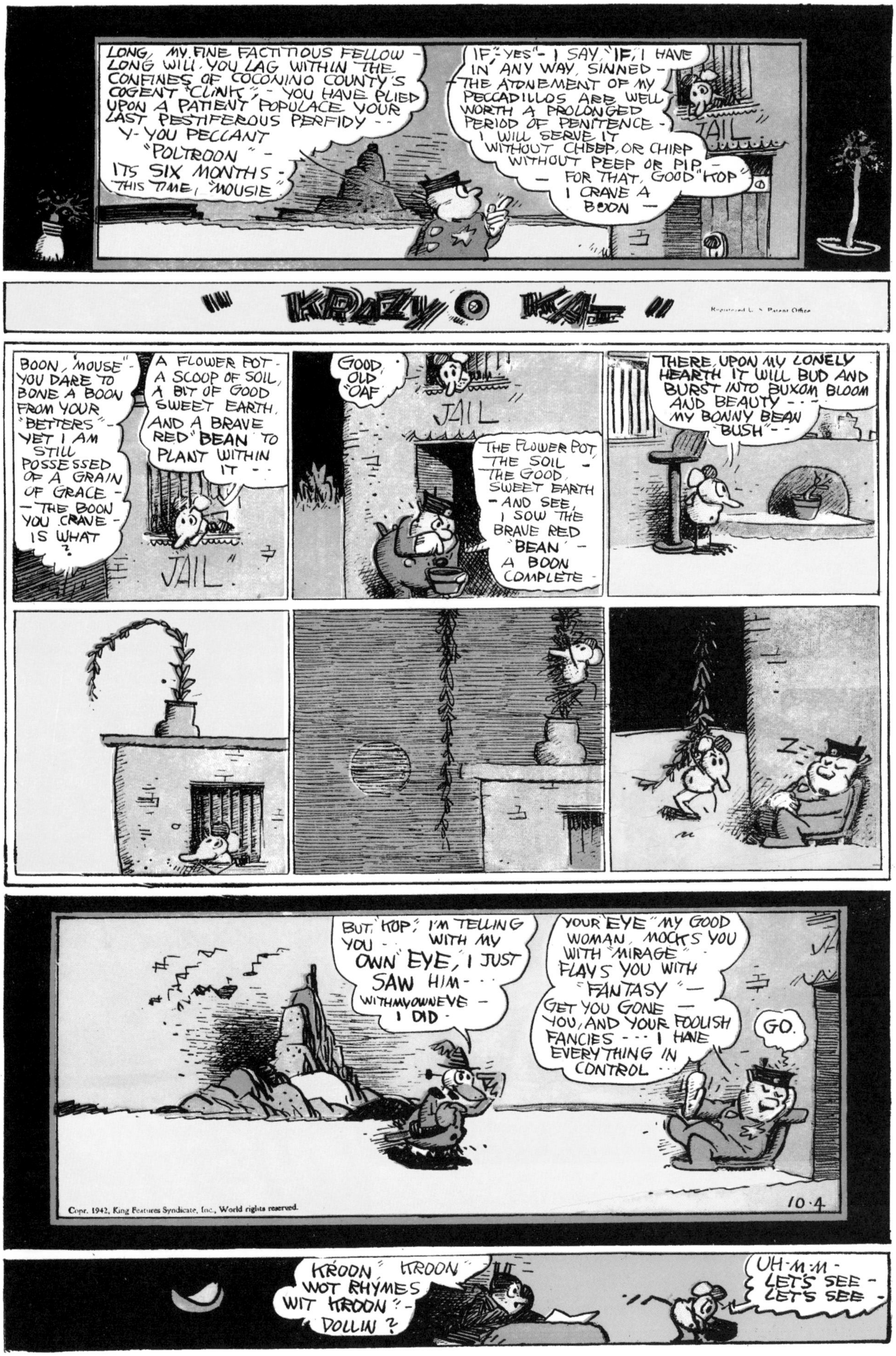
LONG, MY FINE FACTITIOUS FELLOW - LONG WILL YOU LAG WITHIN THE CONFINES OF COCONINO COUNTY'S COGENT "CLINK," - YOU HAVE PLIED UPON A PATIENT POPULACE YOUR LAST PESTIFEROUS PERFIDY - - Y- YOU PECCANT "POLTROON" - ITS SIX MONTHS - THIS TIME, "MOUSIE"
IF, "YES" - I SAY, "IF," I HAVE IN ANY WAY, SINNED - THE ATONEMENT OF MY PECCADILLOS ARE WELL WORTH A PROLONGED PERIOD OF PENITENCE - I WILL SERVE IT WITHOUT CHEEP, OR CHIRP WITHOUT PEEP OR PIP, - FOR THAT, GOOD "KOP" I CRAVE A BOON -
JAIL
"KRAZY KAT"
Registered U.S. Patent Office
BOON, "MOUSE" - YOU DARE TO BONE A BOON FROM YOUR "BETTERS" - YET I AM STILL POSSESSED OF A GRAIN OF GRACE - - THE BOON YOU CRAVE - IS WHAT ?
A FLOWER POT - A SCOOP OF SOIL, A BIT OF GOOD SWEET EARTH, AND A BRAVE RED "BEAN" TO PLANT WITHIN IT - -
JAIL
GOOD, OLD "OAF"
JAIL
THE FLOWER POT, THE SOIL - THE GOOD, SWEET EARTH - AND SEE, I SOW THE BRAVE RED "BEAN" - A BOON COMPLETE -
THERE, UPON MY LONELY HEARTH IT WILL BUD AND BURST INTO BUXOM BLOOM AND BEAUTY - - - MY BONNY BEAN "BUSH" - -
Z
BUT, KOP, I'M TELLING YOU - WITH MY OWN EYE, I JUST SAW HIM - - WITHMYOWNEYE - I DID
YOUR "EYE" MY GOOD WOMAN, MOCKS YOU WITH "MIRAGE" - FLAYS YOU WITH "FANTASY" - GET YOU GONE - YOU, AND YOUR FOOLISH FANCIES - - - I HAVE EVERYTHING IN CONTROL - -
GO.
Copr. 1942, King Features Syndicate, Inc., World rights reserved.
10·4
KROON, KROON - WOT RHYMES WIT KROON? - DOLLIN ?
UH-M-M - LET'S SEE - LET'S SEE -

October 4th, 1942.

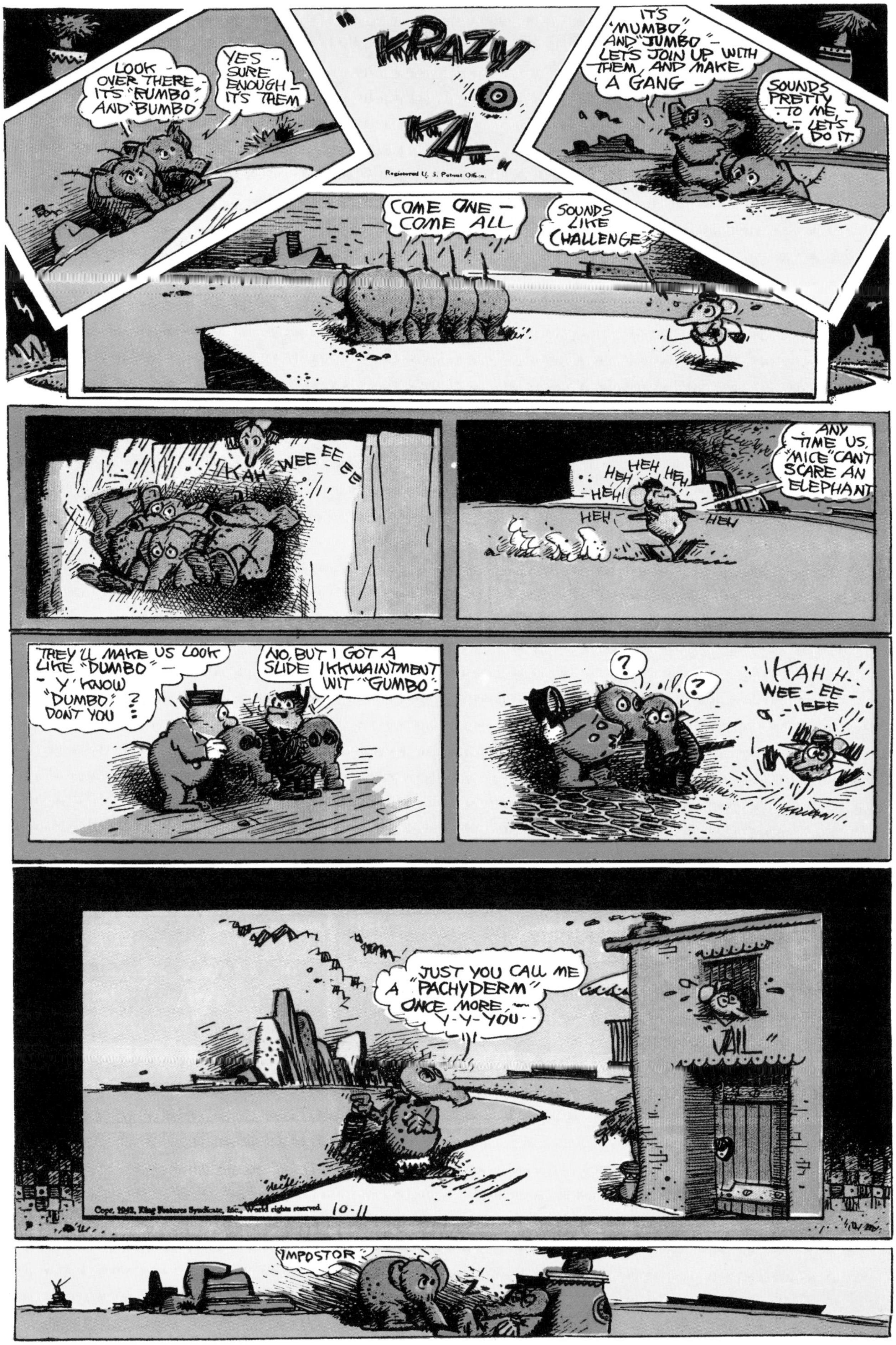
"KRAZY KAT"
Registered U. S. Patent Office.
LOOK OVER THERE ITS "RUMBO" AND "BUMBO"
YES SURE ENOUGH ITS THEM
ITS "MUMBO" AND "JUMBO" LETS JOIN UP WITH THEM, AND MAKE A GANG
SOUNDS PRETTY TO ME, LETS DO IT.
COME ONE - COME ALL
SOUNDS LIKE CHALLENGE
KAH-WEE EE EE
HEH HEH HEH HEH HEH HEH
ANY TIME US "MICE" CANT SCARE AN ELEPHANT
THEY'LL MAKE US LOOK LIKE "DUMBO" - Y' KNOW "DUMBO" DONT YOU ?
NO, BUT I GOT A SLIDE IKKWAINTMENT WIT "GUMBO"
?
?
KAH H- WEE - EE -
JUST YOU CALL ME A "PACHYDERM" ONCE MORE Y-Y-YOU
"JAIL"
Copr. 1942, King Features Syndicate, Inc., World rights reserved.
10-11
IMPOSTOR

October 11th, 1942.

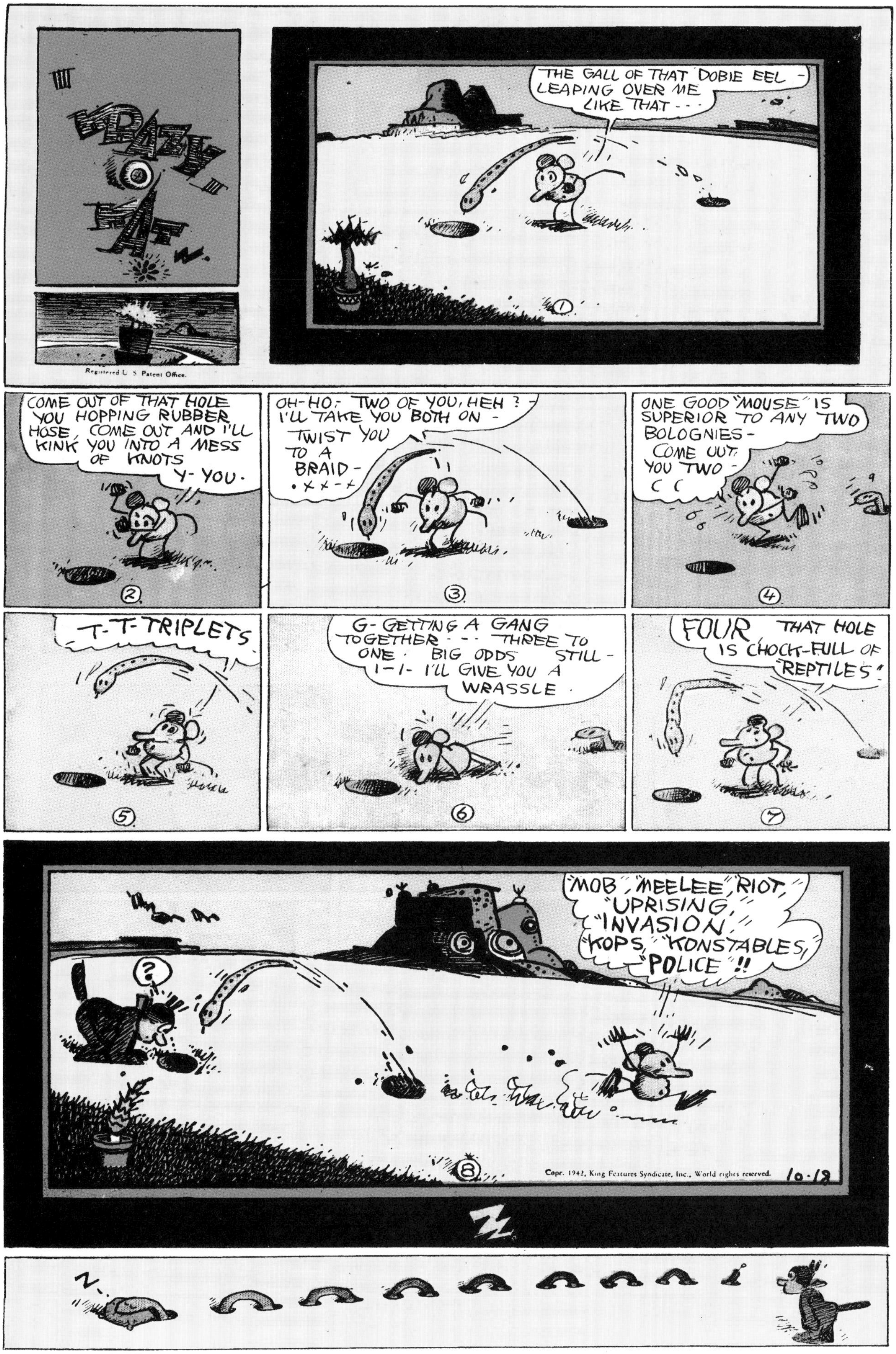
KRAZY KAT
Registered U. S. Patent Office.
THE GALL OF THAT DOBIE EEL - LEAPING OVER ME LIKE THAT - - -
COME OUT OF THAT HOLE YOU HOPPING RUBBER HOSE, COME OUT AND I'LL KINK YOU INTO A MESS OF KNOTS Y- YOU.
OH-HO: TWO OF YOU, HEH ? - I'LL TAKE YOU BOTH ON - TWIST YOU TO A BRAID - • X X - X
ONE GOOD "MOUSE" IS SUPERIOR TO ANY TWO BOLOGNIES - COME OUT YOU TWO - C C
T-T-TRIPLETS
G- GETTING A GANG TOGETHER - - - THREE TO ONE BIG ODDS STILL - I - I - I'LL GIVE YOU A WRASSLE
FOUR THAT HOLE IS CHOCK-FULL OF "REPTILES"
"MOB" "MEELEE" "RIOT," "UPRISING," "INVASION," "KOPS," "KONSTABLES," "POLICE" !!
?
Copr. 1942, King Features Syndicate, Inc., World rights reserved.
10-18
Z
Z

October 18th, 1942.

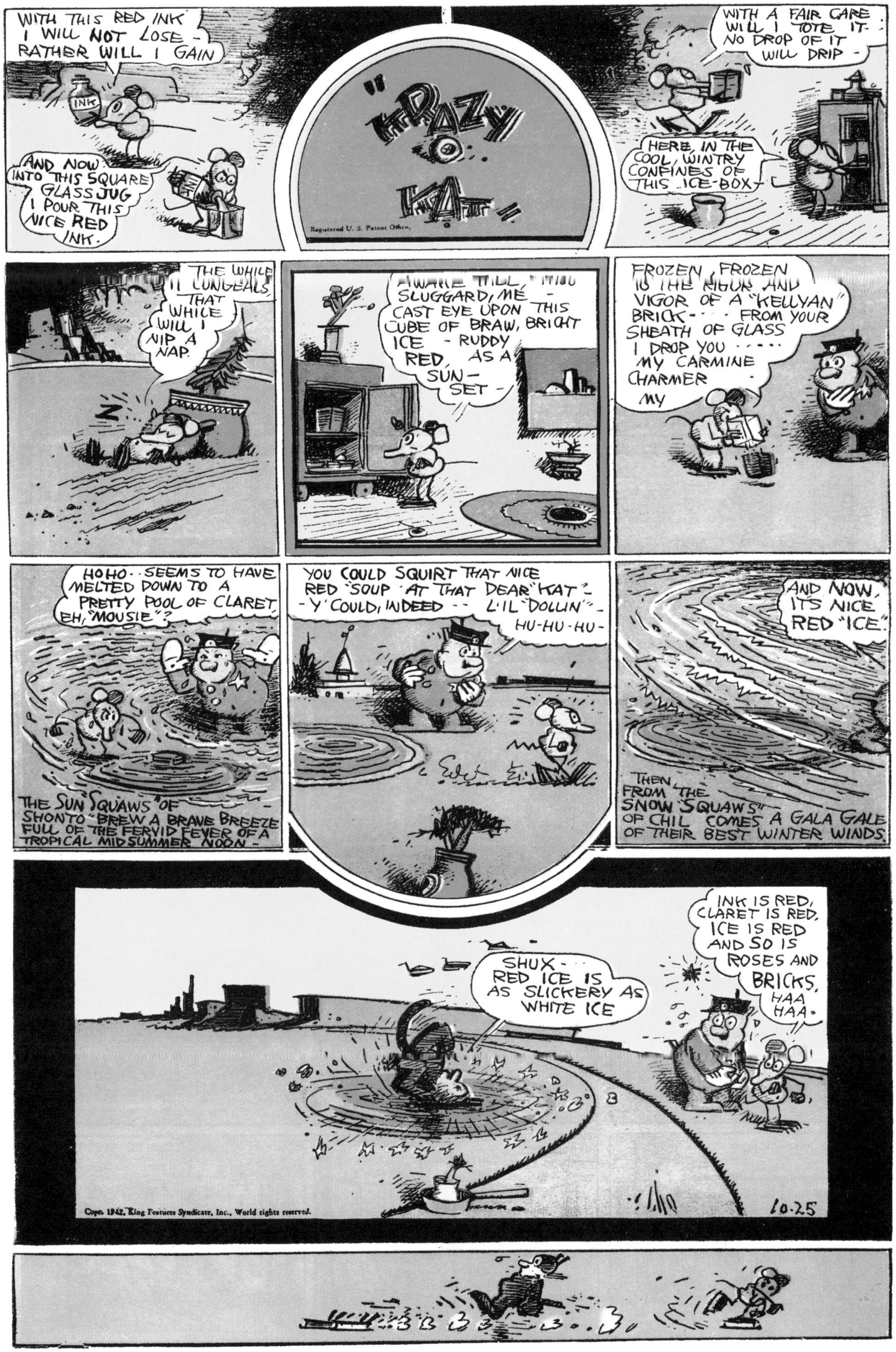

WITH THIS RED INK I WILL NOT LOSE - RATHER WILL I GAIN
INK
AND NOW INTO THIS SQUARE GLASS JUG I POUR THIS NICE RED INK.
"KRAZY KAT"
Registered U. S. Patent Office.
WITH A FAIR CARE WILL I TOTE IT. NO DROP OF IT WILL DRIP -
HERE, IN THE COOL, WINTRY CONFINES OF THIS ICE-BOX
THE WHILE IT CONGEALS, THAT WHILE WILL I NIP A NAP.
Z
AWAKE TILL,
SLUGGARD, ME - CAST EYE UPON THIS CUBE OF BRAW, BRIGHT ICE - RUDDY RED, AS A SUN-SET -
FROZEN, FROZEN
VIGOR OF A "KELLYAN" BRICK - - - FROM YOUR SHEATH OF GLASS I DROP YOU - - - - MY CARMINE CHARMER - MY
HOHO - SEEMS TO HAVE MELTED DOWN TO A PRETTY POOL OF CLARET EH, "MOUSIE"?
THE SUN SQUAWS "OF SHONTO" BREW A BRAVE BREEZE FULL OF THE FERVID FEVER OF A TROPICAL MIDSUMMER NOON -
YOU COULD SQUIRT THAT NICE RED "SOUP" AT THAT DEAR "KAT" - -Y' COULD, INDEED - - L'IL "DOLLIN" -
HU-HU-HU-
AND NOW, ITS NICE RED "ICE".
THEN, FROM "THE SNOW SQUAWS" OF CHIL COMES A GALA GALE OF THEIR BEST WINTER WINDS.
SHUX - RED ICE IS AS SLICKERY AS WHITE ICE
INK IS RED, CLARET IS RED, ICE IS RED AND SO IS ROSES AND BRICKS, HAA HAA -
Copr. 1942, King Features Syndicate, Inc., World rights reserved.
10-25

October 25th, 1942.

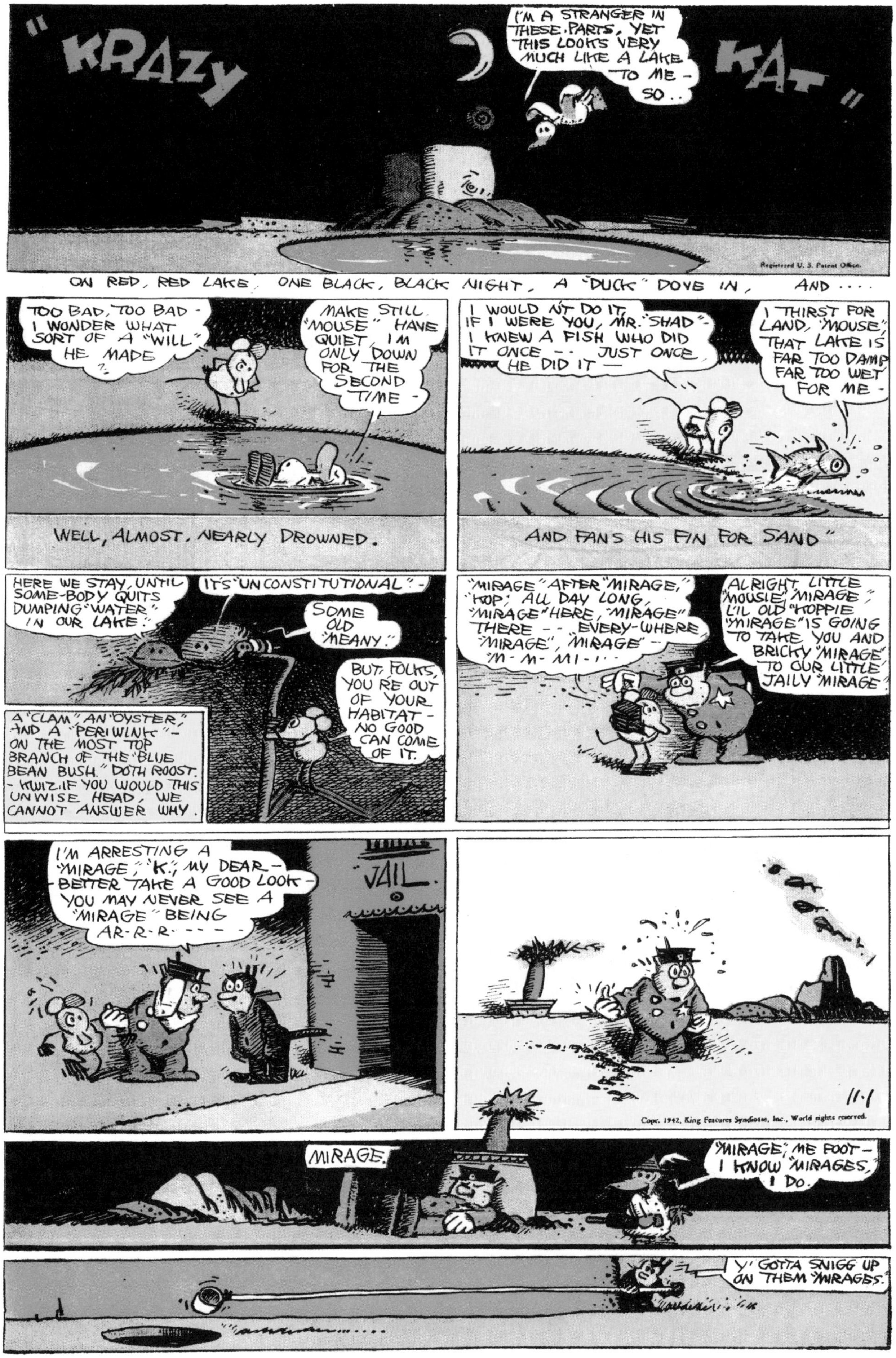
"KRAZY KAT"
I'M A STRANGER IN THESE PARTS, YET THIS LOOKS VERY MUCH LIKE A LAKE TO ME - SO..
Registered U. S. Patent Office.
ON RED, RED LAKE, ONE BLACK, BLACK NIGHT, A "DUCK" DOVE IN, AND....
TOO BAD, TOO BAD - I WONDER WHAT SORT OF A "WILL" HE MADE ?
MAKE STILL "MOUSE" HAVE QUIET, I'M ONLY DOWN FOR THE SECOND TIME -
WELL, ALMOST, NEARLY DROWNED.
I WOULD N'T DO IT, IF I WERE YOU, MR. "SHAD" - I KNEW A FISH WHO DID IT ONCE -- JUST ONCE HE DID IT —
I THIRST FOR LAND, "MOUSE," THAT LAKE IS FAR TOO DAMP FAR TOO WET FOR ME -
AND FANS HIS FIN FOR SAND"
HERE WE STAY, UNTIL SOME-BODY QUITS DUMPING "WATER" IN OUR LAKE."
IT'S "UNCONSTITUTIONAL" -
SOME OLD "MEANY."
BUT, FOLKS, YOU'RE OUT OF YOUR HABITAT - NO GOOD CAN COME OF IT.
A "CLAM," AN "OYSTER," AND A "PERIWINK" - ON THE MOST TOP BRANCH OF THE "BLUE BEAN BUSH" DOTH ROOST. - KWIZ: IF YOU WOULD THIS UNWISE HEAD, WE CANNOT ANSWER WHY.
"MIRAGE" AFTER "MIRAGE," "KOP," ALL DAY LONG, "MIRAGE" HERE, "MIRAGE" THERE -- EVERY-WHERE "MIRAGE", "MIRAGE" - M-M-MI-I...
ALRIGHT, LITTLE "MOUSIE," "MIRAGE," L'IL OLD "KOPPIE" "MIRAGE" IS GOING TO TAKE YOU AND BRICKY "MIRAGE" TO OUR LITTLE JAILY "MIRAGE."
I'M ARRESTING A "MIRAGE," "K.," MY DEAR - BETTER TAKE A GOOD LOOK - YOU MAY NEVER SEE A "MIRAGE" BEING AR-R-R----
JAIL.
11-1
Copr. 1942, King Features Syndicate, Inc., World rights reserved.
MIRAGE
"MIRAGE," ME FOOT - I KNOW "MIRAGES," I DO.
Y' GOTTA SNIGG UP ON THEM "MIRAGES."

November 1st, 1942.

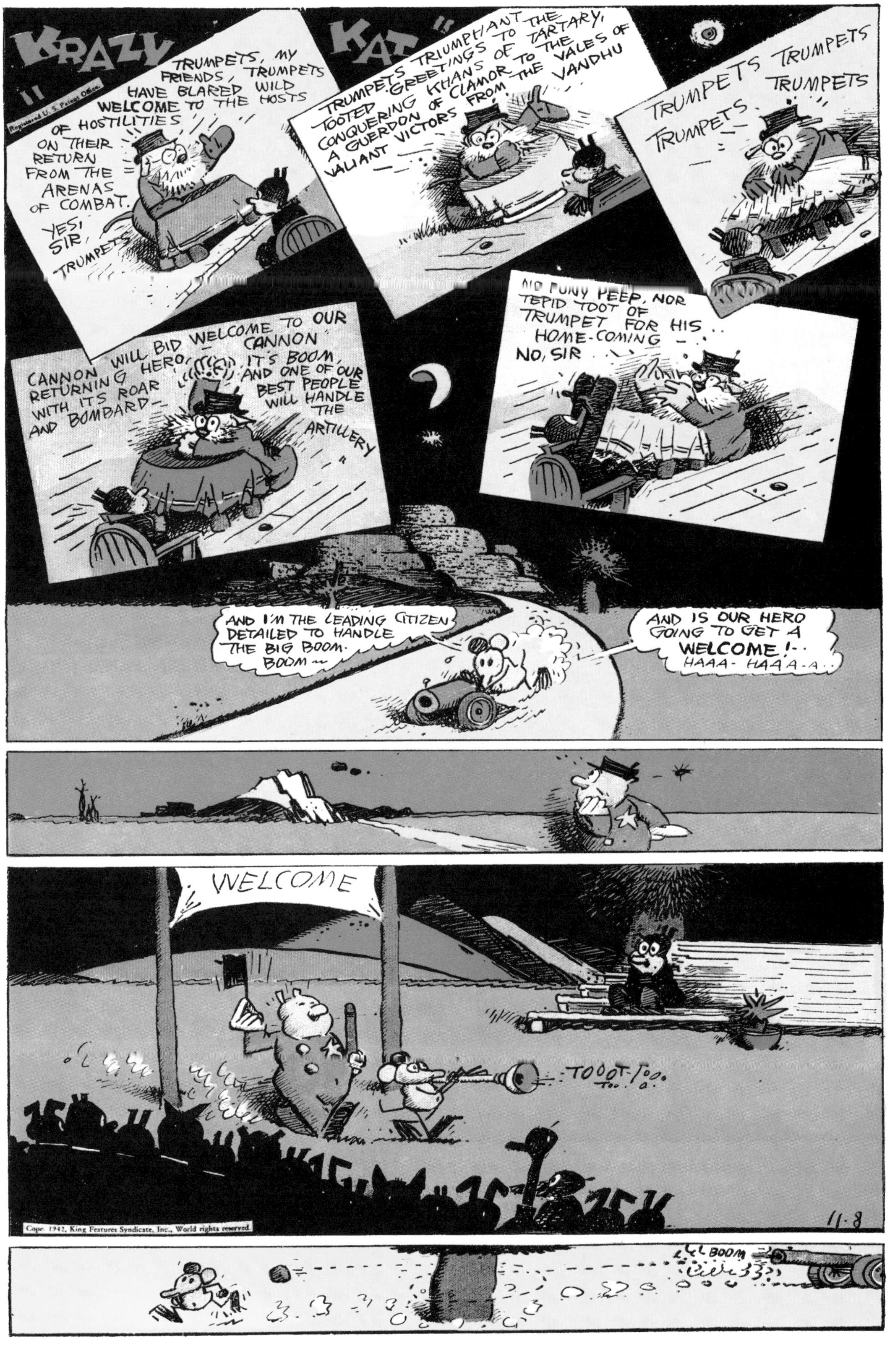
"KRAZY KAT"
Registered U. S. Patent Office.
TRUMPETS, MY FRIENDS, TRUMPETS HAVE BLARED WILD WELCOME TO THE HOSTS OF HOSTILITIES ON THEIR RETURN FROM THE ARENAS OF COMBAT.
YES, SIR, TRUMPETS
TRUMPETS TRIUMPHANT TOOTED GREETINGS TO THE CONQUERING KHANS OF TARTARY, A GUERDON OF CLAMOR TO THE VALIANT VICTORS FROM THE VALES OF VANDHU
TRUMPETS TRUMPETS TRUMPETS TRUMPETS
NO PUNY PEEP, NOR TEPID TOOT OF TRUMPET FOR HIS HOME-COMING
NO, SIR
CANNON WILL BID WELCOME TO OUR RETURNING HERO, WITH ITS ROAR AND BOMBARD— CANNON IT'S BOOM, AND ONE OF OUR BEST PEOPLE WILL HANDLE THE ARTILLERY
AND I'M THE LEADING CITIZEN DETAILED TO HANDLE THE BIG BOOM-BOOM —
AND IS OUR HERO GOING TO GET A WELCOME!— HAAA- HAA'A-A
WELCOME
TOOOT-TOO. TOO.
Copr. 1942, King Features Syndicate, Inc., World rights reserved.
11-8
BOOM

November 8th, 1942.

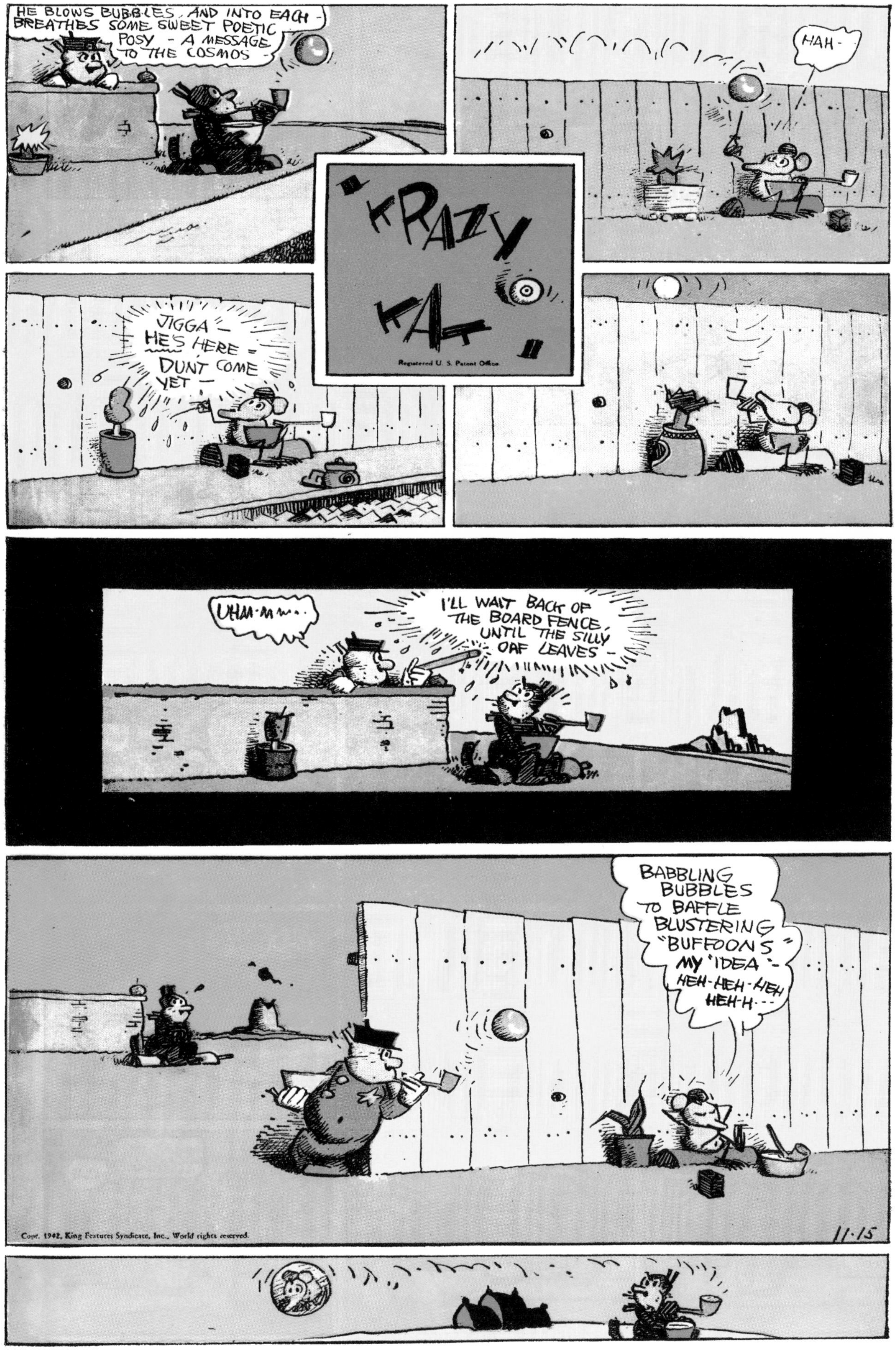
HE BLOWS BUBBLES, AND INTO EACH BREATHES SOME SWEET POETIC POSY - A MESSAGE TO THE COSMOS
HAH-
"KRAZY KAT"
Registered U. S. Patent Office
JIGGA - HE'S HERE - DUNT COME YET
UHM-M-M...
I'LL WAIT BACK OF THE BOARD FENCE, UNTIL THE SILLY OAF LEAVES
BABBLING BUBBLES TO BAFFLE BLUSTERING "BUFFOONS" MY IDEA - HEH-HEH-HEH HEH-H---
Copr. 1942, King Features Syndicate, Inc., World rights reserved.
11-15

November 15th, 1942.

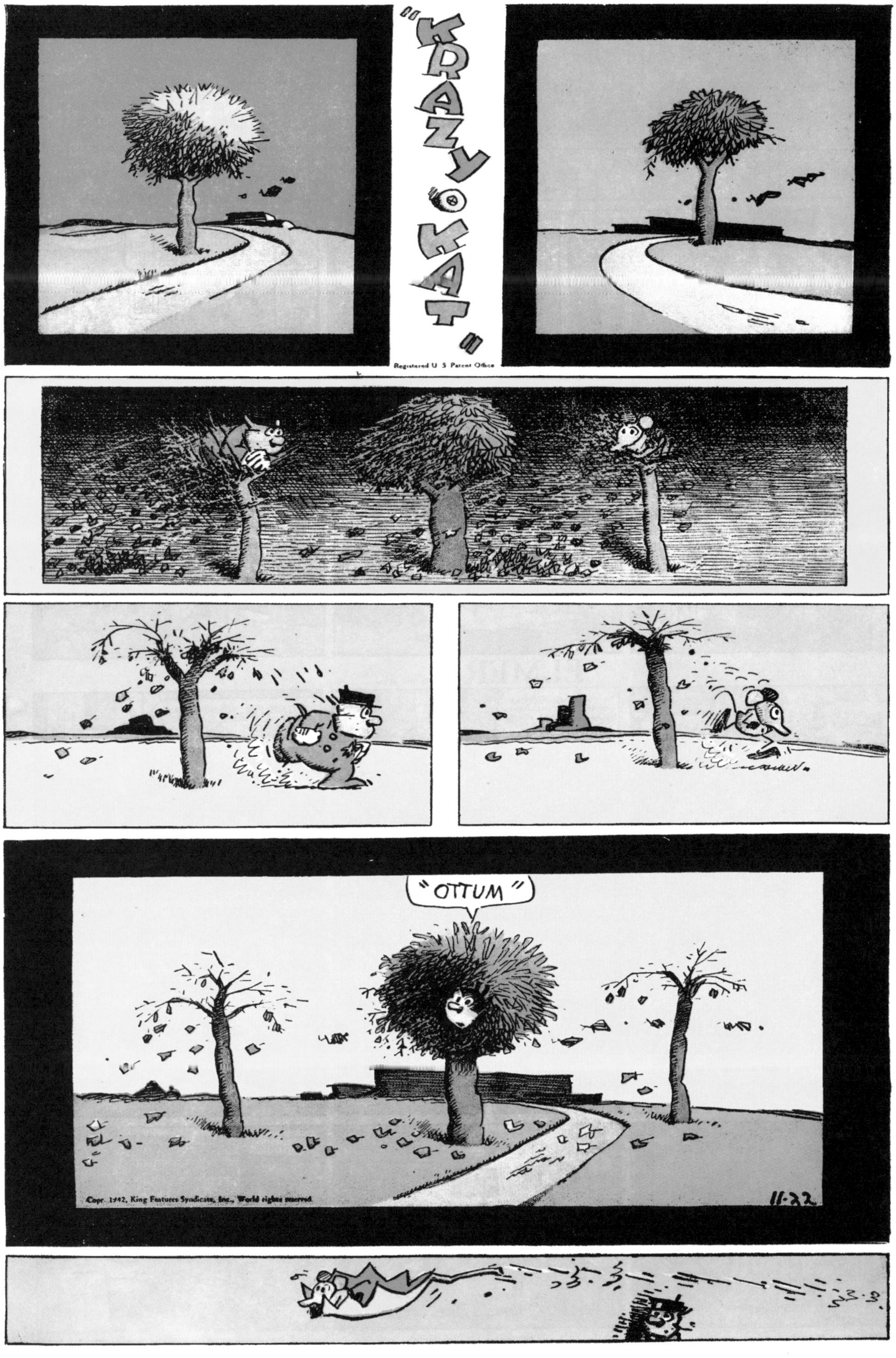
"KRAZY KAT"
Registered U S Patent Office
"OTTUM"
Copr. 1942, King Features Syndicate, Inc., World rights reserved.
11-22

November 22nd, 1942.

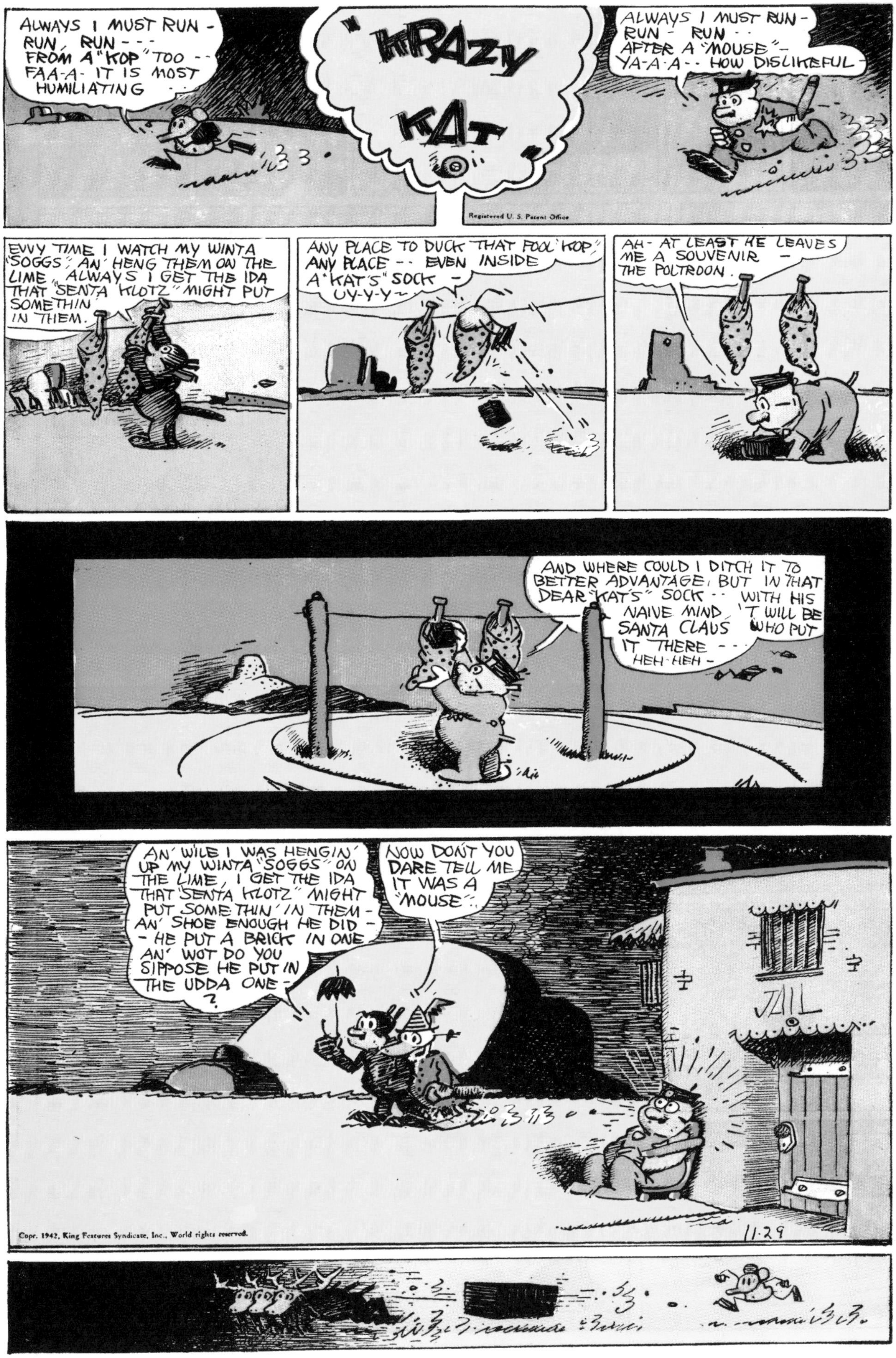
ALWAYS I MUST RUN - RUN, RUN - - - FROM A "KOP" TOO - - FAA-A- IT IS MOST HUMILIATING - -
"KRAZY KAT"
ALWAYS I MUST RUN - RUN - RUN - - AFTER A "MOUSE" - YA-A-A - - HOW DISLIKEFUL -
Registered U. S. Patent Office
EVVY TIME I WATCH MY WINTA "SOGGS" AN' HENG THEM ON THE LIME, ALWAYS I GET THE IDA THAT "SENTA KLOTZ" MIGHT PUT SOMETHIN IN THEM.
ANY PLACE TO DUCK THAT FOOL 'KOP' ANY PLACE - - EVEN INSIDE A "KAT'S" SOCK - UY-Y-Y -
AH - AT LEAST HE LEAVES ME A SOUVENIR - THE POLTROON.
AND WHERE COULD I DITCH IT TO BETTER ADVANTAGE, BUT IN THAT DEAR "KAT'S" SOCK - - WITH HIS NAIVE MIND, 'T WILL BE SANTA CLAUS WHO PUT IT THERE - - - HEH-HEH -
AN' WILE I WAS HENGIN' UP MY WINTA "SOGGS" ON THE LIME, I GET THE IDA THAT "SENTA KLOTZ" MIGHT PUT SOME-THIN' IN THEM - AN' SHOE ENOUGH HE DID - - HE PUT A BRICK IN ONE AN' WOT DO YOU SIPPOSE HE PUT IN THE UDDA ONE - ?
NOW DON'T YOU DARE TELL ME IT WAS A "MOUSE".
JAIL
Copr. 1942, King Features Syndicate, Inc., World rights reserved.
11-29

November 29th, 1942.

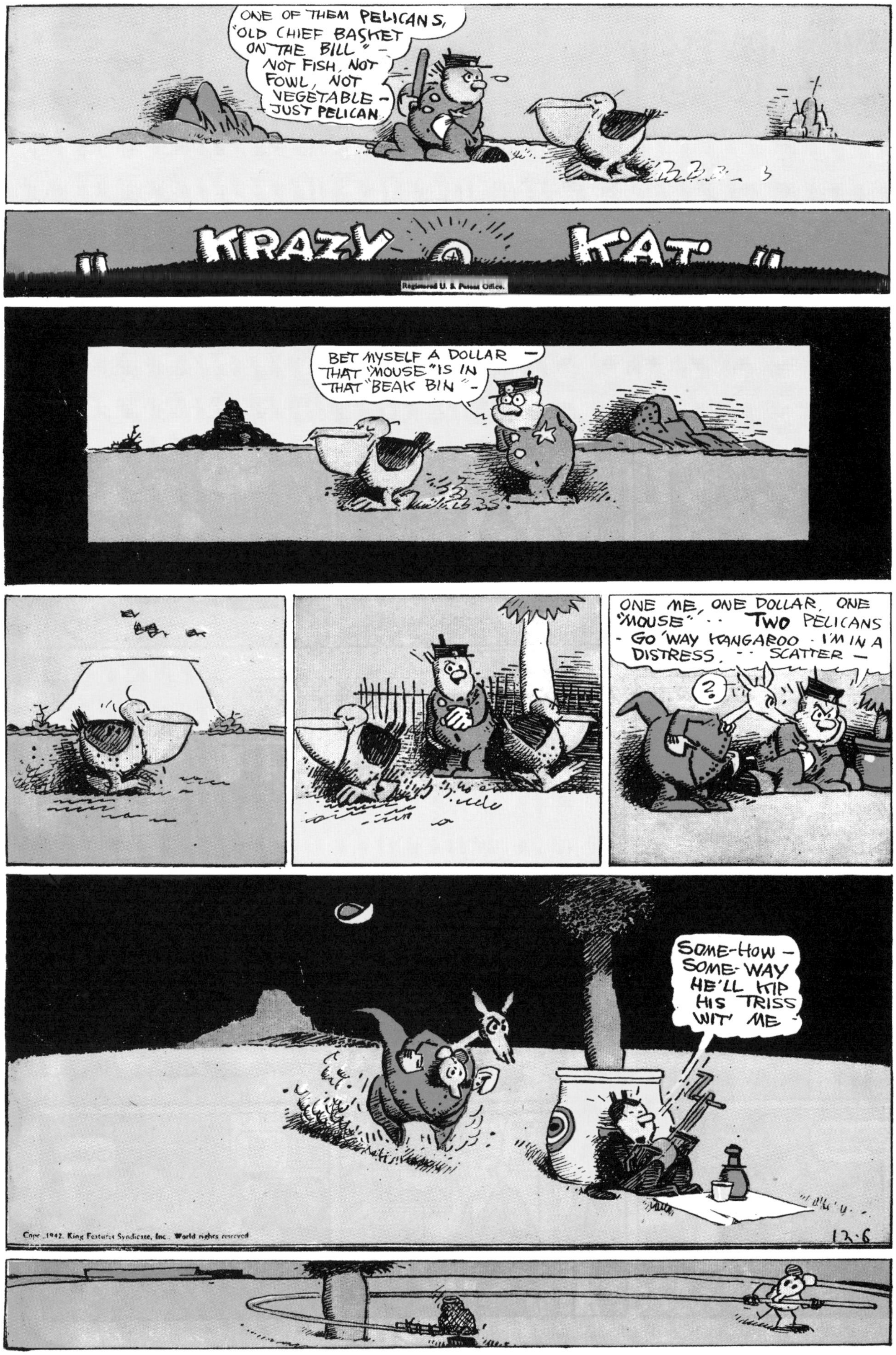
ONE OF THEM PELICANS, "OLD CHIEF BASKET ON THE BILL" - NOT FISH, NOT FOWL, NOT VEGETABLE - JUST PELICAN
KRAZY KAT
Registered U. S. Patent Office.
BET MYSELF A DOLLAR - THAT "MOUSE" IS IN THAT "BEAK BIN" -
ONE ME, ONE DOLLAR, ONE "MOUSE" - - TWO PELICANS - GO 'WAY KANGAROO - I'M IN A DISTRESS - - SCATTER -
SOME-HOW - SOME-WAY HE'LL KIP HIS TRISS WIT' ME
Copr. 1942, King Features Syndicate, Inc. World rights reserved
12-6

December 6th, 1942.

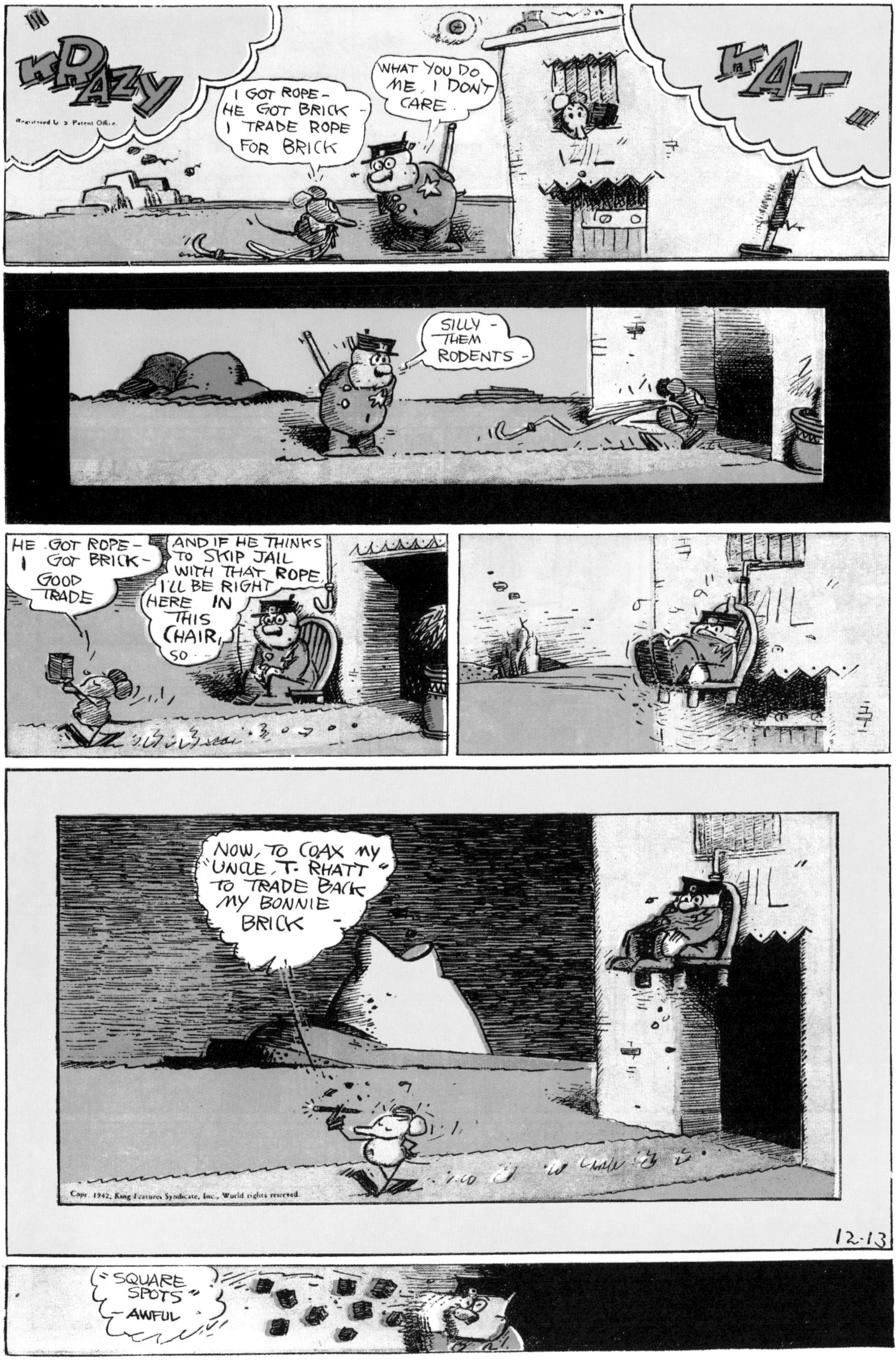
KRAZY KAT
Registered U. S. Patent Office.
I GOT ROPE - HE GOT BRICK - I TRADE ROPE FOR BRICK
WHAT YOU DO ME, I DON'T CARE.
SILLY - THEM RODENTS -
HE GOT ROPE - I GOT BRICK - GOOD TRADE
AND IF HE THINKS TO SKIP JAIL WITH THAT ROPE, I'LL BE RIGHT HERE IN THIS CHAIR, SO -
NOW, TO COAX MY UNCLE, T. RHATT TO TRADE BACK MY BONNIE BRICK -
Copr. 1942, King Features Syndicate, Inc., World rights reserved.
12-13
"SQUARE SPOTS" - AWFUL

December 13th, 1942.

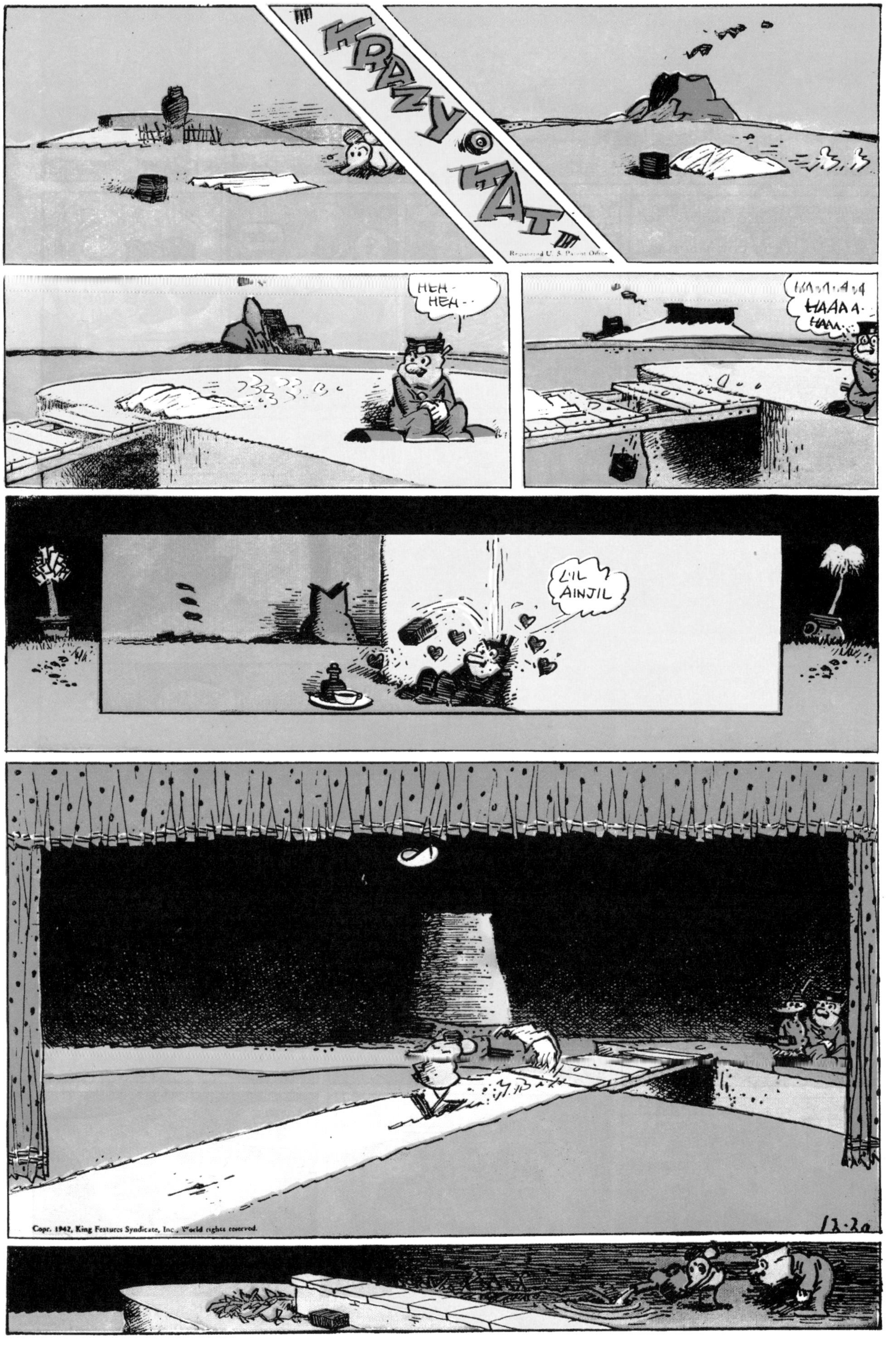
KRAZY KAT
Registered U.S. Patent Office
HEH HEH - -
HAAAA
HAAA-
L'IL AINJIL
Copr. 1942, King Features Syndicate, Inc., World rights reserved.
12-20

December 20th, 1942.

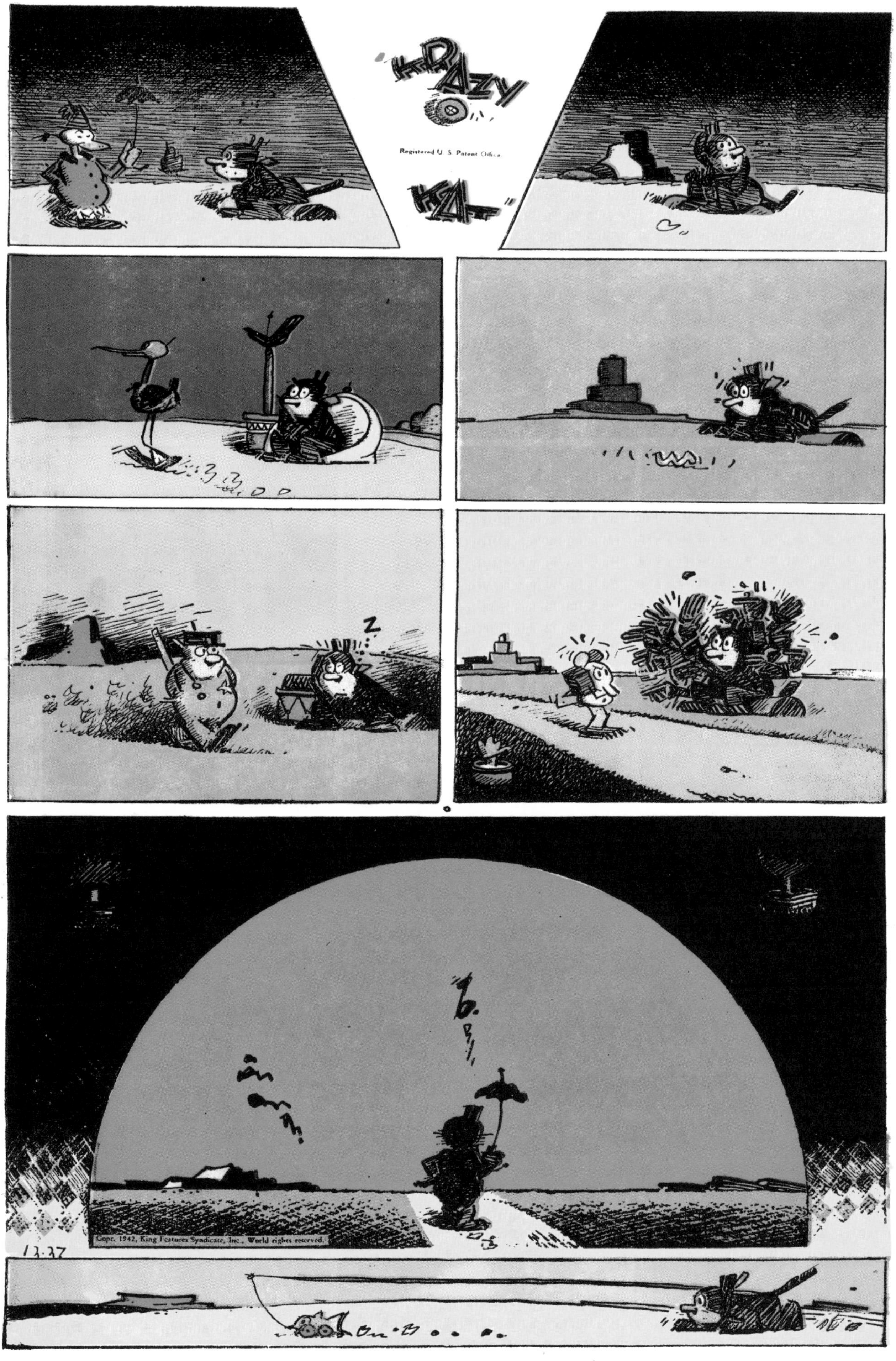
"Krazy Kat"
Registered U. S. Patent Office.
Copr. 1942, King Features Syndicate, Inc., World rights reserved.
12-27

December 27th, 1942.

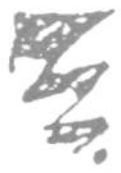

The IGNATZ MOUSE DEBAFFLER PAGE.

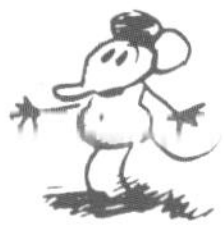

6/1/41 - 6/8/41: Rare instance of Herriman Sunday page continuity, spread over two weeks.

9/21/41: Mrs. Kwakk Wakk wants to pass along some hot rumors to "Cholly Kokonino," who is obviously the real life counterpart to Cholly Knickerbocker, the pseudonymous gossip columnist for the Hearst papers.

11/16/41: Ignatz says, "I've been a bad ba-a-ad 'mouse'." He's echoing the signature catchphrase of Lou Costello, "I've been a bad, bad boy." Abbott and Costello were then at the height of their popularity. Interestingly, Harold Gray was also an Abbott and Costello fan.

2/1/42: Throughout this and the following year, we see evidence of the Second World War changing life in Coconino. On this particular day, Ignatz can't buy a brick because of wartime rationing. On June 28, 1942, there is a blackout. And August 2nd 1942 features a very funny satire of wartime censorship: In the name of freedom and democracy Officer Pupp tries to suppress Ignatz's favorite activity.

3/8/42: One can only hope that somewhere somehow Walt Kelly saw this page.

11/8/42: Certainly the most inexplicable of Gawge's Kat tabs actually appears to have been drawn to baffle, confound and utterly madden, chiefly because it seems to have no other purpose. Do what you can with it, and enjoy. You're being teased by a master.

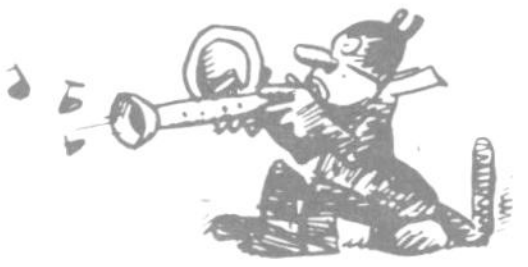

KALLING ALL KAT KOLLECTORS!

Our next volume, scheduled to be released during the Summer of 2008, will bring to a close the project launched many years ago by Eclipse Comics of reprinting every single *Krazy Kat* Sunday page. Partly to celebrate this, and partly because Herriman's untimely death in the Spring of 1944 (and the consequent midyear cessation of the strip) leaves the editors with some room to fill, this final volume will be extra jam-packed with extracurricular goodies. We are especially interested in running as many of Herriman's hand-colored strips, but anything *Kat* fans have they would like to share would be warmly received. Please contact kimt@fantagraphics.com if you have anything you'd like to contribute.

— k.t.

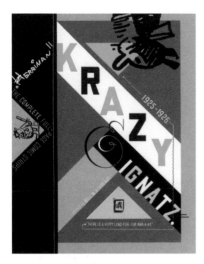

HERRIMAN
THE COMPLETE FULL PAGE COMIC STRIPS
KRAZY
1925-1926
IGNATZ.

Krazy + Ignatz 1925-1926.

"There Is a Happy Lend Fur-Fur Away." The first release in the series, with a gallery of supplements. $14.95.

HERRIMAN
THE COMPLETE FULL-PAGE COMIC STRIPS
Krazy
1927 1928
"LOVE LETTERS IN ANCIENT BRICK"
and Ignatz
EDITED by BILL BLACKBEARD

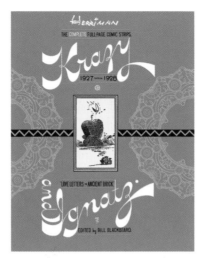

Krazy + Ignatz 1927-1928

"Love Letters in Ancient Brick." Two more years plus "Embarrassing Moments." CURRENTLY OUT OF PRINT.

KRAZY
1929
1930
IGNATZ

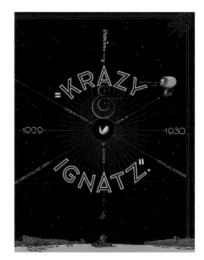

Krazy + Ignatz 1929-1930.

"A Mice, a Brick, a Lovely Night." A more flexible layout replaces the "grid" format of earlier Sundays. $19.95.

Krazy
Ignatz
"A Kat a'Lilt with Song"
The Complete Full-Page Comic Strips
1931
1932
by Herriman
Edited by Bill Blackbeard & Derya Ataker.

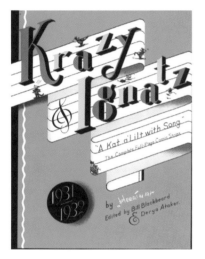

Krazy + Ignatz 1931-1932.

"A Kat A'Lilt With Song." Includes a 20-page portfolio of the 1931 daily strip. CURRENTLY OUT OF PRINT.

KRAZY
IGNATZ

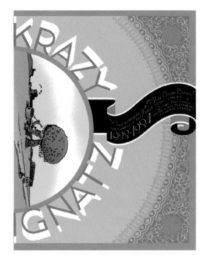

Krazy + Ignatz 1933-1934.

"Necromancy by the Blue Bean Bush." Includes the most obscure and hardest to find full-page strips. $14.95.

KRAZY
The Complete Full-Page
by Geo Herriman
COMIC STRIPS.
IGNATZ.

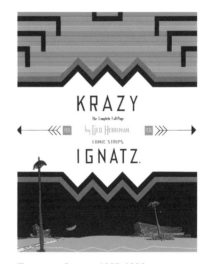

Krazy + Ignatz 1935-1936.

"A Wild Warmth of Chromatic Gravy." The first in color, plus Jeet Heer's article on Herriman's ethnicity. $19.95.

Krazy
by George Herriman
1937
1938
Ignatz

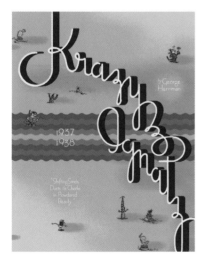

Krazy + Ignatz 1937-1938.

"Shifting Sands Dust Its Cheeks in Powdered Beauty." The second volume of full-color strips. $19.95

1939
KRAZY
IGNATZ
1940

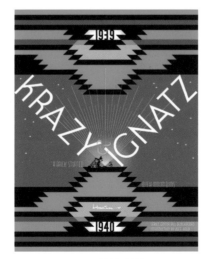

Krazy + Ignatz 1939-1940.

"A Brick Stuffed with Moom-bims." Jeet Heer's analysis of Herriman's use of color printing in his work. $19.95.

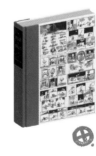

Krazy + Ignatz 1925-1934 hardcover.

This library hardcover binds the signatures of the first five books, but without the paperback covers. $75.00.

All available at a fine comics shop near you, or, to order by mail, send a cheque or money order to

Fantagraphics Books
7563 Lake City Way NE
Seattle, Washington, 98115.
1 800 657 1100

international calls, please dial 001 206 524 1967.
or order from our website
www.fantagraphics.com
Please enclose $3.00 shipping and handling for the first book and $1.00 for every book thereafter.